On Lingering and Being Last

On Lingering and Being Last

Race and Sovereignty in the New World

Jonathan Elmer

FORDHAM UNIVERSITY PRESS
NEW YORK 2008

Library of Congress Cataloging-in-Publication Data is available from the publisher.

Printed in the United States of America
10 09 08 5 4 3 2 1
First edition

CONTENTS

ACKNOWLEDGMENTS

I began work on this book a decade ago, during a year's residence as a Fellow at Cornell's Society for the Humanities. I thank the Society for its support, and especially Dominick LaCapra, Lyndsey Stonebridge, and Mary Jacobus for their advice and intellectual generosity during that year. I have also benefited over the years from the chance to share my work at many conferences and gatherings, and I thank hosts and interlocutors from Bielefeld, Germany, to Eugene, Oregon. I also spent several wonderful days at Dartmouth's Futures of American Studies Institute. I thank Don Pease for the invitation, and for his encouragement and advice.

I wish to thank Helen Tartar, for her continued interest in my work, and Fordham University Press. Some of what is now Chapter 4 was first published in *diacritics* 28.4 (1998) as "The Archive, the Native American, and Jefferson's Convulsions." Parts of Chapter 5 have also appeared in print, in *NOVEL: A Forum on Fiction* 40.1/2 (2007). I thank Len Tennenhouse for the invitation to contribute to this issue, and for general support.

Indiana University was a wonderfully supportive institution during the writing of this book, twice offering me release time: I am grateful to the President's Arts and Humanities Fellowship Committee, as well as the College Arts and Humanities Institute, for their support. Indiana is also an encouraging environment in which to pursue interdisciplinary discussion, and I have grown immeasurably through my conversations with colleagues at the Center for High-Energy Metaphysics, and at the Center for Eighteenth-Century Studies, this last generously supported by the College of Arts and Sciences at Indiana. I have shared work-in-progress several times with the remarkable group of scholars and students at the Center. I wish to express a global thanks to this group and to the various visitors we have hosted at our annual May Workshops, for all the intellectual ferment they have provided. But I must also single out, as especially helpful to me at one point or another, my friends Kon Dierks, Constance Furey, Sarah Knott, Deidre Lynch, Richard Nash, Janet Sorensen, and last but not least Dror Wahrman, a dynamo of intellectual energy and institutional creativity.

Other friends at Indiana have read and responded to earlier drafts of portions of this book and have offered essential companionship. I thank Ed Comentale, Jen Fleissner, Paul Gutjahr, George Hutchinson, Josh Kates, and Bill Rasch. I am especially grateful to Susan Gubar for her friendship, her encouragement, and the humane guidance she has offered over the past seventeen years at Indiana.

I want to acknowledge four friends with whom I have shared not just ideas but life itself over the last decade and more. Mary Favret and Andrew Miller have been the best of colleagues, and much, much more, my entire time at Indiana: we have grown up together. I have enjoyed the consistently invigorating intellectual conversation of Elizabeth Maddock Dillon since graduate school days: without it, and all her encouragement and good advice, this book would not have been completed. Michel Chaouli I have known even longer, and for the past seven years I have been lucky to have him as a colleague at Indiana. Our weekly lunches, in which we talk about family and friends, jobs and writing, but mostly about ideas, have been a joy.

This book has taken shape during a period of momentous change in my life. My parents, Glenn and Felicia Elmer, both passed away after I had begun this book and before I finished it. I am lucky to have two brothers, Tad and Jamie, with whom I can share all ups and downs, and who always manage to convey their belief in me, even when they have no idea what I am talking about. My wife, Alexandra, is an essential part of everything I am and do, my daily guide in the search for balance and perspective. Nathaniel was in kindergarten and Lydia only two when I began work on this book in Ithaca. They are both now teenagers, and both already striking out on their own paths. They make me incredibly proud, and I dedicate this book to them.

On Lingering and Being Last

Introduction

Sovereignty seems to be everywhere these days, and no one is very happy about it. Political theorists, cultural observers, historians, scholars of international relations, lawyers, anthropologists, literary critics—all approach the dilemmas of sovereign power with a mixture of urgency and frustration. Social theorist William Rasch titles his book *Sovereignty and Its Discontents*, and anthropologist Aihwa Ong worries about sovereignty's "mutations."[1] Political scientist Stephen D. Krasner uses the same phrase as Rasch to begin his exasperated introduction to what he calls the "organized hypocrisy" of sovereignty.[2] His discontent with sovereignty is that we never seem to know what we're talking about when we use the term. Is sovereignty about (formal) legitimacy or (practical) authority? Does sovereignty require the ability to control the flow of people and goods across a territorial border, is it primarily a principle of international recognition, or does its essence lie in its power to regulate the lives and welfare of a state's citizens? According to Krasner, even the so-called Westphalian model, according to which sovereign states—originally the European absolutist states of the seventeenth century—tolerate and recognize each other internationally on the condition that each states' internal affairs are protected from outside intervention, is of dubious analytical use: "The most important empirical conclusion of the present study," he writes, "is that the principles associated with both Westphalian and international legal sovereignty have always been violated" (24). In other words, sovereignty names a fiction of state integrity that has never coincided with practice.

Historian James J. Sheehan, dedicating his 2005 Presidential Address to the American Historical Association to "The Problem of Sovereignty in European History," also points to the mystifications surrounding the concept of the state: "*The* state was and is not history's natural telos. The emergence of states was neither inevitable nor uniform nor irreversible." He urges that we "move beyond the handful of Western European states whose quite exceptional experience provides both our political vocabulary and our historiographical models."[3] Sheehan thus joins a chorus of other voices who say that the fictions of state sovereignty have absorbed us for too long. "We all know the fascination that the love, or horror, of the state exercises today," wrote Michel Foucault in 1977.[4] It is a "fascination" ultimately with a poetic trope, Foucault suggests, with the personification of the "cold monster we see confronting us" (220). Foucault's attempt to extricate himself from this fascination is the burden of most of his research after *Discipline and Punish*. But even as he developed his analyses of biopower and governmentality as efforts to historicize and denaturalize the "cold monster" of state sovereignty, Foucault acknowledged that "sovereignty is far from being eliminated by the emergence of a new art of government . . . ; on the contrary, the problem of sovereignty is made more acute than ever" (218).[5] Foucault confirms Sheehan's view that because our very "political vocabulary" and "historiographical models" are bound up with this conceptually vague notion, it is well-nigh impossible to evade it altogether.

Much of the criticism of the concept of sovereignty has come from those who, like Sheehan, see it as an expression of Eurocentrism. Having pointed years ago to the "New World origins of nationalism," Benedict Anderson professes to have been "startled" that the "Eurocentric provincialism," according to which "everything important in the modern world originated in Europe," "remained quite undisturbed" by his evidence.[6] It seems, however, that this misrecognition may be structural. The conceptual history of sovereignty encrypts a dynamic of modernity in which Western thought develops in, and as, a misunderstanding of Europe's relation to the wider world. Political philosophers Michael Hardt and Antonio Negri, for example, understand sovereignty as constitutive of a political modernity defined by European colonialism: "Modern sovereignty . . . functioned as the cornerstone of the construction of Eurocentrism. Although modern sovereignty emanated from Europe . . . it was born and developed in large part through Europe's relationship with its outside, and particularly through its colonial project and the resistance of the colonized. Modern sovereignty emerged, then, as the concept of European reaction and European domination both within and outside its borders. They are two coextensive and complementary faces of one development: rule within Europe and European rule over the world."[7] Edward Keene and Antony Anghie, coming at the problem from the disciplines of international relations and legal history respectively, agree that the orthodox theory of sovereignty, and the international law structured by that theory, can only be understood in relation to the history of European colonialism, a history that both enabled the European theory of state sovereignty and is consistently misrecognized or ignored by that theory.[8] Keene is especially cogent on this point, suggesting that our current uncertainty about the right to international intervention, even in the name of shocking violations of human rights by a sovereign regime, exposes an ideological fissure several centuries old. On the one hand, a principle of *toleration* governs the Westphalian model: a toleration of other states' inviolable right to govern as they see fit within their territorial borders. To this principle of toleration is opposed an ideal of *civilization* that developed in the context of European colonialism; this principle had its roots, ironically, in the extension and elaboration of international individual rights *on behalf of colonizers*, an extension initially advocated by Hugo Grotius. "The pattern of order that is challenging the idea of state sovereignty today is as old as the society of states itself," and it is an order that focuses less on territorial control than on ideas of "economic progress" and "individuals' rights" (Keene 148). International human rights and racist colonial ideologies of a "civilizing mission" share a genealogy, in other words, one that takes the individual, rather than the state, as its foundational concept.

It is this conjunction of the individual, race, and new world sovereignty that I argue holds a key to understanding some of the deepest strata of the political imagination of Atlantic modernity. *On Lingering and Being Last* explores the fascination exerted on some influential Anglo-American writers by the trope of the racialized sovereign individual. The enduring power of these royal slaves, captive kings, and last chiefs comes from their capacity, in varying measures, to absorb projection, identification, and disavowal. These are mythical figures, in some essential ways, sites of cultural overdetermination: simultaneously instances of radical autonomy and the embodiment of a body politic, these characters are both exalted and abjected, exemplary and exceptional, same and other. The fictions on which I focus, however, are not mere thematizations of the racial other. Rather, they reveal the structuring force of a racialized imagination in the new world, the ways in which the culture's deepest investments are both made available and quite regularly misrecognized through racial categories. In its emphasis on the *structuring* nature of racialization, on the way racial otherness is in play even when, as happens, all the characters are white, this book can be seen as extending and adapting Toni Morrison's great intervention in *Playing in the Dark: Whiteness and the Literary Imagination*.[9] In the first half of the book, I trace a black Atlantic tradition running from Aphra Behn to Herman Melville, a tradition in which the "captive king" is both a symbol of utter abjection and of utopian longing. In the second half of the book, I describe the "logic of the last" as exemplified by the Indian in North America, a racial other that, like the African sovereign, incites both repudiation and adulation in varying measure. That such figurative treatments of racial others are ambivalent at heart should not, in itself, seem like news: Eric Lott's *Love and Theft*, to name one influential example, explores with great sensitivity the intricacies of such ambivalence in what may seem the most repugnant of racial representations, the antebellum blackface minstrel show.[10] One contribution of *On Lingering and Being Last* to this rich scholarly conversation about race and cultural production is that it reveals in greater detail and sharper focus than heretofore what the African and the Indian share in the Euro-American imagination, and where they crucially differ. The modalities of ambivalence at work in each tradition are finally traceable, I argue, to differences in their relation to the problem of space, of symbolic geography and territorialization: the uprooted African presents a limit case for the fundamental experience of deterritorialization in modernity, in all its promise and terror. The Indian, by contrast, consistently poses the limit to a hoped-for reterritorialization and is accordingly subjected to a kind of figurative hyper-territorialization, made to vanish into the very land of the new world itself. *On Lingering and Being Last* argues that race, sovereignty, and the problem of the individual are all intimately implicated in a new spatial imagination in the new world. In the remainder of this introduction I will trace out in more detail the nature of this mutual implication.

The idea that the concept and history of sovereignty encrypts a dynamic of modernity in which Western thought develops in, and as, a misunderstanding of Europe's relation to the wider world is clearly related to the disorienting political realities of the past generation—the end of the cold war, the rise of international terrorism, the increased hegemony of capital at the expense of sovereign state control. We often seem to be in a "post-sovereign" environment in which the most significant actors are either sub-sovereign, like multinational corporations or al-Qaeda, or hyper-sovereign, like the United States, which, as "sole remaining superpower," increasingly flouts international law in its aggression against non-state actors and so-called rogue nations. In pursuing this modern version of *raison d'état*, the United States begins to look like the type and exemplar of the rogue states that it sets out to punish, and thereby brings to light the way in which there is, as Jacques Derrida puts it, "something of a rogue state in every state": "Every sovereign state is in fact virtually and a priori able . . . to abuse its power and, like a rogue state, transgress international law."[11] The implicit acknowledgement of this truism—every state is always potentially a rogue state—causes the postmodern to curve around and meet up with the early modern: the Bush Doctrine, asserting the right to preemptive strikes against a merely *potential* aggressor, revives the notion that it is acceptable to "act on the basis not of justice but of fear," a position held by Alberico Gentili in *De Jure Belli* (1598) and other humanist writers influential on modern Western political thought.[12] Given this alarming curvature of historical space-time, it no longer seems so odd that contemporary scholars eager to expose the *contemporary* confusions of the concept of sovereignty would do so by an assiduous return to centuries-old sources: Keene focuses on Grotius, Hardt and Negri revisit Bodin, and Anghie—in a book largely interested in nineteenth- and twentieth-century developments—reaches all the way back to Vitoria in his attempt to figure out how we have arrived where we have.

Such work suggests the value of returning to textual traditions and conceptual histories that precede the naturalization of the European state form. In the chapters that follow, I too return to the works of earlier authors in an effort to gain greater clarity on contemporary dilemmas of sovereign power, humanitarian ideals, and the legacies of racism and colonialism in the new world. Like the scholars of political thought I have mentioned, I try to discern in my texts the larger logic and set of historical problems in which they participate. My method is not the political philosopher's, probing conceptual arguments for their foundations or inconsistencies, but that of the literary critic: even when I treat a writer such as Jefferson, whom we might think of primarily as a political author, I read first with an eye for trope and image, for the ways conceptual contradiction and affective ambivalence crystallize in literary logics or the work of figuration. While all my writers are more or less explicitly interested in the problems of politics—in the dynamic of power and legitimacy, the problems of slavery and emancipation, of genocidal extermination and humanitarian preservation—they do their political thinking with the tools provided by the literary imagination, as that responds to different urgencies of time and place. I try to be sensitive to the local contextual conditions that bear on my authors and their texts, but tropes and topoi have ways of reconstituting themselves in strikingly different historical locations, and I have also been eager throughout this book to recognize and analyze the meaning of these imaginative continuities, some of which retain considerable power on us today.

In the first half of the book, I examine the trope of the African "royal slave," as it is paradigmatically expressed in Aphra Behn's *Oroonoko; or The Royal Slave* (1688). After showing how Behn's understanding of new world sovereignty finds its fullest expression in her great novella, I go on to trace the ramifications of what I call the *Oroonoko effect* first in the Christian emancipatory idiom of the writers of the black Atlantic, especially Olaudah Equiano, and then in the highly wrought articulation of the topos of the captive king found in the sea fictions of Herman Melville. The second half of the book turns to a complementary figurative tradition of representing the modern racialized sovereign, what I call the logic of the last. Here my paradigmatic case is the melancholy speech of Chief Logan, as recorded by Thomas Jefferson in his *Notes on the State of Virginia* (1787), a speech whose poignant closing phrase, "Who is there to mourn for Logan?—Not one," becomes a touchstone for subsequent American literature. After examining how Jefferson's incorporation of Logan operates within his archiving project in *Notes*, I track subsequent versions of the *Logan effect* in the melancholic investments of the transatlantic romantic novel as exemplified by

William Godwin, Charles Brockden Brown, and John Neal. In my final chapter, I use a contemporary act of ecoterrorism in British Columbia as a prism through which to view the ways in which sovereign legitimacy and traumatic race war converge at a vanishing point emblematized by the extraordinarily durable topos of the solitary tree.

I argue that these textual traditions can help us see how the modern problem of sovereignty, as that unfolds in the new world, exemplifies a racialized logic of personification that conjoins individual and collective identities. Personification is the engine of a program of individuation, and of individualism, a program within which sovereignty becomes a subroutine. Such a thesis implies that there is no way to think through sovereign power without recourse to a metric of the individual. This volatile work of personification takes place, moreover, within a world that is both constituted and fissured by a *concept* of equality, homogeneity, and symmetry, on the one hand—by the powerfully deterritorializing ideal of "the" (liberal) individual, that is—and, on the other, by the *realities* of racial domination and ideology in the era of colonial expansion that everywhere install and maintain inequality, heterogeneity, and asymmetrical extremes of power. When Aphra Behn tells the story of Oroonoko, the African "royal slave," or Thomas Jefferson immortalizes Chief Logan, sole survivor of his line, they bring this logic of personification and its contradictions into high relief. They both use, and are used by, this figurative logic. Behn and Jefferson avail themselves of literary expression, I would argue, not in an effort to overcome or resolve the ideological incoherence of modern sovereignty, but rather to pose the conceptual problems in the figurative and dramatic terms most capable of containing the myriad ambivalences and overdeterminations that inform the trope of the sovereign individual. Precisely because of its solicitation of ambiguity, literature can register ideological and historical contradictions with greater sensitivity and nuance than other discourses.

Let us look further at the constitutive role played by the trope of personification in modern political thought. We have already cited Foucault's impatience with the personification of the state as a "cold monster we see confronting us" (220). But as long ago as 1916, the dangers of such personification were being decried: "The tendency to regard international persons as if they were individuals with a conscience, a sense of honor, a single interest, and a single life, confuses our thinking," wrote Edwin DeWitt

Dickinson in the *Yale Law Journal.* "There is a widespread opinion that the constant menace of war can be mitigated only by the further perfection of international organization. One of the greatest obstacles in this direction will be found in the tendency to personify international persons and attribute to them rights derived from the analogy with human beings."[13] Dick-inson knew he had an uphill battle on his hands, however, and readily acknowledged that as a historical reality such personification had "had an immeasurable influence upon the subsequent development of international law" (564).

Just how immeasurable the influence of such personification is, how deep-rooted, is suggested by Richard Tuck in his searching analysis of the rights of war and peace. Tuck argues that "the international arena has been the laboratory for testing liberal political ideas since their invention" (*Rights of War* 229). This international "laboratory" preceded the work of Thomas Hobbes, but it was he who gave it the lasting name of the "state of nature," a complex and hybrid construction that Tuck describes memorably as the combination of a minimal or "thin" account of "agents . . . possessing an extremely narrow set of rights and duties" (6) with a dramaturgy of conflict that is anything but thin:

> It is impossible to deny that the vividness of this picture of moral agents owed a great deal to the astonishing vividness of the picture of international action in the so-called age of European expansion. It cannot be a coincidence, seen from this perspective, that the modern idea of natural rights arose in the period in which the European nations were engaged in their dramatic competition for domination of the world, and in which there were urgent questions about how both states and individuals adrift in a stateless world behave to one another and to newly encountered peoples. (14)

The logic of personification codified in the fiction of a state of nature encompassed both "states" *and* "individuals adrift in a stateless world": in fact, it made states into the individuals of a stateless world, just as it transformed individuals adrift into the moral equivalents of states. The figures my texts return to again and again—the captive kings, the last Indians—are direct and highly complex literary expressions of this logic. Whether they are the last of their race or the sovereign dislocated from his dominion, the heroes of my book—Oroonoko and his epigones, Logan and his avatars—are always at once a person and a people: they embody the substantial connection between the individual and the collectivity. The settings in which they find themselves, moreover, are at once "thin" and "astonishingly vivid," as Tuck might say. Oroonoko in Surinam, Atufal on Melville's dream-like *San Dominick*, Chief Logan and Edgar Huntly on the Virginia and Pennsylvania frontiers—in each case, a more or less thinly characterized figure finds himself radically isolated in a surreal environment from which much of the mediating social reality has been stripped away. It is precisely in these abstracted, pared-down conditions, however, that there emerge vivid explorations of the most extreme conditions of independence and abandonment. I will return to the question of the extent to which historical conditions in the anglophone new world, and not just literary ones, might aptly be described as "thin yet vivid."

Thomas Hobbes's brilliant investigation "*Of* PERSONS, AUTHORS, *and things Personated*" in Chapter XVI of *Leviathan* (1651) may be the best-known account of the fundamental role of personification in modern political thought, but Tuck argues that it was Hugo Grotius who "fundamentally revised Western political thought itself" with the "single extraordinary idea . . . that there is no reason why an individual should not be thought of as morally identical to a state" (81, 228). The implication of this idea was that individuals could hold certain rights and powers that had before been understood as the prerogatives of political collectivities only. Most specifically, Grotius's arguments gave to non-state actors—commercial trading companies, for instance, or merely individuals on the make—the rights to make "war" as an act of self-preservation and to appropriate "unoccupied" land.[14] The crucial concept in this transfer of political sovereignty to the individual is *autonomy*. We often imagine the state being personified as a human individual, the way Hobbes seems to tell us to do. But the history of the concept of autonomy may indicate that tenor and vehicle were originally reversed. The idea of personal autonomy, it turns out, is derived from the political community; the individual is *personified*, we might say, as a state. As Tuck points out, autonomy in Greek means "having one's own laws," and in the ancient world the term was "almost always used to describe the independence of a political community" (226). But then he quotes a line from Sophocles's *Antigone* where the chorus addresses Antigone: "αυτόνομος you alone of all mortals while yet alive descend to Hades." Tuck proposes that " 'autonomy' here is still a living and poetic metaphor in which a person can be momentarily described as a city" (226). And he goes on to suggest that the "history of autonomy is essentially a history of this metaphor being taken increasingly seriously" (226).

To be autonomous as an individual, Sophocles would seem to say, is to take on the not entirely human traits of the polity, traits of radical exceptionality—"you alone of all mortals"—and of a kind of deathlessness—"while yet alive" Antigone "descend[s] to Hades." One way to describe this book would be to say that it shows this metaphor being taken seriously in anglophone literature from Aphra Behn to Herman Melville and beyond: like Antigone, my royal slaves and captive kings and last chiefs are attempts to imagine the mystery of autonomy; they are figures who bear the meaning of the social collectivity in their very isolation, somehow both mortal like the rest of us and yet able to enter a zone of quasi-immortality, by turns exalted and abjected. I call this mythical existence of the autonomous individual the condition of "lingering and being last." My argument's swerve toward Antigone may be taken to foreshadow the repeated turns toward mythic dimensions in the texts I analyze. One characteristic of the zone of lingering and being last is that historical experience itself becomes a myth-element of some kind. Did Aphra Behn know someone like Oroonoko in Surinam in the 1660s? Did the Mingo warrior John Logan really deliver the speech Jefferson claims he did? Is Gustavus Vassa really Olaudah Equiano, was he really born in Benin and destined to receive the scarification that marked his elevated social status? This equivocation between history and myth recurs throughout this book, a reminder that one thing at stake in the imaginative treatments of sovereignty and race is the nature, definition, and authority of historical experience itself. Michael Warner has suggested that given the incredible variousness and complexity of new world colonial experience, we might find an organizing unity to colonial culture not in a single "shared meaning" or even a general "will to dominate," but rather in novel and shared ways of organizing "spatial and temporal hierarchies."[15] My description of the zone of "lingering and being last," as I unfold it over the course of the book, represents such an effort to describe one complex and striking pattern in the imagination of the new world. This pattern takes spatial and temporal hierarchies—mythic past *precedes* historical present, wilderness lies *outside* clearing and settlement—but then contorts, bends back, or folds over these hierarchies: the frontier is both over there *and* inside here, the movement of peoples is both radically unbound *and* it describes the borders of a space of incarceration, the premodern or mythic is both definitively surpassed *and* carefully harbored within history itself. It is the racialized sovereign that provides the hinge for this operation of folding over, that both asserts the identity of the terms joined by the "and" and allows for the disavowal of that identity.

One profound reason for this doubled-over spatiotemporal pattern, I would argue, is that the new world itself was understood as both historical and mythical: "In the beginning, all the world was *America*," Locke famously proclaimed, and Hobbes before him had similarly appealed to the Americans as empirical examples of the "state of nature." Tuck makes the important point that the "state of nature," as it is deployed by Hobbes and subsequent writers, was not "straightforwardly or wholly hypothetical: there were empirical examples of what [Hobbes] meant" (137). At the same time, it was not purely or straightforwardly a historical datum either: "It may peradventure be thought," writes Hobbes in Chapter XIII of *Leviathan*, "there was never such a time nor condition of war as this; and I believe it was never generally so, over all the world. But there are many places where they live so now. For the savage people in many places of *America* . . . have no government at all."[16] It is not the case, Hobbes admits, that there once was "a time" in which mankind lived "over all the world" in a state of nature. Hobbes and others "did not think that it had to be historically proved," says Tuck, but they *did* think that "the empirical possibility of a state of nature defined in their terms was an important part of their argument" (7, 8). Not precisely historical, then, but not purely theoretical either, the state of nature is what we might call an *empirical myth*, one that can be visited, if one travels to the new world, or one that can be visited upon us, if we are not vigilant, because it is a "principle internal to the State revealed in the moment in which the State is considered 'as if it were dissolved.'"[17] The new world plays a profoundly equivocal role, in other words, in both the historical development and the conceptual structure of the idea of the state of nature: at once exemplary of a universal possibility of humanity, the new world also remains an exception to European contemporaneity and indeed to Europe's own sense of global history. In Hobbes's account, what goes on now, exemplarily, in America, remains a dangerous exception, historically speaking, because "it was never generally so, over all the world."

The new world's status as both exemplary and exceptional vis-à-vis European self-understanding tells us something about the nature and force of this imperial misprision, something more than that Hobbes didn't know what he was talking about when he said that indigenous Americans had "no government." When Tuck writes that the "international arena has been the laboratory for testing liberal ideas since their invention" (229), that arena must be understood to encompass both European interstate rivalries and European expansion into the new world, must apply to both "states and individuals adrift in a stateless world" (14). And in fact the behavior of states toward each other was understood to offer another way to conceive the state of nature. But the equivocation to be found in Hobbes's text implies that what was imagined to take place between *individuals* in the new world was theorized as taking place between *states* in Europe. Is the state of nature that obtains between the European states the same one that is imagined to be visible in the new world? Well, yes and no. And here racial identity enters the picture, silently but fatefully. If the state of nature exists in "America," it is in some sense implied to be a situation in which non-European, racially different individuals are set against one another. The interstate rivalries also imagined as a state of nature, by contrast, involve European, racially similar states in opposition. Grotius's personification of the individual as a state creates a conceptual continuity between the two scenes, the two states of nature (in Europe and in the new world), a continuity that racial difference then intervenes to obscure.

Some of the stakes of this equivocation about the relation between European and new world sovereignty can be approached by a look at Carl Schmitt's *The* Nomos *of the Earth in the International Law of the* Jus Publicum Europeaum (1950). Schmitt was perfectly clear in his mind about the radical transformation of European political thought brought on by the discovery and appropriation of the new world: "Hobbes' *homo homini lupus* . . . was influenced not only by the creedal civil wars in Europe, but also by the New World. He speaks of the 'state of nature,' but not at all in the sense of a spaceless utopia. His state of nature is a *no man's land*, but this does not mean that it exists *nowhere*. It can be located, and Hobbes locates it . . . in the New World."[18] Schmitt's "*no man's land*" is, like Hobbes's "*America*," once again a place both mythical and empirical, but its essential importance lies in its existence "beyond the line": "The line set aside an area where force could be used freely and ruthlessly," writes Schmitt. "Everything that occurred 'beyond the line' remained outside the legal, moral, and political values recognized on this side of the line. This was a tremendous *exoneration* of the internal European problematic" (94). How does this "exoneration" work? By displacing the idea of the state of nature as wholly lawless, as a matter of the free and ruthless exercise of force, Schmitt ends up with the purified state of nature within Europe itself often called the balance of power, a kind of dynamic equilibrium of states opposing one another in respectful and unsubordinated equality—something like a gentleman's club in which the members demonstrate non-submission to a higher legal order by recourse to dueling: "A challenge to a duel was neither aggression nor crime. . . . In its ideal form, this also was true of internal European wars between states in European international law" (143). Even leaving aside the actual history of interstate war in Europe during this time, the picture Schmitt draws cannot help seeming wishful: somehow we have the benefits of a liberal order—the civility, the capacity to "bracket" indiscriminate killing—without the individual members having to submit to the authority of any international sovereign order. In this way, the primacy of conflict, of the "friend/enemy" grouping that for Schmitt constitutes the specific and invaluable political dimension, can be maintained, without having to sacrifice a degree of order and civility.[19] But this is an affair of states: the problematic of the individual—the other polarity in the Grotian personification—has been expelled "beyond the line," to a new world in which Europeans can fight each other, and fight non-Europeans, in an "unbracketed" manner. This new world is literally the *alibi* of Europe, its "elsewhere." Given Schmitt's frank nostalgia for this Eurocentric spatial order, it is perhaps not surprising that he would show almost no interest in the role that the slave trade, for example, played in the developments in world politics, international law, and political theory, developments about which he is otherwise so erudite. I revisit Schmitt's peculiar blindness on this topic in Chapter 3, where I discuss the meaning of his profound identification with Benito Cereno, Melville's great representative of a European order that has been historically surpassed.

One of the most revealing aspects of the fictions I examine in this book is the way that they expose the contradictions entailed by a vision of the new world as Europe's alibi, or elsewhere. The narratives I examine do not segregate races from one another, nor states from individuals: rather than non-European individuals confronting each other in a state of nature, *so that* non-racialized states can do so in Europe, the spaces of lingering and being last in which Oroonoko meets Behn, or Jefferson encounters Logan, are zones in which the distinctions between state and individual, and between races, are in danger of collapse. Rather than serving as a place to which the contradictions inherent in the logic of personification in sovereignty theory can be displaced and quarantined, the texts I examine display those contradictions through superimposition: the captive king just *is* the state and the self in one, and if he is racially other, he is taken up within a world that is not racially homogeneous but quite strikingly one of inescapable racial conflict and encounter. In the imaginative treatments I analyze, the isomorphism between state and individual is more freely acknowledged than in other political discourses, even as the meaning of that isomorphism, by virtue of its being embodied by an African or an Indian, becomes the stuff of literary longing, a melancholia that can never be assuaged, or a vision of emancipation veritably utopian in being always out of reach. The ideological space of the new world that my texts depict is not, in other words, a solution to, or "exoneration" of, a European problematic, but that problematic's more intense and more volatile expression.

In making this last assertion I am following in the wake of many scholars who, over the past generation and more, have immensely enriched our understanding of the historical, experiential, and ideological landscape in the anglophone colonial and imperial world. Moving away from analyses that take the state—whether English or American—as the ultimate explanatory horizon, and toward consideration of the constitutive power of imperial ideologies, the myriad varieties of colonial experience, and the fundamental role of racial difference in the realities of land appropriation and the slave trade, these scholars have given us a new world that is neither a pure reproduction of the metropolitan center, nor some radical break with it, but rather a space in which European ideologies undergo what we could call, after Deleuze and Guattari, a process of "deterritorialization" under the pressure of lived realities on the ground. Without making any attempt to survey the several different bodies of scholarship that have pursued these ideas, I will merely extract a few themes that seem especially germane to the argument of my book. David Armitage, Linda Colley, Eliga Gould, Dror Wahrman, Brendan McConville, and others have offered different and detailed descriptions of the development of English imperial ideologies. This scholarship represents an attempt to rethink the relation between old and new worlds, between the rise of the states system and the progress of imperial expansion, not as two separate narratives, but as a single, albeit multifaceted, dynamic in which empire is the (often misrecognized) truth of the state system: in what may seem a familiar perspective at this point in this introduction, Armitage suggests that "the study of imperial ideologies can clarify the limits of political theory studied on the unexamined principle that it encompasses solely the theory of the state and its ideological predecessors."[20] Gould, McConville, and Wahrman all show how keen many Britons were to understand themselves as citizens not of a state merely, but of an empire, and how desperate some were, on both sides of the Atlantic, to devise means of keeping that empire together.[21] The centrifugal tendencies of this English imperial practice proved too great, however, at least in the North American colonies. McConville's thesis is especially interesting in this light: the decentralizing, eventually revolutionary developments in British North America should not be understood, he argues, as some kind of simple negation of monarchical thought, but rather as the result of the very intensity with which the provincials embraced the ideals of empire, with all its patriarchal hierarchies: "Before the Revolution, Americans wanted more patriarchy and more empire, not less, and, strangely, such desires, held by more and more people, helped unravel the imperial state" (147). McConville offers striking indications that this logic was at work in a variety of locales and episodes, and he convincingly argues that scholars "will better understand eighteenth-century America if we accept that monarchy, hierarchy, and patriarchy were primary forces of change and subversion in certain contexts" (139). In a rich literary-critical confirmation of McConville's basic thesis, Paul Downes has demonstrated, in a study whose careful unpacking of the intersections between political thought and literary form serves as an example for my own study, that the "democratic state and the democratic subject inherit the *arcana imperii* of the absolute monarch."[22]

Here again we can see how colonial North America might have served as a laboratory of liberalism, an environment at once "thin" and "vivid." What McConville calls the "institutional truncation" (143) of provincial life in North America was often compensated, as it were, by the intensification of fantasized connection to the symbols and rites of royalty: "It may be said that, in the provinces, attachment to the monarchy was passionate, created by rites and print culture, whereas in England, it was 'normal,' meaning the social structure, land tenure system, and customs supported it" (106). Aphra

Behn's "new world" productions, *Oroonoko* and *The Widow Ranter*, demonstrate this logic powerfully, as I argue in my first chapter. *The Widow Ranter* is set in Virginia during Bacon's Rebellion, a place that, both in history and in Behn's text, is at once intensely royalist and profoundly subversive of imperial order. Virginia is "more overtly monarchical than England itself" (138), as McConville would say, but because the de facto institutional structure is so thin and flimsy—a situation Behn thematizes by making the governor absent—Bacon's defense of royal values cannot help becoming subversive. In this sense, Behn articulates in her fictions a dynamic that McConville argues was more broadly pervasive in "royal America": as the traits and ideals of sovereignty get transplanted to the new world, they are not so much eroded or negated as they are deterritorialized—unleashed, intensified, submitted to torsion.

The complexity of the political imagination in colonial and early national America has been brilliantly impressed on us by the researches of Michael Warner, Ed White, Peter Onuf, and many others, some of whose specific arguments are taken up in the chapters that follow.[23] David Waldstreicher has reminded us of the "extremes of freedom and unfreedom that characterized the Atlantic littoral," and that volatile reality is everywhere confirmed by the texts I analyze.[24] The superimposition of sovereignty and slavery, the quarantining of the meaning of an entire race, nation, or people in the radically helpless body of the abandoned individual—such dramas form the figurative core of the representations I interpret in the following chapters. And here again we find at work the strange mix of vision and blindness that deforms the political imagination of European modernity when it thinks of its "outside." On the one hand, the texts I discuss offer what amount to literary theorizations of the reversibility of "freedom and unfreedom," a theorization that can on occasion be quite sophisticated. On the other hand, the racial otherness of the figures often—though not always—serves as a kind of screen or blind that keeps many of the authors from fully comprehending how this dynamic reflects the systematic inequities of their political world, as well as how it bears on their own real and ideal political condition. The captive king or the royal slave opens to visibility a fundamental likeness, that is, a likeness understood in this tradition as a basic human condition that makes each of us potentially sovereign or subordinated, makes each of us radically vulnerable to the transpositions of power. But this very visibility is a product of Tuck's "laboratory of liberalism," as it were: the racialized sovereign individual only becomes exemplary of a general condition in the controlled environment created by the projective imagination in the new world. This environment is one in which racial otherness intercedes to render the exemplary at the same time exceptional, an overdetermination that makes it possible for the racialized sovereign to be the focus at once of identification and disavowal.

Some sense of how this dynamic of recognition and denial might have looked on the ground can be gained from the story told by John Wood Sweet in *Bodies Politic*, the story of the Ninigrets, eighteenth-century "kings" of the Narragansett Indians in Rhode Island. Scholars have long deplored the ethnocentrism manifested in the widespread misrecognition of native political structures by Europeans, for example the insistence on identifying and then negotiating with the "kings" of the Indian nations they encountered. It was not just ignorance that led them to do so, however, but clear-eyed expediency as well, because the property transfers they were interested in forwarding required such an agent. And as Sweet points out, both sides often knew they were trading in fictions: "Often common ground had been reached when both sides agreed to accept loose analogies and tolerate a degree of misunderstanding on crucial issues. Everyone knew, for instance, that the Narragansetts' traditional 'sachems' were not precisely like European monarchs, but often individuals had good reason not to press the point."[25] Some of these individuals were the Ninigret sachems themselves, who adopted English styles and increasingly imagined themselves as positioned to exercise "royal" prerogatives, especially when it came to land sales. The dénouement of the story is depressingly familiar, with the Narragansetts forced to sell off more and more of their land to relieve debts, some run up by the Narragansett "monarch," who had been encouraged in his aspirations by various local white authorities. But the larger lesson is somewhat more ambiguous. Sweet describes a convergence of political dynamics, tropes, and ideologies between white and native communities: even the yeoman Narragansett resistance to the Ninigrets' "arbitrary tyranny" quite closely paralleled what was unfolding between the English king and his colonies, as various actors in this drama, including the Crown itself, seemed both to recognize and misrecognize at the same time. But the apparent cross-racial convergence of political experience and idiom also led at a different level to a greater sense of cleavage between white and native worlds.

The more that whites and Indians became "like" each other in certain respects, the more occasion they had to remark how fundamentally unlike they were in fact. It is important to observe how race here is less the cause of this divergence than a means to it, an available lever with which power could be exercised, or a screen, as I have already characterized it, on which sameness and difference could be both acknowledged and denied: "Closeness and intimacy in this late-colonial body politic . . . repeatedly fueled the engine of racialization," as David Waldstreicher summarizes the lesson in his review of Sweet's book.[26] The combination of blindness and insight that I have argued characterizes the macrohistorical relation between European conceptions of sovereignty and their extra-European extrapolation can be seen here operating on the microhistorical level of local racial encounter in the new world.

I take Sweet's story of the Ninigret "kings" and the Narragansett, so familiar in the direction of its historical telos and yet so ambiguous at the level of individual motivation and action, as a reminder not to reach too quickly for the reassurances of the theoretical grasp of symmetries. The abstractions of political theory—what characterizes a sovereign, for example, or what rights inhere in those who work the land—are an essential part of the story Sweet tells, and yet the apparent communication across racial division is fundamentally compromised by the Narragansetts' status as a defeated and diminished power in the region. The way in which theoretical symmetries might both make possible ideological communication across social divisions, and serve as a ground against which the distortion or failure of such communication can be perceived as an emergent figure, is a complex operation my analyses return to time and again. The difficulty is often to know what to do with the symmetries on show. Giorgio Agamben's eloquent *Homo Sacer: Sovereign Power and Bare Life* offers the single most powerful theoretical argument I know for the problems and representations discussed in this book. Building on both Schmitt's theories of sovereign exception and Foucault's analysis of biopower, Agamben argues that "the inclusion of bare life in the political realm constitutes the original—if concealed—nucleus of sovereign power" (6). Bare life is the condition of the *homo sacer* for Agamben; it is a life the significance of which has been reduced to its mere animal mortality. Agamben's analysis is powerfully schematizing, and useful for that reason. In the chapters that follow, I borrow many of his ideas concerning the relation between exemplarity and exception or how to understand the topologies of included exclusions. But Agamben's approach is ultimately too schematic, I think, as when it asserts an absolute symmetry between the figure of the sovereign and the abandoned object that is the *homo sacer*: "At the two extreme limits of the order, the sovereign and *homo sacer* present symmetrical figures and have the same structure and are correlative: the sovereign is the one with respect to whom all men are potentially *homines sacri*, and *homo sacer* is the one with respect to whom all men act as sovereigns" (84).

Agamben is fully aware of how such a notion of the "correlative" relation between sovereign and *homo sacer* conforms to the theory of the state of nature, in which each individual is always both figures *in potentia*. (Locke: "The *execution* of the law of nature is, in that state, put into every man's hands.")[27] Agamben argues, for example, that the "state of nature" and Schmitt's "state of exception" are in fact "two sides of a single topological process" (37). For all his cogency, however, Agamben's theoretical apparatus looks to me more like a mutation of state-of-nature theory than a real critique of it. This is not in itself a damning observation. Tuck's work is convincing in its reminder of how many of our deepest political convictions, especially the fundamental right to self-preservation, a right that for liberal theory remains in force even after one has "contracted" to enter a state, remain most fully explained by such theory. The problem is merely that Agamben takes the Schmittian idea of politics too seriously, insists too rigorously on its distinction from every sort of private, social, or other collective organization. In returning again and again to a kind of face-off between the sovereign and *homo sacer*, Agamben saves the specificity of the political, seizes on it as a kind of frozen tableau, but only at the cost of simplification. Jacques Rancière makes the point well: "The attempt to preserve the political from the contamination of private, social, apolitical life . . . depopulates the political stage by sweeping aside its always ambiguous actors. As a result, the political exception is ultimately incorporated in state power, standing in front of bare life—an opposition that the next step forward turns into a complementarity. The will to preserve the realm of pure politics ultimately makes it vanish in the sheer relation of state power and individual life."[28]

The textual traditions I examine in this book—the remarkably durable tropes of captive kings and last Indians—clearly demonstrate the allure of such stark performances on the political stage. Indeed, it is one of my recurring points that the authors of these fictions, and the characters within those fictions, often think that they have seized some fundamental political truth when it has been presented in such vivid colors by the embodied performance of a racial other. But as I have suggested, and as I elaborate in much more detail through the course of this book, the racial difference of an Oroonoko or an Atufal, a Logan or a Chingachgook, may be most useful when it serves a desire to disavow what audience and actors in fact share. The conviction that one is seeing a complete structure, or observing an entire dynamic, from a position exterior to it, is perhaps the greatest pleasure of theoreticism. It is a pleasure regularly proffered by the fictions examined in this book. It is a pleasure to which Agamben succumbs as well when his certainty that sovereign power and the *homo sacer* are correlative and inextricable leads him to dismiss as the corrupted value of "bare life" the non-transcendent animal existence that we all truly share.[29] Despite my conviction that abstract analysis has much to tell us about how literature thinks through the materials of history, I have tried to maintain respect for all the "ambiguous actors" still on the stage, even after their entanglement in deep theoretical logics has been brought to light.

ONE

On Lingering and Being Last: Aphra Behn and the Deterritorialized Sovereign

By April 1677, Nathaniel Bacon had been dead for half a year, and many of his fellow rebels had been hanged or had their holdings confiscated. The king's commissioners were in Virginia to try to make sense of things and put the profitable colony back on track. Charles II was irritated at Governor Sir William Berkeley's savage reprisals, and his commissioners were there, in part, to recall Berkeley to England. When they visited Green Spring House, the governor's mansion, to take their leave, they found themselves unwitting players in a bizarre little spectacle. When the commissioners made their farewells, the governor's wife, Lady Frances Berkeley, "pressed them to ride, instead of walking down to the river where their barge was moored. As the commissioners left the house, they saw an African come forward and 'boldly' replace the postillion, taking the latter's place astride one of the horses. The commissioners declined to ride in the coach, but nonetheless it trundled behind them down to the James. Later they learned that the new postillion was one of the colony's hangmen."[1]

What are we to make of this strange and sinister scene? I will shortly be using it to launch an argument about the volatile relations between race and sovereignty in the new world, with particular reference to Aphra Behn and her late works, one of them a treatment of Bacon's Rebellion. But for now I want this unnamed African postillion to take center stage on his own. A *postillion*, the *OED* tells us, is a kind of mounted guide for a coach, specifically "one who rides the near horse when one pair only is used and there is no driver in the box." Postillion is etymologically linked to the *post*: postillions are sometimes post-boys, and in that sense, they become, figuratively, messengers, forerunners, even harbingers, as in the citation from Sydney's *Arcadia* provided by the *OED* ("But when he strake . . . his arm seemed still a postillion of death").[2] The African hangman riding behind the commissioners, beside a coach with no driver and no passengers, might well have seemed an eerie harbinger and "postillion of death." The postillion/hangman concentrates with figurative intensity much of what will preoccupy me in the rest of this book. In the new world, I will be arguing, there is a formal sovereignty that is in some sense always an empty formality—call it a coach with no drivers or passengers—unless and until it is supplemented or accompanied by a different sovereign figure—a racialized figure, who is spatially and temporally dislocated, off to the side, both trailing behind and running ahead, *foreshadowing*, a figure who embodies a volatile commingling of helplessness and power, sovereignty and servitude, autonomy and slavery. Let the image of this postillion who is a hangman linger in your mind: he is cousin to an array of characters, African and Indian, we will encounter in this book, from Aphra Behn's "royal slave," Oroonoko, to the "black pagod" Melville encounters on the docks of Liverpool.

There is another, more immediate, reason to begin this chapter on Aphra Behn with this hovering hangman. For we might say that Behn's career itself unfolded in the shadow of the executioner—Charles I's executioner. Born in 1640, Behn came of age after the execution of the king, and her final works—she died in 1689—are agitated by the uncertainties surrounding James's precarious position during the Exclusion Crisis and the years leading to the Glorious Revolution. Behn was fascinated throughout her career with the figure of sovereignty, but her notorious "royalism," her commitment to the absolutist ideology of the Stuart court, is everywhere accompanied by the implicit acknowledgement, forced on her by history, that such values and prerogatives are neither natural nor eternal, but have been violently abrogated, and may soon be again. A kind of double vision thus characterizes Behn's investigations of the figure of sovereignty, especially in her late works: the intensity of her image of a "right order" of things is more than matched by the ingenuity she exercises in describing that order's ruination. Sometimes the failure of sovereignty is purely comic, as in the "Memoirs of the Court of the King of Bantam" (1698), with its gleeful cuckolding of the "Wou'dbe King." *The Fair Jilt* (1688), on the other hand, is more troubled. Prince Tarquin, "the last of the race of the Roman kings," plays a supporting role in this tale to the monstrous Miranda. But it is the grotesque pageantry of Tarquin's failed execution that occupies the close of the tale and allows for the dissonant reversal of fortune for the murderous couple.[3] In Behn's two "new world" productions, *Oroonoko* (1688) and *The Widow Ranter* (1689), the geopolitical displacement and its introduction of racial difference brings the tensions in her vision to a breaking point. These texts are tonally hybrid and notoriously ambiguous about their values. In Virginia and in Surinam something new is revealed to Behn's eyes: sovereign authority exists as empty form only—both stories have absent governors—and the disarticulation of power and embodiment is complete. A kind of spatiotemporal distortion has gripped the entire legitimating apparatus. Janet Todd tellingly describes Behn's frame of mind at the time of her American works as a kind of spatial disorientation: "With the state shuddering [in 1688], she saw that there was really no inside in England, no safe place and she felt in London a similar sense of duplicity and instability to that experienced years ago in Surinam. Everywhere was 'America.'"[4]

What would it mean for everywhere to be "America"? If there is no "inside in England," it must be because it has been evacuated, exposed, emptied out as something called "America," as if the latter were the lining of a glove that had been turned inside out. I am playing with the topological weirdness of Todd's imagery because I want to stress that the relation between England and America in Behn's imagination is more complex than a metaphor like center and periphery can capture. Todd's image suggests rather that America represents an ideological intensification vis-à-vis England, a "deterritorialization" of England in the form of, say, Virginia. I use "deterritorialization," with the gloss provided by Deleuze and Guattari in mind, as signifying "the operation of a line of flight," the "movement by which 'one' leaves the territory," or, more abstractly and less colorfully, the process by which codes, or territorializations, become loosened, unmoored, uprooted, such that elements and energies escape and become transformed.[5] Deterritorialization is always a process of fragmentation, then, but it is also always the prelude to new reterritorializations, often enough the intensification of certain elements and codes in its new configuration. We can take the terms of the gloss quite directly: the "movement by which 'one' leaves the territory" means that it is the "one" itself—the "one" as a basal unit, always edged by its quotation marks, always announcing its factitious, citational aspect—that is at stake in the de- and reterritorializations made manifest in Virginia. I will call this "one" the "sovereign individual," a shorthand phrase meant less to designate an identity than index the dynamic, essentially unstable relation between the individuality of the sovereign—a deterritorializing force—and the sovereignty of the individual, which always tends toward reterritorialization. Virginia might therefore represent both a deterritorialization of royalist England *and* its more intense, more volatile version. We might adapt a Lacanian motto and say that "Virginia is in England more than England itself."

Consider again the scene with which we began. Dubbing the little drama "The Scandalous Postillion," historian Susan Westbury argues that it reveals a profound cultural continuity across the Atlantic: "Virginians like other English people" had a keen sense of the "capacity of their countrymen and women to understand public affairs as drama" (69). The Virginia colony was, indeed, a well-known royalist stronghold throughout the century. Governor Berkeley had fought alongside the king before his appointment to Virginia, and when news of Charles I's execution reached him, Berkeley publicly proclaimed allegiance to Charles II. One crucial indication of this shared royalism, argues Westbury, was the self-conscious mixture of theater and politics on display in "The Scandalous Postillion."[6] Berkeley himself had achieved some notoriety years before for his play *The Lost Lady* (1637), and the recent rebellion had been notable for overt and self-conscious histrionics on the part of both the governor and his well-born antagonist, Nathaniel Bacon. A central venue for such theater was, of course, "the spectacle of the scaffold."[7] As the king's representative in Virginia, Berkeley wielded the royal prerogative to order executions. And he did so: thirteen rebels were hanged, three of them on the grounds of the governor's mansion. Charles II was irritated at Berkeley's excessive savagery in meting out punishment to the rebels: he is reported to have complained,

"That old fool has hang'd more men in that naked Country, than he had done for the Murther of his Father!"[8] If the spectacle of judicial punishment and execution is a special kind of political theater, in other words, Charles was in effect expressing disapproval of Berkeley's over-the-top staging.

But Westbury argues convincingly that it was not the governor, but Lady Frances Berkeley who stage-managed the scene at the mansion. It was she who had urged the coach so insistently on the governors, and it was she "who could not resist watching the denouement from her window" (80). For Westbury, as for Kathleen M. Brown, Lady Frances's behavior throughout the rebellion and its aftermath epitomizes the heightened visibility and power of women, on both sides of the conflict. Lady Frances had traveled to England to lobby on behalf of her husband, while on the other side of the conflict women such as Sarah Grendon had proved effective propagandists for the Baconians.[9] Women were unusually visible in the public sphere, in other words, both as actors and as props, even at one point serving as a human shield for the rebel forces: in their report to the king, the commissioners describe how having "planted his great Guns, [Bacon] takes the wives and female Relations of such Gentlemen as were in the Governor's Service against him (whome hee had caused to be brought to the workes) and Places them in the Face of his Enemy, as Bulwarks for their Battery."[10] Perhaps this is another way of remarking on the shared culture of theatricalized politics on both sides of the Atlantic: if with the reopening of the theaters in the Restoration, women could now be both playwrights and actresses, in Virginia they might find themselves, like Lady Berkeley, transforming their home into a theater from which to view their own productions. On the other hand, they might find themselves transported onto a different stage, to serve as a "white-aproned" bulwark.[11] It seems very unlikely that Behn would have heard about this little spectacle by the James River, but it's a shame, because Lady Frances seems like a close cousin to Behn's women impresarios, whether we think of Miranda in *The Fair Jilt* stage-managing her own false rape, Behn's narrating self participating in odd dumb shows with Oroonoko, or, perhaps closest of all, the Widow Ranter herself, effecting the comic resolution in that play with her spirited breeches role. Lady Frances has more than a little of the Widow Ranter in her, having outlived two governor husbands and married a third.[12]

"The Scandalous Postillion," then, like Bacon's Rebellion itself, both typifies and intensifies royalist political theater. More specifically, it mobilizes for its own ironizing ends a volatile interdependence between servitude and power, between domestic and public arenas. The commissioners were apparently particularly alarmed by the idea that the African postillion was a house servant at the governor's mansion. They felt it necessary to assume that the man had been "sent for specially to humiliate them" (79), despite the fact that they had themselves seen the man emerge from the mansion, and that they later wrote that this postillion was "the same hangman 'that was every day at Green Spring, and put the Halters about the Prisoners necks in Court, when they were to make in that posture their submission for their Crimes at the Barr of Justice'" (79). The commissioners were, in other words, particularly intent on drawing a line between the governor's private home and affairs, and his public role, for which the hangman stands as a symbol. But the drama concocted by Lady Berkeley was meant precisely to use the blurriness of that line to aggressive ends. To have a hangman in the role of a house servant, to demonstrate so perversely the labile relation between servant and sovereign, was to draw attention to Berkeley's own position, at once the king's representative in Virginia, invested with the prerogatives of royal power, and his servant, subject to recall at any moment. In a way, Berkeley's ambiguous position is performed in blackface in this little scene with his African surrogate. Just as Berkeley is at once servant and sovereign, so the postillion conflates submission and sovereign vengeance. "The Scandalous Postillion" suggests that the colony is a place where you are likely to find harbored within the sovereign power a position of servitude, and where the servant and the slave can find themselves symbolizing the sovereign. In Aphra Behn's late works, to which I now turn, the ironic, and agonistic, energies so intensely on display in "The Scandalous Postillion" find a fuller and more elaborated form. Especially in *Oroonoko* and *The Widow Ranter*, her American works, sovereignty becomes a value somehow both exacerbated and evacuated, subject at once to racialized embodiment and to a dissemination among competitive individuals. But we will depart for America via Antwerp, where Behn stages a strange fantasy about sovereignty's power to linger.

A Small Matter of Flesh

The Fair Jilt, Behn tells us, was based on "eye-witness" (74, 77) experience in Antwerp, when she served as a spy for the king there. This autobiographical presentation is not all it shares with the much more familiar *Oroonoko*.

The Fair Jilt, like *Oroonoko*, describes the fate of a "last" sovereign—in this case one Tarquin, "who owned himself, and was received, as the last of the Roman kings" (74). Also like *Oroonoko*, at the center of the story there is a powerful and imaginative woman who both loves and admires the royal personage, but who nevertheless betrays and sacrifices him. Unlike the grisly ending of *Oroonoko*, however, here the prince survives his execution and is able to provide asylum for his murderous (though now putatively penitent) wife. At a deeper level, both texts also evince a moral agnosticism that produces dissonance between theme and tone, form and rhetoric. Thus, in *Oroonoko*, what is sometimes called Behn's "realism" disappoints any expectations of an idealized, "tragic" death: as George Starr has it, "Behn treats [Oroonoko's] execution as a kind of legal murder without aggrandizing it as a martyrdom."[13] In *The Fair Jilt*, any "comic" satisfaction we might expect from our lovers surviving their trials to live happily ever after is more than undercut by the "evident zest" (Starr 368) with which Behn retails the amoral machinations of Miranda. In both texts, in other words, the extremity of the sovereign's position—his physical extremity as he undergoes torture and execution, but also his symbolic extremity as a last, and lingering, sovereign—produces an intense pressure placed on form itself, to the point that the conventions of tragic or comic resolution, with their appropriate tonal modulations, are not so much ignored as rendered simultaneously virulent and ineffectual: it is not just sovereignty, in other words, but form itself that is deterritorialized.

Miranda, the fair jilt of the story's title, is well-to-do and beautiful, but her lust for "quality" (80) and the prerogatives it bestows leads her to sexual and criminal depredations that send three different men to prison, one falsely accused of attempting to rape her, and the other two for attempting to murder her sister at her behest. She is presented as a shameless actor by Behn: at one point Miranda is so concerned to "put on a world of sorrow" that she "refused to eat or sleep or see the light" (108), about which Behn remarks dryly that "here she almost overacted" (108). Miranda's means and her ends are, however, in agreement, because her life of pure show is entirely directed toward securing the equally formal and insubstantial attributes of "quality." She was "not so passionately in love with Tarquin as she was with the prince," we are told, "not so fond of the man as his titles and of glory" (108). Rank and title and glory all exist, in this logic, in a purely theatricalized realm, as distinct from real men and women as stage characters are from the actors who play them.

Behn suggests, in other words, that there is a clean separation between actors and roles, between theater and life, but she also doubts it. In fact, the tale seems less interested in enforcing its anti-theatrical lessons than in dramatizing the decisive role played by "the people" in the fate of the actors who embody "quality."[14] This dynamic is brought home most forcefully in the two separate "spectacles of the scaffold" Behn provides. In the first, Van Brune, Miranda's page, is hanged for his attempted murder of Miranda's sister Alcidiana:

> The following Friday was the day of execution, and one need not tell of the abundance of people who were flocked together in the market place. All the windows were taken down and filled with spectators, and the tops of houses, when, at the hour appointed, the fatal beauty appeared. She was dressed in a black velvet gown, with a rich row of diamonds all down the fore part of the breast, and a great knot of diamonds at the peak behind, and a petticoat of flowered gold, very rich and laced, with all things else suitable. (106)

Behn clearly emphasizes the theatricality of the scene. One has the sense here that Miranda's ostentation is a cagey attempt to undercut, or outshine, the other spectacle she is forced to perform, namely "to stand under the gibbet with a rope about her neck, the other end of which was to be fastened to the gibbet where the page was hanging and to have an inscription in large characters upon her back and breast of the cause why" (106). How better to distract from an "inscription" on the breast than by having it compete with a "rich row of diamonds"? But both diamonds and inscription, in the final analysis, mark Miranda as a pure semblance, a creature of "constant outer display" (Pearson 195); that is, both the inscription and the diamonds suggest that Miranda's position in a social order is what is most essential about her. Thus, while Miranda's merely symbolic hanging seemed to many a sentence "too favourable for so ill a woman," others were inclined to understand the coincidence of opulence and degradation as representing a punishment "infinitely more severe than the death itself" (106).

How can there be a punishment "infinitely more severe" than death? It is not such an uncommon idea, after all, and it represents an aggrandizement of the symbolic realm to the point that it is beyond measure altogether. A body is countable, and its death of finite severity: a symbolic death is not so circumscribed, and thus opens up the social order to dimensions understood to be immortal or infinite. In Van Brune's real and Miranda's symbolic execution, this ideological division is distributed between the players and along lines of gender and class. Van Brune is susceptible of being the countable body, by virtue of being male and a mere page, while Miranda can represent a symbolic—theatrical—infinity.

In *The Fair Jilt*'s other scene of execution, the drama of the two bodies plays out differently. Tarquin, the last of the line of Roman kings, survives his own execution, not just in the way a "kingly" body might do according to two-bodies theory, but as a mortal man.[15] What is striking about Tarquin's execution is that he totalizes "the people" twice over, first when he is killed and then when he survives. After the "headsman gave him his last stroke, and the prince fell on the scaffold," the "people, with one common voice, as if it had been but one entire one, prayed for his soul, and murmurs of sighs were heard from the whole multitude, who scrambled for some bloody sawdust to keep for his memory" (116). Here we have the populace brought together by the royal martyrdom: it is as though the removal of his head leads to the distribution of his symbolic oneness throughout the collective, a distribution symbolized by handfuls of bloody sawdust. But in fact Tarquin has not been killed: "The headsman, going to take up the head, as the manner is, to show to the people, he found he had not struck it off, and that the body stirred" (116). The headsman tries a second time with an "engine they always carry with 'em to force those who may be refractory, thinking . . . to have twisted the head from the shoulders, conceiving it to hang but by a small matter of flesh" (116). This "small matter of flesh" is precisely what secures the passage between Tarquin's ability to totalize the people symbolically (that is, after his bodily death) and his ability to actually embody "one entire one." Struggling "between life and death" (117), Tarquin has "found himself yet alive, or rather . . . past thinking, but [with] some sense of feeling left" (116). Falling backward off the scaffold, Tarquin lands "upon the heads and shoulders of the people," who "with one accord, as if the whole crowd had been but one body and had but one motion . . . bore the prince on their heads about a hundred yards from the scaffold" (117). This scene begins to look like Behn's troping of the famous frontispiece to the Head edition of *Leviathan*—a "crowd [of] but one body"—with the sovereign physically surmounting it. But this "head" is not exactly a thinking head; it is rather in a zone of "feeling" between life and death. Tarquin's "head" is somehow both severed and not severed, linked merely by a "small matter of flesh," and his sovereignty is thus neither fully embodied nor sufficiently abstract. Tarquin is the sovereign individual as survivor, lingering in a zone characterized by "flesh" and feeling, separated from both the "thinking" head and the "one body" with "one motion" by which he is carried away.

In *Leviathan*, the sovereign's absolute authority cannot force an individual, no matter how guilty, to accept the legitimacy of his own execution. It is the condemned man's immitigable right to resist being put to death. This may seem a surprising limitation on the sovereign authority, but we can surmise that without it Hobbes saw no way to maintain the universality of his system's fundamental premise—that the one essential right is the right to self-preservation. It's not exactly correct, however, to say that Tarquin resists his execution. Rather, he *is* executed, but imperfectly, after which point resistance belongs to the people, who "now had a right to protect him and would do so" (117). Tarquin represents a deterritorialized version of the sovereign individual, I would say: he embodies neither the individuality of the sovereign (he who must resist his execution) nor the sovereignty of the individual (he who must not fail to put to death in the name of absolute right and legitimacy), but rather a narrow passage between the two, the hinge of their union and their instability, here called a "small matter of flesh."

What is Behn's political point in *The Fair Jilt*? The figure named Tarquino, whose abortive execution in Antwerp was recorded by the *London Gazette* in 1666, and who "was generally regarded as an impostor,"[16] must have seemed to Behn too good an opportunity to pass up when she returns to it more than twenty years later. By that point, after the Exclusion Crisis, the story of Tarquin, the rape of Lucretia, and Tarquin's overthrow by Lucius Junius Brutus, who installs the first Roman republic, had become a highly overdetermined Whiggish allegory in the political theater. Nathaniel Lee's *Lucius Junius Brutus* (1680), for example, was "suppressed for its republican content by order of the Lord Chamberlain after at most six performances."[17] By having Tarquin survive to live happily ever after with his self-styled Lucretia—Miranda was "resolved to be the Lucretia that this young Tarquin should ravish" (98)—Behn is taking a poke at the Whiggish triumphalism of the story of Tarquin's overthrow. Jacqueline Pearson observes that Behn was adept at sending signals "designed to gratify Tory readers without decisively alienating others," but *The Fair Jilt* does not seem a clear-cut case of Tory propaganda either, because "a prince with a debatable title, honourable but easily manipulated by the woman he loves, a failed murderer, victim of an abortive execution, is an uneasy model of the Stuart monarchy" (190). What, then, is Behn's point? I would suggest that, as with the late "American" works to which I am about to turn, Behn is trying to capture in *The Fair Jilt* a political condition that exceeds the opposition between Whig and Tory. And one register of that condition is a kind of theatrical self-presentation about which Behn remains agnostic:

> He was all the discourse of the town; some laughing at his title, others reverencing it; some cried that he was an impostor, others that he had made his title as plain as if Tarquin had reigned but a year ago. Some made friendships with him, others would have nothing to say to him, but all wondered where this revenue was that supported this grandeur, and believed, though he could make his descent from the Roman kings very well out, that he could not lay so good a claim to the Roman land. Thus everybody meddled with what they had nothing to do, and, as in other places, thought themselves on the surer side if, in these doubtful cases, they imagined the worst. (98)

It is rather remarkable that Tarquin can "make his descent from the Roman kings very well out," given that his namesake Tarquin was (legendarily) deposed in the sixth century BCE. But perhaps Behn asks us to take him as a kind of modern stateless sovereign, equipped with a title, substantial "revenue," but no "claim to . . . land." In that sense, too, Tarquin is deterritorialized, a lingering remnant, neither living nor dead, neither legitimate nor clearly illegitimate, neither purely body nor clearly abstractable. His adventures in Antwerp seem to presage the fate of the sovereign individual in the modern age, especially as that age unfolds itself in the new world: lots of revenue supporting grandeur, indexing title and right, but no territorial fixity to anchor it. Behn's "comic" conclusion, letting Tarquin survive his execution so that he can care for the devious Miranda, might be seen as either a last wishful embrace of a world in which "quality" survives, or as a sour and ironic send-up of such a dream. Whatever the case, the tonal ambiguities affecting her exploration of the deterritorialized sovereign individual are only exacerbated once she begins to set her explorations in the new world.

The Good Subject in Virginia

There is a tendency to minimize the difference Virginia or Surinam makes in Behn's late, "American" works, to insist that their explorations of tragedy, race, and the dilemmas of sovereign authority are ultimately reducible to reflections on contemporary conditions in England. In its extreme form, happily no longer credible, this bracketing of America took the form of dismissing Behn's claims to having been in Surinam at all—it all becomes fantasy.[18] But less extreme versions of this reduction are still in force. Elliot Visconsi concludes, for example, that Behn's "American texts, which are so critically concerned with forms of government, are not primarily warnings against colonial dissolution, miscegenation, or imperialism," but rather "represent Behn's more local warnings tuned to a fever pitch."[19] But the fever itself, I would argue, is proof of the irreducibility of the American encounter, a kind of imaginative and figural intensification or delirium that is neither English nor American, but rather the distorting result of their interaction. If *The Widow Ranter*, in the words of Todd and Derek Hughes, "reflects and fragments royalist values," we need to understand how these two verbs work together.[20]

Let us ask first about the role of race in *The Widow Ranter*. At first glance race seems to be a mere theatrical prop in a way that it is not in *Oroonoko*, for example. The real Bacon's Rebellion, on the other hand, turned largely on the question of race war, whether it presently existed (as one clearly did in contemporary New England), or whether one *should* exist. Nathaniel Bacon's standing with his followers lay in his willingness to lead reprisals against the Indians without the governor's approval. As the king's commissioners explained in their report, Berkeley's frontier defenses had been a miserable failure: he favored the building of forts, for which the people were taxed heavily, and which were easily attacked or simply circled around by Indians making incursions. This failure had led to a demand for racist simplification, a redrawing of the friend/enemy distinction: their desperation "made the people expostulate and say how shall we know our enemyes from our Friends, are not the Indians all of a colour. . . . Nor would the people understand any distinction of Friendly Indians and Indian Enemyes, for at that tyme it was impossible to distinguish one nation from another, they being deformed with Paint of many colors. . . . Soe the common cry of the

Vulgar was, away with these Forts, away with these distinctions, wee will have warr with all Indians."[21] And so it was. Bacon's men did, in fact, wage "warr with all the Indians," even attacking the Pamunkey Indians, long-standing allies of the Virginia colony, whose queen, Cockacoeske, seems to be the model for Semernia in *The Widow Ranter*.

But Behn's Bacon does not want to kill the Pamunkey Queen (along with all the other Indians): he wants to win her away from Cavarnio, the young king of the Pamunkey. At first glance this love plot looks like the convention according to which imperial aggrandizement is both effected and mystified through dynastic intermarriage, though in the new world setting the European male is *founding* a dynasty rather than merely extending it—think of Cortes and Cydaria in Dryden's *The Indian Emperor* (1667). Behn may also have the John Rolfe-Pocahontas union in mind. Whatever the case, Bacon must have seemed to Behn to have arrived from central casting, just the type of adventurer-hero to secure legitimacy for conquest through winning a native queen's hand. "Strange Newes from Virginia" (1677), a pamphlet Behn could well have seen, emphasizes Bacon's "Birth and Acquisitions," and while it deplores his role as "Molestor of the quiet" in Virginia, it also argues against disregarding his "former honours and dignities."[22]

The royal commissioners are less overtly ambivalent about Bacon himself, though their report is reasonably sympathetic to the discontent of the rebelling faction. They describe Bacon as "a person whose erratique fortune had carryed and shewne him many Forraigne Parts, and of no obscure Family": "Hee was said to be about four or five and thirty yeares of age, indifferent tall but slender, blackhair'd and of an ominous, pensive, melancholly Aspect, of a pestilent and prevalent Logical discourse tending to atheisme in most companyes, not given to much talke, or to make suddain replyes, of a most imperious and dangerous hidden Pride of heart, despising the wisest of his neighbors for their Ignorance, and very ambitious and arrogant. But all these things lay hidd in him till after hee was a councillor" (110). The "melancholly Aspect" of Bacon makes him seem a version of the baroque stage prince, that "paradigm of the melancholy man."[23] But this "black-hair'd" prince does not merely brood, steeped in his black bile; on the contrary, he is on the go. The commissioners offer here a succinct sketch of what I have been calling the deterritorialized sovereign individual: an "imperious . . . Pride of heart," a spirit both "ambitious and arrogant," lies dangerously "hidd" in this character until a change of conditions releases his "pestilential" energies. These conditions are the movement out to "Forraigne parts," or up into the ranks of the councilors (or perhaps, younger sons like Bacon being a dime a dozen in the colony, merely into landholding status). Bacon's "erratique fortune," in other words, is a typical description of "the movement by which 'one' leaves the territory."

Our question, however, is whether Behn's transformation of Bacon from a killer of Indians into a lover of one indicates her ignorance of, or indifference to, racial realities in the colony. I don't think so. Behn's investigation of Bacon's "imperious" individualism reveals his love making and his war making to be complementary rather than opposed undertakings. Early in the play, the question of Bacon's motives in fomenting with the Indians comes up. One of the craven buffoons, Whimsey, opines that "under pretence of killing all the Indians [Bacon] means to Murder us, Ly with our Wives, and hang up our little Children, and make himself Lord and King" (I.ii.7–9). But "Lord and King" of what or whom? After he kills all the Indians as well as the whites and their "little children," over whom will he rule? The more sensible councilor, Downright, also sees pretense in Bacon's aggressive posture toward the Indians: "'Tis most certain that Bacon did not demand a Commission out of a design of serving us, but to satisfy his Ambition and his Love, it being no secret that he passionately Admires the Indian Queen, and under the pretext of a War, intends to kill the King her Husband, Establish himself in her heart, and on all occasions make himself a more formidable Enemy, than the Indians are" (I.ii.21–27). In both scenarios, and as the play bears out, Bacon's personal ambition wreaks havoc on the friend/enemy distinction, pushes it to its limit. The government faction "fear[s] his siding with the Indians" (III.ii.45–46), and when Bacon finally has Cavarnio in his grasp, his insistence on treating the king according to the protocols of honor—he wants to resort to dueling—exasperates his lieutenants: "'Sdeath, his Romantick humour will undo us" (IV.ii.47). The colony in general, we might conclude, is a scene in which friend and enemy become indistinguishable: thus the internecine strife between the colonists is echoed in the scene in which the Indians, retreating from Bacon's group, are pursued by their own King Cavarnio, "who shoots them as they fly" (IV.ii). Bacon's amorous "ambition" does not escape this generalized dissolution of distinctions. Rather, having first provoked it, it then becomes engulfed in it: when a fleeing Semernia appears "dress'd like an Indian Man" (V.iii), Bacon cuts her down because she looks like the enemy.

But Behn's deepest point, I take it, is that for a deterritorialized sovereign like Bacon, *everyone* looks like the enemy. If war is a pretext for love, the reverse is necessarily also true: the "conquest" of Semernia is a metaphor for an act of dominion so total in its self-aggrandizing force that it leads ultimately to a radical isolation. Bacon becomes a sort of universal antagonist, "on all occasions . . . a more formidable Enemy, than the Indians are." Bacon's prowess as a conquistador is nowhere doubted, least of all by himself: Friendly claims that he has heard Bacon asking himself, "Why cannot I conquer the Universe as well as Alexander? Or like another Romulus form a new Rome and make my self Ador'd"? (I.i.129–31). Behn does not dispute the principle that "great Souls are born in common men, as well as Princes" (I.i.132–33). After his death, Dareing reiterates this judgment but also makes a crucial qualification: "See where the General lyes—that great Soul'd Man, no private Body e're contained a Nobler, and he that cou'd have conquer'd all America, finds here only his scanty length of Earth" (V.iv.37–40). Nobility of soul is, indeed, harbored within "private" bodies, but if that cannot be wedded to another "public" dimension, an abstracted authorized body, then the essence of sovereign power cannot be exercised. Instead of "all America" becoming Bacon's corporeal extension, his private body becomes absorbed in it.

It is this disjunction between the "private Body" and the abstracted body of authority that constitutes the general political crisis explored in the play. As several commentators have noted, Behn's decision to excise Governor Berkeley from her depiction of the rebellion, having the colony awaiting an absent governor (as in *Oroonoko*), serves to foreground the instability of a situation in which there is no undisputed representative of authority to suture private bodies to the abstract concept of the law. According to Todd and Hughes, "Behn is here addressing one of the most crucial political questions of the seventeenth century: should the power of law be absolute, or does it need to be tempered by the prerogative of a monarch not subject to it? For the opponents of James II, the king was subject to legal compulsion; for his followers, it was dangerous to bind the king in this way since the royal prerogative of mercy could mitigate the mechanical rigour of a usually corrupt law" (93–94). Virginia, in Behn's imagination, is a place in which private bodies and a "mechanical" and senseless legality both run amok. The low comedy of the play depends on the perverse conflation of these two unregulated domains in the behavior—lewd, drunken, and cowardly—of the "Justices of the Peace" Timerous, Whimsey, and Whiff. It is grotesque Whimsey who announces the logic of a law ungrounded by a sovereign's transcendence to it: "Though [Bacon] fought like Alexander and preserv'd the whole world from perdition, yet if he did it against Law, 'tis Lawful to hang him. . . . These things are not to be suffer'd in a Civil Government by Law Establish'd" (I.ii.120). The authority of the sovereign, as we know, is based on the same right to self-preservation as that of the individual. Alexander, preserving the "whole world from perdition," should presumably present the limit case to law's power to curtail sovereign authority, and that he does not for Whimsey is a sure sign of his having become unhinged. Bacon defends his own behavior on the same principle: "Is it unlawfull to defend my self against a Thief that breaks into my doors?" (II.iv.94–95). But Bacon does not understand the assertion of this right to self-preservation—the higher authorities having failed to provide it—as anything other than loyalty: "The height of my Ambition is to be an honest Subject" (II.iv.109–10). In this world, however, a world neither wholly lawless nor wholly dishonorable, but one in which the values both of law and of honor find themselves in a kind of drifting and fevered condition, the *Good Subject* is only the name of a ship in the James River, upon which rebels intent on setting fire to Jamestown have become too drunk to prosecute their plans (III.ii.81–83).

The Fair Jilt had managed to imagine a sovereign surviving his own execution (as well as his historical surpassing), and who is thereby able to provide protection for his beloved Miranda. Miranda's amoral and theatrical manipulation of a gendered patronage system is, in that sense, rewarded. Something similar happens in *The Widow Ranter*. If there is a "private Body" who exemplifies the vulgarity of new world competitive individualism, it would seem to be the Widow. And yet despite Behn's evident scorn for such a vulgar world, the Widow, too, is rewarded. Semernia is killed for having dressed as a man, but Ranter's cross-dressing does not announce in the same way the breakdown of the crucial symbolic distinctions. On the contrary, Ranter's appearance in breeches, playing at battle and dueling, fools no one and is all the more charming for that fact. Ranter's feminine appeal to Dareing is not obscured, but rather enhanced by her breeches: "Nay, prithee, take me in the humour, while thy breeches are on—for I never lik'd thee half so well in Petticoats" (IV.iii.81–82). What is in play here is the complex interplay and identification between prostitution and acting that Catherine Gallagher has so compellingly analyzed in Behn's dramatic works. Ranter is, we can see, a figure for Behn, a character who stages herself as something she is not, and who thereby both reveals herself more lewdly, as breeches do compared to petticoats, and keeps herself in reserve as different from her self-presentation: as Gallagher writes, "The mask that hides the face"—or the breeches the calves—"signals the availability of the body but also implies the impenetrability of the controlling mind."[24] Just as in *The Fair Jilt*, then, the fate of the female character is tied in essential ways to the success of a kind of theatricality. But in *The Widow Ranter* it is only the *acknowledgement* of a role for fiction and impersonation in the sociosexual order that allows the violable body and the impenetrable mind to appear together, to come as a single package. In the more overtly political register, theater is what allows for the "private body" and the disembodiment of sovereign authority to be sutured to one another. Bacon and Semernia take their theater too seriously, as it were: the two "heroic" characters represent an archaic mode of playacting that, because the social-theatrical order of a stable sovereign state can no longer underwrite it, is doomed to misprision and failure. Ranter and Dareing, on the other hand, seem able to recreate on a more intimate level what the rest of the play exposes as missing at the level of society itself: a consensus about how the sovereign's theatrical self-presentation is both transparent—it is clear enough that he is neither a mere "private body" nor a purely abstract body of the state—and rendered more powerful and desirable for that very transparency.[25]

We have circled back to where we began, with the issue of the status of "political theater" across the Atlantic. It could be said that Lady Berkeley, with her little play "The Scandalous Postillion," rivals Aphra Behn as first female playwright of the new world. Berkeley is arguably as sophisticated as Behn in her grasp of the key theatrical paradoxes of power in the new world, even if her play lacks the nuance and verbal wit of Behn's. But "The Scandalous Postillion" is also neither tragic, nor comic, nor even, like *The Widow Ranter*, tragicomic. It is just sinister, in a way that even Behn shies away from. In both *The Widow Ranter* and *The Fair Jilt*, we find Behn whistling in the dark, as it were: in both texts, the problems of a deterritorialized sovereignty are inventively explored, a sovereignty more dead than alive, historically out of date, lingering. But with the fate of her female characters, both of whom are morally ambiguous, she settles on resolutions that leave a place for satisfactory regulations of power and care, sovereignty and protection. All the same, the tonal ambiguity of both texts suggest that Behn's "comic" conclusions are finally inadequate. It is only in her influential, breathless novella *Oroonoko* that these issues reach both their greatest analytic sharpness and their most agonized affective pitch, and it is this text that most powerfully anticipates the contradictory career of race and sovereignty in the new world.

Oroonoko *and the Deterritorialized Sovereign*

Like *The Widow Ranter* and *The Fair Jilt*, *Oroonoko; or The Royal Slave: A True History* (1688) both records the end of a world and imagines it lingering on in a new configuration. Putting it more pointedly, I would say that it is Behn's fidelity to an archaic value system, the very intensity of her elegiac gaze, that allows her to discern what was most definitively modern in the new world. Her vision seems at once blinkered and prescient: perhaps it is this combination that has made Behn, and especially *Oroonoko*, such a magnet for contemporary criticism, as though in our powerful investment in her work and example we are implicitly acknowledging both our fear of being blinkered and our wish to achieve prescience.[26] Her work has the charisma of the originary—"earliest American novel," "first play . . . set in colonial America"—even as its complexities seem to announce a future into which we still have not yet entered.[27] These complexities, I will suggest in what follows, concern the vicissitudes of a deterritorialized sovereignty in a new transatlantic and interracial world. In exploring the paradoxes of the royal slave, the possibility of the superimposition of sovereign power and abjected humanity, Behn's text speaks quite directly to a contemporary condition in which imperial power, racialized violence, and humanitarian intervention share a theater of crisis.

The problem of the relation between sovereign power and the logic and history of humanitarianism discloses itself first as an interpretive dilemma, "the utter lack of critical consensus about whether Behn's book supports or attacks the institution of slavery."[28] Behn's text frankly endorses natural hierarchy and royal prerogative. Oroonoko is a king, perhaps even "the" king: awaiting the arrival of this prodigy, Behn remarks that "if the King himself (God bless him) had come ashore, there could not have been greater expectations by all the whole plantation" (40). The slave name he is given is "Caesar," which is at once ironic and apposite, because " 'tis most evident that [Oroonoko] wanted no part of the personal courage of that Caesar, and acted things as memorable" (40). The African himself endorses a royalist position on the English Civil War, referring to the "deplorable death of our great monarch . . . with all the sense, and abhorrence of the injustice imaginable" (11). Laura Brown has read these details as indicating that the execution of Charles I casts its long shadow over this text as well: "The political endpoint of Behn's narrative is the reenactment of the most traumatic event of the revolution, the execution of Charles I."[29] The pathos of Oroonoko's destruction would ultimately derive from this subtext: "The sense of momentous loss generated on behalf of the 'royal slave' is the product of the hidden figuration in Oroonoko's death of the culminating moment of the English Revolution" (58).

But the pathos, according to Brown, has another source as well. She suggests that it was Behn's very royalism that enabled her to sympathize with Oroonoko *as a slave*, and not just as a king: the forces of "antiabsolutist mercantile imperialism" (59), Behn is argued to have understood, victimize Charles I and Oroonoko alike. The prolonged and grisly scene of Oroonoko's death thus displays "not merely a fascination with . . . brutality . . . but a sympathetic memorialization of those human beings whose sufferings these words recall" (60). It is according to this historical logic that Behn's text, with its openly absolutist sentiments, can also serve as a "crucial early text in the sentimental, anti-slavery tradition that grew steadily throughout the eighteenth century" (42).[30]

There are, however, a number of problems with this view. Behn nowhere really shows much concern for slaves as a class, nor indeed any horror of mercantile imperialism. In fact, she seems rather fascinated with the mechanics of the slave trade, with its talk of "contracts," "bargains," and "lots":

> Those who want slaves make a bargain with a master, or captain of a ship and contract to pay him so much a piece, a matter of twenty pound a head for as many as he agrees to pay for 'em when they shall be delivered on such a plantation. So that when there arrives a ship laden with slaves, they who have so contracted go aboard and receive their number by lot; and perhaps in one lot that may be for ten, there may happen to be three or four men, the rest, women and

children. Or, be there more or less of either sex, you are obliged to be contented with your lot. (9)

Caveat emptor! Behn does draw attention to the ways in which a trade in flesh defined by "lot" renders other ways of organizing people—by sex or by generation—more or less irrelevant. But she does not seem to judge it, and later when she describes the practice of "not putting any two [noble slaves] in one lot . . . not daring to trust 'em together" (37), her tone seems descriptively neutral. Wylie Sypher's succinct judgment of sixty years ago still seems persuasive: "Mrs. Behn is repelled not by slavery, but by the enslaving of a prince."[31]

But perhaps there is a different way to describe the link between Behn's absolutism and her proto-sentimental stance toward Oroonoko's sufferings. George Starr has made the intriguing suggestion that one should view sentimentalism "as a working out of Hobbes's principles from a victim's standpoint," that sentimentalism explores "what it means to be powerless in a society where . . . power is everything," and "turning the other cheek merely doubles the available target area" (362, 370). Hobbes's theory begins with the dialectical relation between power and vulnerability: what defines the equality of all in a state of nature is each person's equally radical exposure to the reversibility of power and victimization. It is, Starr argues, "Behn's insight into this paradoxical linkage" that constitutes "her greatest contribution to the rise of sensibility. She recognizes that apparent strength may be bound up with real weakness, and seeming impotence with genuine power" (363). Behn does make use in places of the discourse of "heroic tragedy" (Brown 57) that had been mobilized to describe Charles I's death. But Starr insists, and I think correctly, that Behn finally "puts greater emphasis on the linkage between heroism and weakness" (363) than on the conventions of heroic romance.

When Oroonoko discovers that his executioners have no intention of whipping him (merely torturing and then drawing and quartering him), he experiences vast relief: "'My friends, am I to die, or to be whipped?,' and they cried, 'Whipped! No, you shall not escape so well.' And then he replied, smiling, 'A blessing on thee'" (72). Dismemberment allows for the display of the stoical contempt for the body requisite for a heroic death: thus the "mangled king" seems directly to call forth Behn's conventional scruple as to whether "the reputation of [her] pen is considerable enough to make his glorious name to survive to all ages" (73). But why, then, does Behn characterize Oroonoko's death, in her preface to Lord Maitland, not as heroic, but as "inglorious"?

> This is a true story of a man gallant enough to merit your protection; and, had he always been so fortunate, he had not made so inglorious an end: the royal slave I had the honour to know in my travels to the other world; and though I had none above me in that country, yet I wanted power to preserve this great man. If there be anything that seems Romantic, I beseech your Lordship to consider these countries do, in all things, so far differ from ours, that they produce unconceivable wonders; at least they appear so to us because new and strange. (5)

If Oroonoko's death can be viewed as "inglorious" despite his obviously heroic fortitude, that anomaly is here made to seem the effect of a world without "protection." I think we need to hear Behn as both anguished and puzzled at a situation in which "though I had none above me in that country, yet I wanted power to preserve this great man." This, perhaps, is the absolutist's nightmare: a world in which having equal stature and authority with all others means not an accession to power, but power's dispersal and diminishment. Having "none above" changes the very essence of power: it becomes destructive, and no longer preservative. The co-implication of power and victimization that characterizes the Hobbesian state of nature is not evaded in "that country"; on the contrary, it is experienced all the more directly in its disorienting instability.

This invocation of the power to preserve and protect is, I would argue, the essence of Behn's royalist project in Surinam, and it is precisely the power that fails her. Parham, the plantation at which her party gathers, is an asylum for Oroonoko. Trefry argues that it is "exempt" from the acting governor's authority:

> Trefry then thought it time to use his authority, and told Byam his command did not extend to his Lord's plantation, and that Parham was as much exempt from the law as Whitehall, and that they ought no more to touch the servants of the lord (who there represented the King's person) than they could those about the King himself, and that Parham was a sanctuary, and though his lord were absent in person, his power was still in being there, which he had entrusted with him, as far as the dominions of his particular plantations reached, and all that belonged to it—the rest of the country, as Byam was lieutenant to his Lord, he might exercise his tyranny upon. (66)

The complexities of this passage are symptomatic of a world in which there "are none above." Byam is the acting governor on behalf of the absent Willoughby, the king's representative. Trefry is Willoughby's overseer on the latter's personal plantation, Parham Hill. The duplication of authorities, the disputes as to whether personal possessions retain the exemptions and protections of the Crown's public properties, the semi-legal wrangling about whether, though the "lord were absent in person, his power was still in being there"—all these uncertainties characterize a world struggling to adapt absolutist concepts of the relation between property and authority to a context in which sovereignty is, quite obviously, divided. This world in crisis, in which power is present, absent, and (merely) represented all at once, is recognizably the same world that Behn explored in *The Widow Ranter*. It is also the theater of crisis that Lady Berkeley put to ironic use in her little spectacle of "The Scandalous Postillion."

There are indications that the party of Trefry, to which Behn belongs, has put itself in special peril through its decision to exert its authority to protect rather than punish:

> When the news was brought on Monday morning that Caesar had betaken himself to the woods and carried with him all the Negroes, we were possessed with extreme fear which no persuasions could dissipate that he would secure himself till night, and then, that he would come down and cut all our throats. This apprehension made all the females of us fly down the river to be secured, and while we were away they acted this cruelty. For I suppose I had authority and interest enough there, had I suspected any such thing, to have prevented it, but we had not gone many leagues but the news overtook us that Caesar was taken, and whipped like a common slave. (64)

Behn's headlong prose contributes here to the sense that we are in a topsy-turvy world. Both Caesar and the "females" are busy "securing" things in the above passage, but there is no security. We might suspect that the "cruelty" mentioned is the threatened throat cutting, but in fact the "authority" Behn "supposes" she had, but failed to exert, can be exercised to prevent cruelty against the slave, but not the slave's cruelty against her. But why would Oroonoko be so ready to cut Behn's throat, or Behn so ready to believe him capable of it? At Parham, "He was received more like a governor than a slave" (40). Although he is given "his business up in the plantation . . . it was more for form than any design to put him to his task" (40).

In fact, "he endured no more of the slave but the name" (40). In an earlier encounter, Behn indicates that she did not consider Caesar's condition at Parham plantation one of "confinement," because she warns him of this unpleasant possibility should he occasion further anxiety in the whites (46).

It turns out, however, that to have to "endure" merely the "name" of slave is no easy task, and the burden is rendered even greater if it entails having to endure the name of king as well—Caesar. I think we need to honor Behn's concern to observe forms ("it was more for form") and investigate to what extent Caesar is himself an essentially formalized creature. To endure the name is a way of saying that Oroonoko is made to *embody* the *form* of the slave and the king at once. Catherine Gallagher's brilliant interpretation of Oroonoko's blackness helps us see what is at stake here. Citing the famous description of Oroonoko's appearance as European in all ways save the "perfect ebony" (12) of his skin, Gallagher observes that "Oroonoko's blackness must therefore be seen at once as authentically and unnaturally black" (70–71). What she means is that Oroonoko must be seen as both an example of his people and an exception to them. His blackness is more perfect than his fellow Coramantiens' "brown, rusty black" (12), which at once signals his superiority to them and clarifies his formal otherness to the "white world." But his doubleness is itself doubled, because in this white world, too, he is both example—of natural royalty—and exception—as black.

Gallagher points out how the overdeterminations of Oroonoko's blackness can be ultimately reduced to a single contradiction: "'Black,' then, is connected to bodies but is also an abstraction from them signifying exchangeable value. It is not so much descriptive of the skin as of the difference between African skin and all other skin that has arbitrarily come to take on the meaning of exchange value per se" (77). At once real and fictive, "authentic and unnatural," black signifies an equivocation about the possibility of abstracting from bodies. In the case of slavery, this abstraction is called "exchange value." Laura Brown had suggested that absolutism and mercantile imperialism were opposed ideological systems in Behn's text, but Gallagher's analysis suggests a deeper structural intimacy between them: "Exchange value and kingship are both realized in *Oroonoko* at the vanishing point of African bodies, the moments when the king sells his subjects" (78). Gallagher reads Behn's absolutism as being of the reactionary, "Filmeresque" (80) variety, that is, an ideology that "re-imagined the king's sovereignty as an absolute property right in the bodies of his subjects" (79). This

Filmeresque argument is self-consciously reactionary and archaic (Filmer, we recall, looked all the way back to Adam, much to Locke's exasperation). But the radicality of its vision, its atomizing focus on the sovereign/subject dyad, also perversely causes it to join up with the corrosively modern ideology of commerce, commodification, and exchange. Thus it is that "slavery is presented [in *Oroonoko*] not as a semifeudal but as a fully commercial institution. That is, exchange, rather than mere ownership, is its essence" (79). On the one hand, then, we have the "imaginative pattern informing centuries of monarchist thought" according to which the "mystical body of kingship continues to represent even that against which it is defined, the physical bodies that constitute the realm" (75). But on the other hand, we have the same bifurcation expressed in the logic of the commodity. As king, Oroonoko must both be his body and bear the abstraction of that body, and as slave he is similarly split between body and value. It is Oroonoko's blackness, Gallagher argues, that serves as the site for the superimposition of the slave and the king: "The intrinsic, non-negotiable kingship of Oroonoko is thus paradoxically figured in the same blackness that designates the principle of exchange itself. . . . Kingship, the right of ownership, and the act of exchange entail each other so closely in *Oroonoko* that they are virtually identical" (77, 81). This virtual identity is that of the deterritorialized sovereign, and it is what makes *Oroonoko* such an ideologically unstable text: "Sovereignty keeps sliding into self-alienation, and keeping someone entails the renunciation of property claims" (82).

Such are the paradoxes of the "royal slave." Behn's volatile text anticipates, as it were, Giorgio Agamben's thesis about the inextricable relation between the sovereign and the *homo sacer*. Indeed, Behn goes further, in that she does not so much display the "correlative" or "symmetrical" aspects of the two figures as she exhibits the *short circuit* between them. Agamben argues that the essential political relation in play here is only disclosed in a liminal space, a "zone of indistinction" that can be called either the "state of nature" or the "state of exception" (37). As I have begun to argue in this chapter, it was the "new world" that proved to be the most significant stage for the exhibition of this liminal space in which sovereign power and "bare life" square off. It is a space, as Behn's Oroonoko explores in detail, in which exception and example, the different-than-all-others (while still being one) and the same-as-all-others (and hence no longer being [merely] one), converge in their shared anomalousness. In both example and exception, as

Agamben argues, following Alain Badiou, nuances of membership are being negotiated:

> The example is thus excluded from the normal case not because it does not belong to it but, on the contrary, because it exhibits its own belonging to it. . . . The mechanism of exception is different. While the example is excluded from the set insofar as it belongs to it, the exception is included in the normal case precisely because it does not belong to it. . . . In every case . . . exception and example are correlative concepts that are ultimately indistinguishable and that come into play every time the very sense of the belonging and commonality of individuals is to be defined. In every logical system, just as in every social system, the relation between outside and inside, strangeness and intimacy, is this complicated. (22)

Agamben's remarks are ambitiously general—"in every social system"—but I would like to stay focused on the difference that race and the new world make to this structure. The logic of sovereignty after Hobbes in itself already displays this co-implication of exception and example: both sovereign and subject can only "belong" to the social field by carrying their convertibility into each other, their exemplary exceptionality, with them at all times. But what Behn's text shows us is that this doubleness is itself doubled in the new world, and that it is Oroonoko's racial difference—his "blackness" as analyzed by Gallagher—that serves as "vanishing point" for this deterritorialized sovereignty.

Let us return to *Oroonoko* and the specific figural logic it brings to bear on these questions. How does Behn represent Surinam as an Agambenian "zone of indistinction"? In some ways, the new world is familiar. once landed in Surinam, Oroonoko must be called "Caesar" because he now lives in "our Western world" (40). But Surinam also has an extramundane quality for Behn: she calls her trip there her "travels to the other world" (5). Behn calls the colony an "obscure world" (40), almost as if she were an epic traveler making her requisite tour of the underworld. Oroonoko himself seems to invoke a theological sense when he rallies his fellow slaves with a call to "see if we can meet with more honour and honesty in the next world" (38). But these stray phrases finally amount to little more than metaphors of estrangement. Surinam is less a purely other world than it is a world in which same and other are held in suspension. There are aspects of its physical properties that indicate as much. If you wanted to find a natural habitat for a "gleaming vision of disembodied value" (Gallagher 77) such as Oroonoko presents, choose a place where " 'tis the nature of that country to rust and eat up iron, or any metals but gold and silver" (57). Indeed, the land itself seems productive and destructive in equal measure, to figure a kind of creepy composting power that blurs the line between life and death. Consider in this regard an apparently minor incident where Oroonoko manages to kill a tiger that has been terrorizing the area: "But I shall now relate a thing that possibly will find no credit among men, because 'tis a notion commonly received with us, that nothing can receive a wound in the heart and live; but when the heart of this courageous animal was taken out, there were seven bullets of lead in it, and the wounds seamed up with great scars, and she lived with the bullets a great while, for it was long since they were shot" (51). In the final agonizing pages dedicated to the death of Oroonoko, Behn reverts to this strange curative power: "In six or seven days [Oroonoko] recovered his sense, for you must know that wounds are almost to a miracle cured in the Indies" (71). Given that by this point Oroonoko had been flogged to within an inch of his life, had pepper rubbed into his wounds, and undergone a series of self-mutilations, including disemboweling himself and cutting a piece of his throat out to use as a missile, "miracle" is probably not too strong a word. If *Oroonoko* presents the black body of the royal slave as a "vanishing point," then, we have to admit that this vanishing takes a really long time. The clean divide between embodiment and abstraction that the ideological structure leads us to expect is precisely blurred and distended in the twilit, lingering "zone of indistinction" that is Surinam.

Let us conclude, then, that Surinam is a place that can keep you alive against all odds. In the end, of course, neither the tiger nor Oroonoko are imagined capable of evading their inevitable deaths: the land's power to keep alive is better described as a power to *cause to linger* in a zone that is not quite living and not quite dead. Oroonoko's repulsive behavior with his wife's body conforms to the same logic: "first cutting her throat, and then severing her yet smiling face from that delicate body, pregnant as it was with the fruits of tenderest love. As soon as he had done, he laid the body decently on leaves and flowers, of which he made a bed and concealed it under the same coverlid of nature; only her face he left yet bare to look on" (68). What we witness here is an act of literal prosopopoeia: Imoinda gives face to the land's suspension between life and death, her own womb-become-tomb merging with that of nature, which is always bringing forth "flowers" from its general decay, the "leaves that lie thick on the ground by perpetual falling" (69). It might seem that Oroonoko's idiosyncratic obsequies are meant to keep Imoinda alive by abstracting value (the personality) from decay, like gold from the iron that rusts. But even this desperate act is overtaken by what can only be called the vital energy of decay. Imoinda's smiling face may be what distinguishes her for Oroonoko, but for those who have come to seek his capture, it is her bodily corruption that identifies her: "They had not gone very far into the wood, but they smelt an unusual smell, as of a dead body, for stinks must be very noisome that can be distinguished among such a quantity of natural sweets as every inch of that land produces" (69). It is perhaps this suspension of the difference between life and death, this short circuit between body and value, that Behn signals with her characterization of Surinam in her preface: "I beseech your Lordship to consider these countries do, in all things, so far differ from ours, that they produce unconceivable wonders; at least they appear so to us because new and strange" (5). Imoinda, with her own power of conceiving cut off, comes to symbolize Surinam's ability to "produce unconceivable wonders." This wonder, neither body nor value, caught in a "zone of indistinction" between life and death, merely lingering, has a name: "the last of the race."

For it is of course Oroonoko's unwillingness to submit his unborn child to a condition he detests that initiates the series of actions that conclude the novel: the rebellion and subsequent capture, his murder/sacrifice of Imoinda, his self-mutilations, recovery, and final dismemberment. But the last of the race can neither live nor die. Oroonoko might kill his wife and unborn child, but that merely leaves *him* as "the last." (This is an isolation Oroonoko almost anticipates, for who is the "he" in the following sentence? "And in a very short time after, she conceived with child, which made Caesar even adore her, knowing he was the last of his great race" [44].) To be last is to be reduced not just to one's personal mortality: it is also to be required to sustain an immortal social value past the destruction of its significance. In such a state, as Oroonoko claims, one is neither dead nor alive: " 'Tis not life I seek, nor am I afraid of dying" (72). Much is made, in Behn's novel, of Oroonoko's disdain for the notions of the Christian afterlife: as he says, "Punishments hereafter are suffered by oneself, and the world takes no cognisances whether this god have revenged 'em or not, 'tis done so secretly" (35). What is truly eternal is not the afterlife, but the life of society: "Let him know I swear by my honour, which to violate would not only . . . give myself perpetual pain, but it would be eternally offending and diseasing all mankind, harming, betraying, circumventing, and outraging all men" (35). To live dishonorably is to "die every day" (36). But to live in a world in which the social values are not honor and fame, but survival and promises, is another kind of eternity on earth, what Oroonoko calls, in his speech to the slaves, the "infamy of life" (58).

Given the sinister qualities of the lingering life in Surinam's "zone of indistinction," we can perhaps understand why Tuscan, who is stabbed in the arm by Oroonoko in the last battle, "neither pulled it out himself, nor suffered it to be pulled out, but came down with it sticking in his arm, and the reason he gave for it was, because the air should not get into the wound" (71). Having one's wounds attended to in this locale is not something to seek. It is certainly an open question whether the humanitarians at Parham are doing Oroonoko much of a favor in their efforts to protect and heal him. These operations of sustenance are ambiguously medical and moral:

> They brought him to Parham, and laid him on a couch, and . . . the chirurgeon . . . dressed his wounds and sewed up his belly and used means to bring him to life. . . . For some days we suffered no one to speak to him, but caused cordials to be poured down his throat, which sustained his life. . . . He besought us we would let him die and was extremely afflicted to think it was possible he might live. . . . We said all we could to make him live, and gave him new assurances, but he begged we would not think so poorly of him, or of his love to Imoinda, to imagine we could flatter him to life again. (71)

It seems that Oroonoko's reference to "assurances" and "flattery" is directed at the Parhamites' readiness to treat him as slave in "name only," and indeed to "feed him day to day with promises" (45) of attaining his liberty, in an act morally cognate to "caus[ing] cordials to be poured down his throat." But this time, Oroonoko must be definitively abandoned, because the short circuit has finally shorted out: "We were all (but Caesar) afflicted at this news, and the sight was gashly; his discourse was sad and the earthly smell about him so strong that I was persuaded to leave the place for some time" (71). "Gashly" here evokes both the wound and the ghost, the unsettling convergence between "discourse" and the "earthly smell" of death.

So Oroonoko is abandoned. The final act of the Parhamites, those who feed and protect and sew him up, is to abandon him to his death at the hands of Byam's party. We might argue that it is the Parhamites, with their solicitude for Oroonoko's dignity, who exhibit the latest refinements in sovereign power: when Colonel Martin, one of the humanitarians allied with Behn, refuses one of the "quarters" of Oroonoko's corpse, he does so not from outrage, but because he claims "that he could govern his Negroes without terrifying and grieving them with frightful spectacles of a mangled king" (73). Long before Foucault's Damiens met his end, before Beccaria's strictures on overly cruel punishments, Behn's text invites us (quite against her apparent intentions) to look for the "trace of torture" (*Discipline* 13) lingering in the apparently more humane treatment of Oroonoko by the Parhamites.

With this final image of the "spectacle of a mangled king," we can return a last time to the question of theater, and its failure, in the new world. I argued about *The Widow Ranter* that Behn's comic hopefulness there, such as it is, depends on an endorsement of a kind of post-heroic political theater. Oroonoko, whose fate is both heroic and "inglorious," seems to foreclose even that possibility. Here it is the better part of valor to *refuse* the political theater staged by Byam's quartering of Oroonoko. When the royal commissioners complained to Governor William Berkeley about the incident of the African hangman, Berkeley offered to give them a black servant to torture, that they might discover the source of the insult. The commissioners refused. Berkeley (and his wife, Lady Frances), like Byam, seems to revel in the control of a new kind of post-heroic political theater, one in which the substitutability of (racialized) sovereigns for servants is exhibited so that some position outside that volatile "zone of indistinction" can be imagined as secure for the white governors. In *Oroonoko*, Behn gives us the "spectacle of a mangled king," to be sure. But perhaps her decision *not* to make a stage drama of it indicates her conviction that the new world of deterritorialized and racialized sovereignty was no longer expressible in terms of the theatrical unities, but leeched and drifted into ambiguous spaces and twilit times, only graspable by a spasmodic—"I writ it in a few hours" (5)—and "inglorious" prose.

TWO

The Future Perfect King: Olaudah Equiano and the Poetics of Experience

Is a life after death possible for Oroonoko, Aphra Behn's royal slave? He shows no interest at all in Christian conceptions of an afterlife. To be honest, Behn herself does not show much interest in the issue either, but at one point the narrator tries to do her duty with regard to Imoinda, "endeavouring to bring her to the knowledge of the true God" (45). But we are told that "of all the discourses," Oroonoko "liked that the worst" (45). For Oroonoko, it seems, the only conceivable afterlife would be one of honor and reputation, and such an immortality can be secured only in the context of a society ready to receive and sustain such a reputation for glory. But Oroonoko's end is "inglorious" (5), as Behn admits, and thus does heroic romance run aground in the new world. Behn does not save Oroonoko's life, nor does she secure his immortal fame according to conventional measures, but she does tap into what I argued in the last chapter was a strange "power to preserve" (5) specific to the new world, as well as its fateful conjunction of race and a deterritorialized sovereignty. For despite the severity of Oroonoko's end, despite his absolute abandonment by both home and host cultures, despite his dismissal of any Christian principle of immortality, Oroonoko does have an extensive afterlife—as a character or type.

The influence of Behn's hero on subsequent European literature—especially in England and in France—has long been recognized.[1] But what is its specificity? After all, as Barry Weller has pointed out, the "conjunction of noble birth and social abjection dates back at least as far as Homer."[2] Numerous other African nobles and royal slaves followed in Oroonoko's wake, whose stories were meant to affirm an older, romance-like recognition—all the more powerful for being cross-racial—of certain essential character traits associated with "noble" status.[3] But these are not, I submit, Oroonoko's most significant heirs. It is an odd fact that despite *Oroonoko*'s equivocal message about both slavery and Christianity, "the historical fate of the text was emancipationist" (Weller 68). It is in the context of the Christian emancipationist discourse of the latter eighteenth century that the most profound implications of Behn's treatment of race and sovereignty are revealed and extended. The writers of the black Atlantic—John Marrant, James Albert Ukawsaw Gronniosaw, and above all Olaudah Equiano—take up the conjunction of sovereignty and slavery, noble birth and social abjection, within a Christian, especially Pauline, idiom. These writers' status as hyperbolically deterritorialized subjects—abducted, transported, itinerant—makes them especially sensitive to the ambiguities of Paul's metaphorics of slavery and salvation. The explorations of the rootless sovereign self offered by these Christian writers reveal new configurations of event and experience, facticity and historicity, in modernity.

Weller surmises that *Oroonoko*'s influence has finally to do with historicity, or with the desire for historicity, what he calls a "prestige of origins": "It seems possible," he writes, "that this prestige of origins inflects our reading of Equiano and later African-American narratives as the tradition of the 'royal slave' affected that of his contemporaries. Is it not, in particular, tempting to accord a special value to Equiano's representation of his African past as marking the success of his autobiographical enterprise?" (69). If, as Weller suggests, we read and value Equiano's *Interesting Narrative* in ways that mimic how Equiano and his contemporaries read and valued *Oroonoko*, this may well have to do with a probabilistic attitude toward historical truth: *Oroonoko* and texts that followed caused readers to be "sufficiently persuaded that a slave could be royal to make fictions which exploited this premise acceptable and even attractive" (66). It was this "sufficiently persuasive" historicity that Equiano borrowed from the example of Behn's text, Weller argues, and to which we still respond today.[4] Behn's text mobilizes a "prestige of origins" not only in Oroonoko's African, and innate, nobility, but also in her own firsthand experience in Surinam (the feather headdress worn by Anne Bracegirdle in *The Indian Queen*, she tells us, was brought back from Surinam by Behn herself). At the same time, *Oroonoko*'s modernity lies in its revelation that such prestige now comes framed by contingency, that origins are henceforth taken up as essentially contingent facts to be worked on, revised, disputed, undone. Oroonoko lives on, we might say, as a textual character about whom we cannot be sure that he ever existed, but about whom we cannot simply decide that his historicity is irrelevant, either. In this sense, one of Oroonoko's afterlives or avatars is Gustavus Vassa, about whose "African origins" as Olaudah Equiano—called into question by the recent research of Vincent Carretta—we might say the same thing: we cannot be sure that Olaudah Equiano ever existed as a child in Benin, but we also cannot simply decide that whether he did is irrelevant to his claim on our attention.[5]

Equiano's *Interesting Narrative*, I will argue, completes and inverts Oroonoko's example: where the royal slave discloses a zone of lingering through the dramatic submission of his body to extended suffering, Equiano's text provides a remarkably sophisticated deconstruction of such a concept of the wound of experience. Oroonoko's contradictory status as at once sovereign and slave is dramatized in terms of his stoic capacity to sustain a suffering existence that is neither life nor death, but merely lingering, beyond the distinction between mortal and immortal that organizes the political imagination of the relation between subject and sovereign. But Equiano's use of the royal slave topos is, as it were, in default, a matter less of a past that can never be entirely surpassed than a future that can never be entirely joined. For Equiano's mark of distinction is forever deferred: the entirety of *The Interesting Narrative* unfolds in the space opened up by such a wound or scar having *failed* to appear:

> My father was one of those elders or chiefs I have spoken of, and was styled Embrenché; a term, as I remember, importing the highest distinction, and signifying in our language a mark of grandeur. This mark is conferred on the person entitled to it, by cutting the skin across the top of the forehead, and drawing it down to the eye-brows; and while it is in this situation, applying a warm hand,

> and rubbing it until it shrinks up into a thick weal across the lower part of the forehead. Most of the judges and senators were thus marked; my father had long borne it: I had seen it conferred on one of my brothers, and I was also destined to receive it by my parents.[6]

In keeping with the emancipationist idiom he shares with Gronniosaw and others, and in distinction to Behn's hero, Equiano will present this destiny both as something of which he was robbed, *and* from which he was emancipated. His childhood in Benin and his destiny as marked for greatness form a conceptual and experiential dyad: the interruption of the one entails the structural postponement of the other. It is the Christian idiom, as we will see, that shows Equiano how to superimpose on this structure of deferral a narrative that *achieves* a childhood rather than merely tries fruitlessly to *retrieve* one. In this way, as we will see, the Christian emancipationist discourse aims to transpose the sovereign selfhood formerly emblematized by royal status onto an "innocence" of childhood that is both immemorial, forever lost, and transcendent, forever approached.

But the possibility that Equiano *fabricated* his African childhood altogether adds another layer of complexity to his example, and makes this destined-but-unconferred mark an emblem of historical experience itself as something that both does and does not happen, does and does not leave a mark. In this regard, Equiano speaks quite directly to some of the debates about historicity in our own day. In *The Interesting Narrative*, Equiano's deferred scarification, his circumcision, and the ambiguous presentation of his own flogging constitute a symbolic network that points to another form of temporal lingering, in which the full achievement of an emancipated, sovereign selfhood is always deferred, always only available through the future perfect tense—a "will have been." In both the intricate workings of its own figurative logic, and in its historical reception, Equiano's text demonstrates that our concepts of event and experience—the very stuff of historicity—are at once aggrandized and eroded in modernity. In what follows I will first look at the Christian transformation of the topos of the royal slave, a textual tradition Equiano takes up, in order to give it another turn of the screw. I will then turn to a consideration of the intricacies of Equiano's text and conclude with some general remarks about what Equiano's story has to tell us about our understanding of the relation between experience, selfhood, and history.

Kings, Christians, and the Ambiguities of Emancipation

In place of the king, Jesus puts the child: "At the same time came the disciples unto Jesus, saying, Who is the greatest in the kingdom of heaven? And Jesus called a little child unto him, and set him in the midst of them, And said, Verily I say unto you, Except ye be converted, and become as little children, ye shall not enter into the kingdom of heaven" (Matthew 18:1–3). What does it mean to "become as little children"? It cannot mean simply to embrace an innocence given at birth. One could say that, on the contrary, it demands the *negation* of any given childhood, or at the very least the transformation and transposition of the notional innocence of childhood from its position as origin to one of end. The spiritual autobiographers of the black Atlantic are especially sensitive to this double movement away from and toward an innocence of childhood that determines access to, and greatness within, the kingdom of heaven. Jesus's words surely lie behind the scene in John Marrant's *Narrative*, for example, in which the convertibility of sovereign and slave in Cherokee country becomes a scene of child's play: "The king would take off his golden ornaments, his chain and bracelets, like a child, if I objected to them, and lay them aside."[7] Improbable as this scene is as historical reportage, however, its power of persuasion lies in the way that the trope of the sovereign child allows Marrant to image a version of the deferred Christian homecoming on this earth.

But such an entry into the kingdom of heaven can only arrive *after* Marrant has alienated himself from his original home and family through his uncompromising piety. Having been saved literally at the hand of Whitefield, Marrant soon decides that "it was better for me to die than to live among such people" (115), that is, his family. Undertaking a spiritual journey and trial in the "desart" (115), he is eventually taken captive in Cherokee country, where he is condemned to be put to the torture: "It was the law, and it must not be broken" (117). This law, like the Jewish law Paul so insistently submits to reversal in his epistles, fails in its rigidity and its incomprehension of the invisible effects of grace. After having once saved himself from execution by converting the executioner, Marrant is brought to the king: "He asked me how I was supported before I met with this man? I answered by the Lord Jesus Christ, which seemed to confound him. He turned round, and asked me if he lived where I came from? I answered, yes, and here also. He looked about the room, and said he did not see him. . . . I then pointed to the sun, and asked him who made the sun, and moon, and stars, and preserved them in their regular order; He said there was a man in their town that did it" (119). The king expects powerful agents to be physically locatable, "about the room," "in their town," and does not comprehend how this Lord can be in two places at once. But through a series of conventional events—intercession of a Pocahontas-like daughter, talking books, and so forth—the king is eventually "awakened, and the others set at liberty": "A great change took place among the people; the king's house became God's house; the soldiers were ordered away, and the poor condemned prisoner had perfect liberty, and was treated like a prince. Now the Lord made all my enemies to become my great friends. . . . I had assumed the habit of the country, and was dressed much like the king, and nothing was too good for me. The king would take off his golden ornaments, his chain and bracelets, like a child, if I objected to them, and lay them aside" (120). On the one hand, Cherokee country is a place that combines benightedness and spiritual infancy with the violent imposition of a sovereign, irrational law. On the other hand, once this world has been saved, once it has submitted to the power of the invisible agency of grace, both the infancy and the sovereignty can be reclaimed as sources of delight, precisely because they are now versions of one another. There is a jubilantly childish sense of playacting in this scene: the king becomes "like a child" in his willingness to "take off his golden ornaments," but the former child—Marrant was fifteen at the time—also can enjoy his aggrandizement as he is "treated like a prince" and "dressed much like the king" (120).

Marrant was the child of free black parents, and so is not equipped, as Gronniosaw and Equiano were, with an African past on which to work a Christian negation and subsumption: this may account for the scene in Cherokee country. But for other writers of the black Atlantic, the symbolic sovereignty of childhood was complicated by its African origin: childhood for Wheatley, Gronniosaw, and Equiano is a condition that they must both convert to and be converted from. Perhaps the most formulaic and succinct expression of this ambiguous African origin is the opening of Phillis Wheatley's "On Being Brought From Africa" (1773):

> 'Twas mercy brought me from my Pagan land,
> Taught my benighted soul to understand

> That there's a God, that there's a Saviour too:
> Once I redemption neither sought nor knew.[8]

Wheatley's enslavement was a "mercy" because it also constituted her awakening to the need for Christian redemption. The poem implies that without enslavement (here below), there would be no emancipation (in the beyond). This intimacy, almost a symbiosis, between slavery and emancipation is a consistent feature of these Christian texts of the black Atlantic. On the other hand, the innocence of the African origin also has a somewhat positive connotation: to neither seek nor know redemption may be a spiritually "benighted" condition, but Wheatley comes by her ignorance of the spiritual interdependence of bondage and redemption honestly, as it were, through being wholly unacquainted with this-worldly slavery and its blameworthy horrors. Africa lies outside the dialectic of redemption in the logic of this poem, an emblem of a lost innocence about which Wheatley (and her readers) cannot but feel ambivalent.

A similar but more complex treatment of the dialectic of slavery and emancipation can be found in *A NARRATIVE OF THE MOST REMARKABLE PARTICULARS IN THE LIFE OF JAMES ALBERT UKAWSAW GRONNIOSAW, AN AFRICAN PRINCE, AS RELATED BY HIMSELF*, a text "committed to Paper" by Hannah More, and eventually published in 1772 in the hope that its readership might be able to help alleviate the poverty of Gronniosaw's family.[9] Like Oroonoko, Gronniosaw is the beloved grandson of the local African king, and like Equiano, he is also especially close to his mother. But the alienating effects of his spiritual yearnings undermine these signs of social and familial election: "I had, from my infancy, a curious turn of mind; was more grave and reserved in my disposition than either of my brothers and sisters. I often teased them with questions they could not answer: for which reason they disliked me, as they supposed that I was either foolish or insane. 'Twas certain that I was, at times, very unhappy in myself: it being strongly impressed upon my mind that there was some GREAT MAN of power which resided above the sun, moon, and stars" (34). With typographical insistence, Gronniosaw keeps up his search for an invisible "GREAT MAN" and "SUPERIOR POWER" (35). Alarmed at a violent storm, he approaches his mother: "My dear mother, says I, pray tell me who is the great MAN of POWER that makes the thunder? She said there was no power but the sun, moon, and stars; that they made all our country.—I then enquired how all our people came? She answered me, from one another; and so carried me to many generations back.—Then says I, who made the *First Man*?" (35). Young Gronniosaw's hankering after first things, the child's recursive "Why?" is meant to stand as a sign that he is destined for salvation: the Reverend Walter Shirley, who prefaces the *Narrative*, refers to this scene as the "First-Fruit of the Display of Gospel-Glory" (33). But Gronniosaw's experience seems rather focused on *non*-display to me, committed to a negation of present forms of power—very much including the power to which Gronniosaw himself might accede in the fullness of time—and their replacement by invisible versions of the same thing.

In truth, Gronniosaw can't wait to give up the marks of his nobility, his destining to power. In what could be described as the political conversion scene that precedes and prepares his later spiritual one, Gronniosaw is brought to a neighboring kingdom, where he is accused of spying and sentenced to death:

> The morning I was to die, I was washed and all my gold ornaments made bright and shining, and then carried to the palace, where the King was to behead me himself. . . . I went up to the KING alone—I went with an undaunted courage, and it pleased GOD to melt the heart of the King, who . . . being himself so affected . . . dropped [the scimitar] out of his hand, and took me upon his knee and wept over me. I put my right hand round his neck, and pressed him to my heart.—He sat me down and blessed me; and added that he would not kill me, that I should not go home, but be sold for a slave. (37)

What are we to make of this scene, in which slavery appears as a mercy, a reprieve, perhaps even an emancipation? The competition for sovereignty between king and God is once again implied typographically (indeed it almost seems that once the "KING" appears in all the magnificence of his capitals, "GOD" *must* enter the text). In plot terms, the scene completes Gronniosaw's extrication from his homeland, from his entanglement in a system of power that he had been questioning since "infancy," a fact brought home by his relief at having his royal gold confiscated: "When I left my dear mother I had a large quantity of gold about me, as is the custom of our country, it was made into rings, and they were linked one into another, and formed into a kind of chain, and so put round my neck, and arms and legs, and a large piece hanging at one ear, almost in the shape of a pear. I found all this troublesome, and was glad when my new Master took it from me" (38). The royal gold, the mark of his destined position of sovereign authority, is in itself a kind of shackling from which he is glad to be free. Gronniosaw's enslavement is a release from the beginning—"I should not go home"—and from an immediate end—"He would not kill me." Gronniosaw's being "sold for a slave" is an emancipation into a suspended state of radical individuation, a species of freedom from immediate mortality as well as from the grip of the past, but this is an individuation that has nothing to do with autonomy, nothing to do with the sovereignty of self understood as self-appropriation, self-belonging.

From what perspective does sovereignty look like slavery? How do royal ornaments become the shackles emblematic of the Middle Passage? From a perspective in which one becomes the slave of God: "When you were slaves of sin, you were free in regard to righteousness," Paul writes to the Roman believers. "But then what return did you get from the things of which you are now ashamed? The end of those things is death. But now that you have been set free from sin and have become slaves of God, the return you get is sanctification and its end, eternal life. For the wages of sin is death, but the free gift of God is eternal life in Christ Jesus" (Romans 6:20–23). Paul's metaphors of slavery are more than a little puzzling, as Christians across the centuries have found. Dale B. Martin, whose *Slavery as Salvation: The Metaphor of Slavery in Pauline Christianity* offers a discerning survey of some of the more recent, specialized literature on the question, has stressed the extent to which Paul made use of the variety and complexity of the social reality of slavery in the Roman world for his own rhetorical ends.[10] In absolute terms, being free, or being a freedman, was, of course, of higher status than being a slave, but given the pervasiveness of the patronal social structure, such an absolute hierarchy was regularly compromised by the rank order among the houses themselves. Being a slave was not therefore incompatible with social status: one could have a higher status being a slave in a great house than being a freedman of a lesser one. Thus even in terms of this-worldly calculation, being a slave to Christ, as Paul characterizes it, could be a step up from being a freedman to however great a lord, or indeed to being a free Roman citizen.

The dialectic of slavery and emancipation in Paul is tightly bound to the problem of the law, especially the Jewish law. Both accepting and revising the concept of slavery allows Paul also to negotiate his complex relation to the law. In Romans 6, for example, Paul "realizes, rightly, that his statements about the law could lead to charges of libertinism," writes Martin: "He avoids libertinism not by reintroducing the law—or any law—but by setting up an either/or situation: one must live either in the sphere of sin or in the sphere of God. As each sphere entails its own obligations and returns, Paul can contrast the two by comparing them to slavery to two different masters, a good one and a bad one. But in order for this strategy to work, Paul must presuppose that in early Christianity the image of slavery functioned to depict not just moral obligation but also salvation" (61). In other words, certain forms of slavery must be actively appreciable as promising a kind of salvation, if only a step-up in social status, *in the here and now*, for Paul's strategy of endorsing slavery to Christ to be effective proselytizing. His audience needs to be able somehow to see continuity *and* rupture between human and divine patronage simultaneously. In the passage from Romans 6:20–23 cited above, for example, "end" (*telos*), "return" (*karpos*), and "wages" (*ta opsonia*) are all perfectly active economic terms, and "one need not decide whether *telos* means 'spiritual reward' or 'payment rendered.' For Paul's readers it meant both at the same time" (62). That the terms of slavery, emancipation, redemption, wages, payment, and so forth were both less and more than metaphorical in Paul's text is a useful reminder when looking at what can seem to modern readers a puzzling, and even disturbing, blend of the theological and the economic registers in writers like Gronniosaw and Equiano.

At the deepest conceptual level, slavery and emancipation are about belonging, and self-belonging, about subordination to the sovereignty of an other versus the autonomy of self-sovereignty. In Paul's politico-theological project, this problem of belonging is most fundamentally urgent with respect to the Jewish law. And here, again, we see a similar equivocation at work, in which what has been given—the law; the mark of circumcision—is both accepted and rendered irrelevant:

> Was any one at the time of his call already circumcised? Let him not seek to remove the marks of circumcision. Was any one at the time of his call uncircumcised? Let him not seek circumcision. For neither circumcision counts for anything nor uncircumcision, but keeping the commandments of God. Every one should remain in the state in which he was called. Were you a slave when called? Never mind. But if you can gain your freedom, avail yourselves of the opportunity. For he who was called in the Lord as a slave is a freedman of the Lord.

> Likewise he who was free when called is a slave of Christ. You were bought with a price; do not become slaves of men. So, brethren, in whatever state each man was called, there let him remain with God. (1 Corinthians 7:18–24)

On the one hand, this passage celebrates the power of the Christian inversion. In Christ's household, the former slave becomes "a freedman of the Lord," that is, of higher status than the formerly free man who is now "slave of Christ." On the other hand, there is an instruction to embrace the status quo: "Every one should remain in the state in which he was called." The general drift of the passage seems to be Stoic in emphasis: what counts, that is, is not your outward condition—"Were you a slave when called? Never mind."—but the inward state of your will. But whereas "will" would be the crucial category for the Stoic, for Paul it is of course faith, and this makes a huge difference: for Paul, there is no absolute autonomy, there is only freedom in Christ, which is also a superior form of servitude. And this embrace of a model of slavery to Christ oddly has the effect of rendering the posture toward this-worldly conditions ambiguous. The *possibility* of change here below is readily admitted—you *could* add or remove the "marks of circumcision"—but such changes of belonging do not "count for anything." At the same time, the language of will and voluntary action is still powerfully present, to the extent that Paul seems prepared to endorse efforts to free oneself, even within a discourse suggesting unambiguously that it doesn't matter: "Were you a slave when called? Never mind. But if you can gain your freedom, avail yourselves of the opportunity." It almost sounds as if he had added an afterthought: "If you are a slave when called, it doesn't matter (because you will be a freedman in Christ's household). Then again, if you *do* have a chance to become free (here and now), go ahead and try, because freedom remains the best condition (even when its purest expression is as 'slave of Christ')." Can we be sure that Christ's purchase of us renders Paul's instruction to "not become slaves of men" a purely metaphorical matter? The Christian transformation of the law renders the latter *contingent*, something that is given, imposed, and *could* be changed, and sometimes perhaps *should* be changed, but in general should not be worried about too much.

If I seem to be reading Paul too much against the grain, my central point is simply that slavery and emancipation are subjected in the Christian texts—in Paul as in Gronniosaw—to a rhetorical manipulation that is strange to modern sensibilities. These writers dwell less on the ontological divide between slavery and freedom than on their promiscuous interaction, and emancipation becomes an ambiguous ideal as a result. In a powerful essay called "The Grip (Mainmise)," Jean-François Lyotard also questions the logic of emancipation, in terms that allow us to return to the theme of childhood from which we have digressed. Lyotard believes that we are never free from "the grip" associated with childhood, the taking hold or seizure by the hand. (The metaphor governing the concept of emancipation comes from the hand, *manus*; the *manceps* is "the person who takes hold," *mancipium* is the "gesture of taking hold").[11] Lyotard characterizes this experience of being affected as a wounding or a trauma ("For the child everything is trauma" [150]), availing himself of a figure—expressed as wound, mark, or circumcision, depending on the context—that goes from Paul through Equiano to contemporary trauma theory: we "do not attain emancipation from . . . childhood, either from [the] childhood wound or from the call that has issued from it" (149). Lyotard detects an ambiguity in Matthew 18, "two meanings of the word *infancy*" (154). He refers to the words that Jesus utters after those we have already quoted from Matthew 18:7: "Woe unto the world because of offences! for it must needs be that offences come; but woe to that man by whom the offence cometh!" Lyotard glosses as follows: "He who causes scandal exercises a *mancipium* over the child, which distracts and separates it from the only true *manceps*, the father. This scandal and this distraction are necessary. It is necessary to be *bound*, expropriated, appropriated by humanity, instead of by the father" (154). Jesus invokes a pure innocence to which everyone should seek to return—the innocence of a child unoffended. This innocence is not a condition of simple emancipation, however, because it is a freedom that is purely coincident with being in the grip of the "only true *manceps*, the father," namely God. But Jesus also seems to acknowledge that there is a condition called humanity, in which other kinds of *mancipium* are exercised, and that these are inevitable—"It must needs be that offences come." The logic is like Wheatley's vis-à-vis her "Pagan land": woe to those that bring the offence of enslavement to the innocence of the African child! But there is, in a sense, no child against whom some form of offence will not come. It is an offence for a child to be "*bound*," as Lyotard says, "by humanity," but it is all the same necessary, for without such expropriation redemption would be, as Wheatley says, neither sought nor known.

Lyotard's sympathies in his essay are clearly with the Judeo-Christian attitude toward emancipation, an attitude that does not pretend that any of us could ever get free from being bound by our humanity, from having been a child, wounded and traumatized by our natal helplessness: for Lyotard, the concepts of faith and salvation in these great religions are accommodations to the *mancipium* of the past, the call, the "grip" of history. Against this, "modernity," as Lyotard characterizes it, dreams of emancipation:

> The West does not accept gifts. It takes up, elaborates, and gives back to itself whatever is assumed to be given, but it treats the given as only a possible case of the situation. . . . Other cases are thus possible. They are conceived and carried out. That is called development or complexification. What was held to be the essence of the situation (political, economic, epistemological, mathematic, etc.) ceases to be essential. Situational *axiomatics* are installed. . . . We acknowledge instances of being grasped or seized only in order to deny them. They are thus conceived as cases, represented and treated according to scenarios. One frees oneself from the other by locating it as an exteriority and then taking a grip on it. (151)

But as our selective survey of the Christian use of the metaphors of slavery indicates, there is a radical embrace of contingency in the Christian message, an acceptance that the childhood that one is given is exactly that which is worked on, developed, exchanged: in the hands of a writer like Paul, Christianity "takes up, elaborates, and gives back to itself whatever is assumed to be given." To the extent that the Christian texts invoke—as mythic origin *and* as telos of salvation—an innocence unoffended, a *mancipium* by God alone and absolutely detached from family or nation, and situate that innocence athwart the givenness of our bound humanity, we can say that Christianity also promotes the deterritorializing effects of modernity. What the writers of the black Atlantic reveal, with their concrete understanding of the dialectic of slavery and emancipation, is that the Christian approach does not necessarily oppose the erosion of historicity implicit in modernity's ideal of emancipation, the relativizing, revisionist momentum of Western modernity. Equiano's *Interesting Narrative* is exemplary for us, in fact, precisely because it so subtly, but so thoroughly, deconstructs such a distinction between Christian experience and the deterritorializing drift of modernity. It is to that text, then, and its implications about memory, history, and the sovereignty of the modern, rootless self, that I now turn.

The Particular Favorite of Heaven

> The break with tradition, uprooting, the inaccessibility of histories, amnesia, indecipherability, and so on: all of these unleash the genealogical drive, the desire of the idiom, the compulsive impulse to anamnesis, and the destructive love of the interdict . . . the madness of a hypermnesia.
>
> —JACQUES DERRIDA[12]

One might well conclude, looking at the contemporary recuperation of Equiano's *Interesting Narrative*, that we are witnessing what Derrida calls "hypermnesia," the "genealogical drive" unleashed. A. E. Afigbo, in his 1981 study *Ropes of Sand (Studies in Igbo History and Culture)*, dates the "rehabilitation" of Equiano to 1960, when the "celebrated Africanist, Mr. Thomas Hodgkin . . . included an extract . . . in his selection of documents on Nigerian history."[13] Afigbo notes that Chinua Achebe published some remarks on Equiano in 1964, and that *The Interesting Narrative* enters the academy with Paul Edwards's edition of 1967, a scholarly work contemporary with a series of abridgements and school editions that formed part of an early attempt to institutionalize at least some black history in secondary schools.[14] In the mid-1980s, Equiano figured prominently in Gates and Davis's important collection *The Slave's Narrative*, and then again later offered Gates, in *The Signifying Monkey*, a paradigmatic account of the trope of the talking book.[15] More recently still, Abiola Irele has placed Equiano in a pan-African literary historical context—that is, a context neither exclusively African American nor Anglophone. Irele describes *The Interesting Narrative* as "the most significant African work to emerge from this early period" of African literary production after the European incursion.[16] The critical work has run parallel with Equiano's extensive anthologization: I first became acquainted with *The Interesting Narrative* in the *Heath Anthology of American Literature* (Equiano as American?), and he has of course been included in other, newly multicultural anthologies as well.

The revival of Equiano is, then, part of the multicultural moment. On the one hand, he is African, or claims he is, and this elicits what Weller calls the "prestige of origins." As Carretta has said clearly, Equiano's "authority to speak as a victim and eye-witness of slavery in Africa, the West Indies, North American, Europe and the Middle East . . . was dependent on the

African nativity he claimed."[17] But multiculturalism must negotiate its commitment both to the concept of cultural identity and to a description of cultural drift and hybridity across time. This requirement has led the increasingly sophisticated multiculturalism represented by cultural studies and postcolonialism to see Equiano as exemplary not of some kind of original or authentic identity—African or otherwise—but rather of what Derrida might call a "disorder of identity," an experiential witness of "the break with tradition, uprooting, the inaccessibility of histories, indecipherability." Both Paul Gilroy and Srinavas Aravamudan, for example, see Equiano as offering insight into a fundamental condition "between tradition and modernity" (Gilroy),[18] in which the shipboard life shared by Equiano and others becomes an allegory of "unbelonging and placelessness" (Aravamudan 239). Equiano's text becomes exemplary of a modernity, in other words, that solicits simultaneously the "genealogical drive" and its "despair," to quote Derrida again. And this modernity, for reasons we have begun to see in the last section, is especially manifest in Equiano's relation to Christianity: "Conversion," writes Aravamudan, "or Christian behavior . . . is a response to liminal rootlessness but is also occasionally shown up as knowingly self-interested and complicitous. Equiano's conversion enables an inclusive narrative of the rediscovered cultural *simultaneity* of African and Euro-American contexts, one that replaces the initial sense of exclusionary spiritual *development* from one to the other" (241).

But let us begin at the beginning, with Equiano's self-presentation as "neither a saint, a hero, or a tyrant" (31): "I believe there are few events in my life which have not happened to many; it is true the incidents of it are numerous; and, did I consider myself an European, I might say my sufferings were great; but, when I compare my lot with that of most of my countrymen, I regard myself as a *particular favorite of Heaven*, and acknowledge the mercies of Providence in every occurrence of my life" (31). Every autobiographer must negotiate the requirement to be at once unique and representative, but Equiano does so negatively, as it were: he is *neither* unique, *nor* representative. We can see here how the need to refer his experience to two different cultural frames, African and European, at once overdetermines and underdetermines his identity: he becomes an example of an exception. The invocation of Providence—he is the "*particular favorite of Heaven*"—is meant to secure and stabilize this exceptional status from the vantage of an achieved spiritual rebirth in Christianity, but there is some room for interpretation here. The mobilization of providential explanations, I would argue, is less a retrospective clarification of the course of his life than an ongoing strategy, one that is shown to be perfectly amenable to modes and codes other than those of Christianity: long before Equiano experiences his saving grace, he remarks of himself that "I had a mind on which everything uncommon made its full impression, and every event which I considered marvellous. Every extraordinary escape, or signal deliverance, either of myself or others, I looked upon to be effected by the interposition of Providence" (85). Escapes and deliverances come fast and furious in Equiano's eventful narrative, and one of the odd effects of his excessive providentialism—it pertains to "every occurrence" and "every event"—is to reduce the impact of any event taken on its own. Thus it is that even his manumission seems to make less difference to Equiano than we might expect.

For reasons that pertain to both the Christian prism from which he is writing and the hard facts of life, Equiano's text suggests a continuum of occupations and hazards between slavery and freedom where we are inclined to imagine an ontological divide. On the one hand, this is due to a status system that is not entirely coincident with institutionalized slavery; on the other hand, as Carretta points out, it is due to the way that the fact of the African slave system always threatened to violently trump any other status order in which a freedman like Equiano might hope to make his way: "Equiano knew that freedom in the West Indies was not sufficient to guarantee true liberty."[19] While Equiano does not downplay the momentousness of his enslavement nor that of his emancipation, in a variety of ways his narrative works to undermine the incommensurability of chattel slavery to other forms of subjugation by placing his life in that larger Atlantic world of labor and risk studied by Linebaugh and Rediker. This continuum is manifest in a variety of ways: Equiano continues to work much as he had before his emancipation and continues to be implicated in the powerfully stratified labor economy centered around Atlantic trade routes of slaves and sugar. Some of his trade adventures, indeed, are directly contributory to the slave economy, such as his work as overseer on a South American plantation. As a freedman, he must still seek a "master" to undertake to direct and employ him. And having agreed to continue work for Captain King after his manumission, he describes himself as having "consented to slave on as before" (141).

Something like this rhetorical erosion is at work in the narrative of his religious conversion as well. As I have already remarked, Equiano's African religious perspective is presented as more continuous with his post-conversion stance than one might expect in a spiritual autobiography. Readily ascribing "every event" to the interposition of Heaven, we might see Equiano here as merely using Providence as a technique for managing shock and risk. Aravamudan makes a valuable observation in this regard: "The harsh environment in which, or in fear of which, conversion occurred gives the mixture of doctrine, devotion, and superstition a different meaning from terrestrially produced belief. Even though Equiano's qualified Methodism—along with a nominal adherence to the articles of the Church of England—is not a contingent happening aboard ship, it is intimately connected to his maritime experiences, his entrepreneurial vicissitudes, and his physical survival" (240). The risks that Equiano must negotiate are not simply those attendant upon enslavement and sinfulness, they are also—and always more immediately—weather and warfare. The convergence of religious and entrepreneurial idioms is hardly unusual in this period, but it is nevertheless charming in how businesslike a manner Equiano goes about attaining salvation: "I was determined to work out my own salvation . . . and procure a title to heaven" (178), he announces at the beginning of his long chapter on his conversion experience. "Being resolved to be saved, I pursued other methods . . . I asked different people questions about the manner of going to heaven, and was told different ways" (178–79). Like a mariner adrift, every choice of route must be made against the background knowledge that one might also take "different ways"; one cannot escape the sense that one moves within a horizon determined by contingency.

Equiano's eye for the main chance characterizes his religious stance from the beginning:

> I was from early years a predestinarian, [and] I thought whatever fate had determined must ever come to pass; and therefore, if it ever were my lot to be freed, nothing could prevent me; on the other hand, if it were not my fate to be freed, I never should be so, and all my endeavours for that purpose would be fruitless. In the midst of these thoughts I therefore looked up with prayers anxiously to God for my liberty; and at the same time used every honest means, and did all that was possible on my part to obtain it. (119)

Equiano's providentialism, then, is not some final position he arrives at, and from which he reorders and stabilizes his pre-conversion past; it is, on the contrary, a providentialism always on the go. It is a technique for managing risk and contingency, and it thereby participates in the simultaneous aggrandizement and erosion of event that we can suggest is characteristic of modernity: "Modernity is not . . . a historical period," writes Jean-François Lyotard, "but a way of shaping a sequence of moments in such a way that it accepts a high rate of contingency."[20] Lyotard earlier helped us see how the Christian (and Pauline) treatment of the themes of emancipation and childhood both embraced the givenness of one's natal condition and subjected that condition to revision and transformation. Lyotard's sketch of modernity in "The Grip" had invoked a discourse of "development": modernity "treats the given as only a possible case of the situation. Other cases are thus possible. They are conceived and carried out. That is called development or complexification. What was held to be essential to the situation . . . ceases to be essential. Situational axiomatics are installed" (151). It was then suggested that the Christian and the modern were—when one looks at the figural logic of slavery and salvation in the texts we are considering—less antagonistic formations than complementary ones. That Equiano's agility with managing risk and contingency would move so easily between religious and economic idioms confirms that view. This is one way to understand the linkage between Equiano's abolitionism and his endorsement of market capitalism.

What Lyotard calls "situational axiomatics" govern the itinerary of Equiano's personal development. *The Interesting Narrative* is particularly compelling for us in that it demonstrates both the impact of the given and its capacity to be rewritten. Consider in this regard the striking account of Equiano's forcible renaming: "In this place I was called Jacob; but on board the African Snow, I was called Michael" (60). On the next page, he continues: "While I was on this ship, my captain and master named me Gustavus Vassa. I at that time began to understand him a little, and refused to be called so, and told him as well as I could that I would be called Jacob; but he said I should not and still called me Gustavus: and when I refused to answer to my new name, which I at first did, it gained me many a cuff; so at length I submitted, and by which I have been known ever since" (61). Adam Potkay reads this scene of resistance as a retrospective rhetorical insistence on his identification with Jewish patriarchalism before the Exodus, and thus as marking a stage in his spiritual journey.[21] It seems to me more a case of finding resistance where one can: either way, it is a moment that both insists on givenness and resists it, a scene of the workings of a "situational axiomatics." But situations, too, are contingent, and subject to drift, as one can see when one considers the ironies that quickly accumulate around this event. Carretta makes the interesting suggestion that Captain Pascal may have renamed Equiano here—a quintessential expression of the power of the slave master—as an attempt to *hide* his status as a slave, because the "man-of-war [was] a little piece of British territory in which slavery was improper" (252). On the other hand, it is hard to see how the name itself could not help advertising Equiano's status as slave, because a small black boy named after a Swedish freedom fighter could hardly be explained any other way. As Carretta notes, "Slaves were often given ironically inappropriate names of powerful historical figures like Caesar or Pompey to emphasize their subjugation to their masters' wills" (252). But Gustavus Vassa had a particular resonance in the contemporaneous British political lexicon that Pompey, for example, did not, because he stood as a figure of political liberty for the anti-Walpole elements, and their heirs, throughout the eighteenth century. Was Pascal sympathetic to those who admired Vassa? Or was his contempt for such a conception of liberty precisely what was being expressed through the ironic naming of his slave after the freedom fighter? Carretta suggests that Equiano hopes that his readers will see both the irony of the fact that he comes to exemplify his name, in his prominent role as an abolitionist freedom fighter, as well as that he had already, in a sense, exemplified its meaning in his very resistance to its imposition. It seems as if every gesture of this complex discursive event comes equipped with its own ironic subversion: the imposition of identity is resisted in the name of an imposed identity; the naming of a slave may be meant to hide his identity as a slave; the irony of the name chosen extends beyond Pascal's—and perforce Equiano's—control and ends up allegorizing the character it is meant to ironize.

Equiano signs his autobiography, of course, with two names: Olaudah Equiano, or Gustavus Vassa. In contemporary practice, however, we refer to him as Equiano; the front cover of Carretta's Penguin edition, indeed, gives only the African name. This is despite the fact that Carretta himself has been at pains to point out that this was not Equiano's normal practice. In only two documents other than his autobiography did Equiano sign his name as Equiano: he is consistently Gustavus Vassa in all other correspondence, even in personal letters to his wife (103). It is worth remembering that namings are explicitly *events* for Equiano, and not just on shipboard: "Our children," he writes in his first chapter describing his childhood in Essaka, "were named for some event, some circumstance, or fancied foreboding at the time of their birth. I was named Olaudah, which, in our language, signifies vicissitude, or fortunate also; one favoured, and having a loud voice and well spoken" (41). Afigbo, while nowhere questioning the authenticity of Equiano's Africanness—indeed quite the opposite: "There is no doubt that Equiano was an Igbo man to the marrow" (183)—nonetheless cannot make sense of the Igbo here: "Unless we are to assume that between the middle of the eighteenth century and the beginning of the twentieth century the Igbo language had undergone radical transformations, it is impossible to think of any reading of Olaudah which would give it such meaning as 'vicissitude or good fortune,' 'one favoured' by God" (154). Remembering Equiano's hyperbolic providentialism in which "every occurrence" confirms him as a "particular favorite of Heaven," do we have here a kind of retrospective self-naming? Perhaps so, but as with so much else in this autobiography, what might seem an overdetermination of namings and events oddly adds up to an underdetermination. The name, in its proliferation of senses, comes to seem almost a mere promise of the distinction that will convert vicissitude into fortune and favor, that will set him apart, raise his loud voice above the prevailing cacophony, mark him as special. The event of naming never finishes, as it were; it is at once a circumstance and a foreboding. As with Gustavus Vassa, "Olaudah" is a name that exists as a destiny waiting to be fulfilled, even if only ironically.

I am inclined toward this ironizing interpretation of Olaudah because of its close association with that other marking to which he is destined but never receives, the Embrenché. Let me quote the passage again:

> My father was one of those elders or chiefs I have spoken of, and was styled Embrenché; a term, as I remember, importing the highest distinction, and signifying in our language a mark of grandeur. This mark is conferred on the person entitled to it, by cutting the skin across the top of the forehead, and drawing it down to the eye-brows; and while it is in this situation, applying a warm hand, and rubbing it until it shrinks up into a thick weal across the lower part of the forehead. Most of the judges and senators were thus marked; my father had long borne it: I had seen it conferred on one of my brothers, and I was also destined to receive it by my parents. (32–33)

Afigbo asserts that Equiano has scrambled things such that "two institutions appear to have been confused: "Equiano's conception of *Embrenche* combines the two ideas of *igbu ichi*, facial decoration by scarification, and *Ndichie*, the status of an elder, also a form of title and salutation" (152). This confusion, or conflation, brings together social and bodily distinction, but what remains to be thought through is how the overdetermination by conflation of title and mark, name and scar, is in the service, as it were, of an underdetermination of identity, because this is a mark of distinction that he never received but to which he was destined.

What governs the set of associations I am pursuing is the figure of circumcision. The two features of life in Benin emphasized by Equiano are namings and circumcision, and they are emphasized because they secure an identification with the Jews: "We practiced circumcision like the Jews. . . . Like them also, our children were named for some event." Indeed, as he remarks later on, it was through his readings in the Bible about Jewish law and practice that he both recognized and secured for memory the customs of his African past: "I was wonderfully surprised to see the laws and rules of my country written almost exactly there; a circumstance which I believe tended to impress our manners and customs more deeply on my memory" (92). This momentous event of finding his past already inscribed in the great book of the West does not, however, resolve the ambiguities surrounding his identity. Like the Jews, Equiano is structurally included, as it were, while simultaneously remaining an other within. To identify with the Jews is, from the perspective of the Christian West, to find one's identity through a mark of difference that both cannot, and must not, be erased. This is, of course, the theme of Paul's writings on the Jewish law and circumcision in his epistles. Equiano's treatment of this theme, I suggest, positions *The Interesting Narrative* within this symbolic dispute between the Jewish law and its Christian revision. Equiano emphasizes his chosenness—he is a "particular favorite of Heaven"—but the indexes of that chosenness are a series of scars and marks that remain oddly unimprinted, in suspension.

This ambiguity of circumcision—election and wound, assimilation and alienation—distributes its effects everywhere in Equiano's text as the figure for his errant trajectory. Even before he comes into contact with the whites, what Derrida might call Equiano's "experience of the mark" has begun to proliferate its ambiguities.[22] It is as if having been "hurried away even amongst the uncircumcised" (53) now requires that he remain unscarred, that the default represented by his having never received the Embrenché has now become the guarantee of some projected belonging: "I came amongst a people who did not circumcise" and who "ornamented themselves with scars. . . . They wanted sometimes to ornament me in the same manner, but I would not suffer them; hoping that I might some time be among a people who did not thus disfigure themselves" (54).[23] And indeed, when he does come among the Europeans, the scar he did not "suffer" becomes a source of great relief: "As I was now amongst a people who had not their faces scarred, like some of the African nations where I had been, I was very glad I did not let them ornament me in that manner when I was with them" (69). The psychic investment in this missing scar is made the more striking by its juxtaposition to the scene in which the young Olaudah tries to "make my face the same colour as my little play-mate" (69) through vigorous scrubbing. The logic seems to be, I may be (unfortunately) black, but at least I am not scarred. It is as if Equiano realizes that to belong in this new world depends on being able to remain unscarred, or to be able to erase the scars one has had.

Consider in this regard one final set of scars that Equiano bears and does not bear. In abolitionist discourses, the scene of flogging was a powerful rhetorical commonplace, and the display of scars from flogging an irrefutable proof of authenticity.[24] But Equiano is ambiguous on this matter as well. Early on, he quails before a "flogging" to be administered by one of his African masters, because he "had seldom been beaten at home" (49). Once on the slave ship, however, he is terribly beaten: "Two of the white men . . . laid me across . . . the windlass, and tied my feet, while the other flogged me severely. I had never experienced anything of this kind before. . . . I have seen some of these poor African prisoners most severely cut . . . and hourly whipped for not eating. This indeed was often the case with myself" (56). What had "seldom" happened before becomes what had "never" happened before. This may be Equiano pointing out the difference between African and English varieties of slaveholding (in the final edition the first "flogging" is changed to the more excusable "correction"): thus, the flogging at the windlass may quite accurately be called something that he had "never experienced before." In any case, like the "poor African prisoners" with whom he identifies here, such a "cutting" would be far from his last, because it was "often the case with myself." All the more surprising, then, that some years later, in Georgia, when Equiano is a freedman, he describes his experience rather differently: "I was . . . very apprehensive of a flogging at least. I dreaded, of all things, the thoughts of being stripped, as I never in my life had the marks of any violence of that kind" (139–40). Here the emphasis of "marks" makes it just possible that he is not denying having been "often" beaten in his early months as a slave. But is it possible to have been "most severely cut" and to have still escaped the "marks of any violence"? It is hard to see how. This ambiguity about the scars of flogging would seem to be generated by the same aporia between uniqueness and exemplarity that inheres in the figure of circumcision. Like the Embrenché, which at once marks cultural affiliation and promises distinction within it, the "marks of violence" are at once implied by Equiano's cultural identification—he is one of the "poor African slaves" who are hourly whipped, his experience here stands in for theirs—and somehow evaded or erased: "When I compare my lot with that of most of my countrymen, I regard myself as a *particular favorite of Heaven*" (31).

The Future Perfect King

That Equiano has to negotiate a double requirement to be at once unique and exemplary is not, I repeat, anything unusual. I have been arguing that this contradictory demand expresses itself in the form of a metaphoric network of marks and scars that are alternately there and not there, suffered and resisted, borne as sign of distinction and erased as sign of belonging. What we can call Equiano's poetics of experience thereby illuminates a condition in which history is taken up as something to be worked on, both ineluctable in its givenness and inescapably subject to revision, to a kind of textual erosion. On the one hand, such a condition has quite ancient versions: Equiano's play with the tropes of sovereignty and slavery, scars and circumcision, participates, as I have argued, in a rhetoric of Christian revisionism going back to Paul. On the other hand, the ambiguities of Equiano's text speak to contemporary dilemmas as well. One of the confounding things about the contemporary historical imagination is that even as the category of experience has become increasingly important for historical inquiry, its concept has become more obscure and attenuated. The same scholars who emphasize history from the ground up, the recovery of historical experience ignored by official historiography, also hold methodological and interpretive commitments that lead them to undermine any certainty of access to such experience. An interest in historical memory, for example, as opposed to the available archives so massively shaped by the interests of the powerful, cannot evade the indistinct line between what we might call inner and outer experience, where the first names a zone in which the imagination and desire (with their correlates: defense, fantasy, projection) play a central role, and the second names conditions and events that arrive from without. It is precisely by worrying this distinction, by which I mean both keeping it in play and assuming its essential porousness, that much sophisticated work at the intersection of psychology, rhetoric, and history has been produced.[25]

As with experience, so with the notion of the event. Here, the discourse of trauma theory crystallizes the dilemma with the greatest clarity: something terrible has happened, something catastrophic, but it exerts its effects precisely by being unable to be recuperated, by forming a hole in the individual's, or society's, ability to place it narratively and sequentially, or to make it the theme of communication (though its incommunicableness, its unspeakableness, can be communicated quite effectively). In this discourse of trauma theory, we take history so seriously that we don't really believe in it. In a kind of post-historical Kantianism, we endlessly elaborate the critique of historicism, a critique that preserves the very concepts that it declares radically problematic. Thinking historically becomes recognizing that we have no access to "events-in-themselves": "History can be grasped only in the very inaccessibility of its occurrence."[26] Equiano's various wounds and scars that seem all the more determinative for their inaccessibility might be seen as an allegory of trauma theory as a model of history. Derrida's vocabulary of marks, scars, and wounds can serve as an index here: there is, Derrida writes in *Monolingualism of the Other*, "a desire to invent a *first* language that would be, rather, a *prior-to-the-first* language destined to translate that memory. But to translate the memory of what, precisely, did not take place, of what . . . ought, nevertheless, to have left a trace, a specter, the phantomatic body, the phantom-member—palpable, painful, but hardly legible—of traces, marks, and scars" (61).[27] But rather than follow the intriguing resonances between Equiano's story and Derrida's meditations on history and experience, let me turn to a less well-known writer, one more newfangled than Equiano or Saint Paul, to be sure, and yet still not quite of our present moment.

"Is it not strange," asks Maurice Halbwachs in his wonderful book *On Collective Memory*, "that society causes the mind to transfigure the past to the point of yearning for it?"[28] Halbwachs began his book with a thought experiment that may remind us of Equiano's story:

> A child of nine or ten years old possesses many recollections, both recent and fairly old. What will this child be able to retain if he is abruptly separated from his family, transported to a country where his language is not spoken, where neither the appearance of people and places, nor their customs, resemble in any way that which was familiar to him up to this moment? The child has left one society in order to pass into another. It seems that at the same time the child will have lost the ability to remember in the second society all that he did and all that impressed him, which he used to recall without difficulty, in the first. In order to retrieve some of these uncertain and incomplete memories it is necessary that the child, in the new society of which he is a part, at least be shown images reconstructing for a moment the group and the milieu from which the child had been torn. (37–38)

Halbwachs introduces this "extreme case" (38) as an illustration of the irreducibly social and collective dimension of memory. He is "astonished when reading psychological treatises that deal with memory to find that people are considered there as isolated beings" (38). On the contrary, Halbwachs insists, memories are "recalled to me externally, and the groups of which I am a part at any time give me the means to reconstruct them" (38). Indeed, he goes further: it is *only* "to the degree that our individual thought places itself in these [social] frameworks and participates in this memory that it is capable of the act of recollection" (38). It is a stark image of the domination of the individual and his unique history by the collective's code: "One cannot in fact think about the events of one's past without discoursing upon them. But to discourse upon something means to connect within a single system of ideas our opinions as well as those of our circle. It means to perceive in what happens to us a particular application of facts concerning which social thought reminds us at every moment of the meaning and impact these facts have for it. In this way, the framework of collective memory confines and binds our most intimate remembrances to each other" (53). Well before Foucault, we can see Halbwachs reaching for a concept of discourse to indicate a quasi-linguistic, supraindividual, communicative medium. The crucial features of discourse here are systematicity (a "single system of ideas") and the production of examples: "what happens to us" is merely a "particular application" of a larger, more general, and systematic case. "What happens to us" never becomes a memory unless it submits to this process. There is no unique experience unless it is in some way also exemplary, and thus participates in a system that erodes its uniqueness.

This domination of the individual by the collective is admittedly "harsh": "How can one fail to see that if people in society . . . were limited to the groups of their contemporaries . . . if they were constantly forced to behave in conformity with their customs, tastes, beliefs, and interests, they might well bow before the social laws but would endure them only as a harsh and continued necessity?" (51). Halbwachs suggests that it is as a kind of fabricated escape from such "necessity" that society demands the production of history, to the point of yearning for it: "Society from time to time obligates people not just to reproduce in thought previous events of their lives, but also to touch them up, to shorten them, or to complete them so that, however convinced we are that our memories are exact, we give them a prestige that reality did not possess" (51). Our yearning and our revisionism go hand in hand here, at once a retreat from the presentist domination of contemporary social codes of meaning and the performance of an obligation imposed by that same society. Society obliges us to yearn for a touched-up past.

Equiano's account of his acculturation is, in many ways, quite Halbwachsian. Consider this example: when Equiano reads the Bible he "was wonderfully surprised to see the laws and rules of my country written almost exactly here; a circumstance which I believe tended to impress our manners and customs more deeply on my memory" (92). Here it is the biblical account of the time of the patriarchs that gives Equiano "the means to reconstruct" his childhood memories of Benin, or perhaps it is the entire "social framework" (Halbwachs 38) in which the Bible operates as authoritative text that allows Equiano to find his own past there. On the one hand, Equiano characterizes his early memories of life in Benin as an "impression . . . time could not erase" (46). This naturalistic account of memory, in which things happen to isolated individuals that leave permanent traces, would seem to be exactly the model Halbwachs disputes. But notice how Equiano introduces in this very passage an acknowledgement of an ex post facto effect, a force of alteration so pervasive that it even renders it a matter of little import whether certain feelings and memories are "real or imaginary":

> I hope the reader will not think I have trespassed on his patience in introducing myself to him with some account of the manners and customs of my country. They had been implanted in me with great care, and made an impression on my mind, which time could not erase, and which all adversity and variety of fortune I have since experienced served only to rivet and record: for, whether the love of one's country be real or imaginary, or a lesson of reason, or an instinct of nature, I still look back with pleasure on the first scenes of my life, though that pleasure has been for the most part mingled with sorrow. (46)

Equiano here describes a fundamental ambiguation of the way in which experience produces, secures, and complicates memory, to such a point that one cannot decide whether it is "real or imaginary," or affectively separate pleasure from sorrow. The same movement that "rivets and records" also transforms and alters. Equiano considers this process by which one secures memory through a kind of experiential overwriting to be a distinctive feature of the white world:

> From the various scenes I had beheld on ship-board, I soon grew a stranger to terror of every kind, and was, in that respect at least, almost an Englishman. I have often reflected with surprise that I never felt half the alarm at any of the numerous dangers I have been in, that I was filled with at the first sight of the Europeans, and at every act of theirs, even the most trifling. . . . I no longer looked upon them as spirits, but as men superior to us; and therefore I had the stronger desire to resemble them; to imbibe their spirit, and imitate their manners; I therefore embraced every occasion of improvement; and every thing that I observed I treasured up in my memory. (77–78)

The passage describes the process of cultural assimilation as the growth in the ability to transform experience from the registering of affect to the "treasuring up" of memory. To become "almost an Englishman" seems to mean translating experience into memory, a process whereby that which is given (as experience) must be managed and available for transformation (as memory, as a kind of capitalization of the "treasure" of experience). Such a regime does not discount experience; on the contrary, it values it greatly, but only as something that can be worked, transformed, or developed.

But of course we are still considering Equiano's memory, what I have called his poetics of experience, as he presents it in his text. What if we take his African past to have been fabricated, as Carretta has felt obliged to do? Here we must return to what I have argued is the profoundest maneuver in

Equiano's text, his Christian troping of the royal slave, in which he presents himself as having been destined for, but never received, the Embrenché. Equiano presents himself as an unmarked child—already spoken for, in a sense, destined for the mark of distinction, but as yet unscarred by it. Let us say that he was, in a sense, perfect in the past—a child unoffended, Jesus might have said. And in the future, too, he will be perfect, when the suspended mark of distinction, the sovereign greatness that lies latent in his childish past, will at last be conferred. But at that point the mark will no longer be a wound, will no longer be riven by an ambiguity as to whether it indexes exclusion or belonging, exemplarity or exceptionality. To have "become as little children" is to attain a condition in which an immemorial past meets up with a transcendent future, when to be a sovereign and to be a self are no longer conditions that ceaselessly undermine each other. The perfect, as yet unscarred, unoffended child will have become the perfect king, no longer scarred, because at once the "greatest" in the "kingdom of heaven," and no different from all others there. But this condition can only be expressed in the future perfect tense: his past perfection can only be conferred from the vantage of a future still to come. At some point inaccessible to us in the present, Equiano's latent sovereign childish greatness *will have been* vindicated. In the meantime, there is only the work of marking and unmarking, the drift of a world to which "offenses must come." If Equiano continues to exert a kind of fantasy power on our historical imagination, it is because his Africanness is a condition all the more perfect for being suspended by its quasi-fictionality, caught between a past prior to the "offenses" of the slave trade—and to the scars of experience itself that that trade is made to emblematize and a future in which all such traumas will no longer matter, because they no longer divide the mortal self from the immortal sovereignty for which we continue to yearn.

THREE

Was Billy Black? Herman Melville and the Captive King

It sometimes happens, when I am teaching *Billy Budd*, that a brave student will ask, after a day or so of discussion, "Is Billy black?" How could such a misunderstanding come about? It's true that Melville's language is notoriously difficult for students, and *Billy Budd* especially so, with its ornate vocabulary and dense allusiveness. Consider the following passage:

> A barbarian Billy radically was—as much so, for all the costume, as his countrymen the British captives, living trophies, made to march in the Roman triumph of Germanicus. Quite as much as those later barbarians, young men probably, and picked specimens among the earlier British converts to Christianity, at least nominally such, taken to Rome (as today converts from lesser isles of the sea may be taken to London), of whom the Pope of that time, admiring the strangeness of their personal beauty so unlike the Italian stamp, their clear ruddy complexion and curled flaxen locks, exclaimed, "Angles" (meaning *English*, the modern derivative), "Angles, do you call them? And is it because they look so much like angels?" Had it been later in time, one would think that the Pope had in mind

> Fra Angelico's seraphs, some of whom, plucking apples in gardens of the Hesperides, have the faint rosebud complexion of the more beautiful English girls.[1]

Billy goes through a dizzying set of transformations here: he is first a "British" captive (that is, slave) of the Romans, and then a "nominal" Christian whose transportation and review before a different leader in the same imperial capital merges imperceptibly with the earlier enslavement; finally, through wordplay that conjoins racial and artistic determinations (as "Angle" turns to "angel" to "Fra *Angel*ico"), Billy's abjection undergoes an overt aestheticization in his appearance as a seraph and a girl. But even if some students do not have "ruddy" and "flaxen" as part of their working vocabulary, how could they fail to see, once they have read about his "faint rosebud complexion," that Billy is being described as especially beautiful because *especially white*? It may be that what students pick up on here, amid the complexly shifting frames of reference, is simply that being a "barbarian" and being a "captive" both have something to do with race. Billy's transformation from captive slave to pretty girl turns around the pope's admiring gaze, a gaze that, like Behn's toward Oroonoko, both dominates and exalts its object on the basis of its racial difference. Race casts a shadow over the whole passage. Perhaps students grasp this structure of racial domination, but for them such a structure would "normally" have a black person in the dominated position. The question "Is Billy black?" in other words, correctly registers Melville's focus on the relation between domination and racialization, and misrecognizes it at the same time. Somewhat like Amasa Delano, these students' intuitive grasp of a deep structure both grants them access to a profound truth and makes them unable to see what is right before their eyes.

"Was Billy Black?" The question might be rephrased, in order to make its implications clearer: to what extent is there what Toni Morrison called an "Africanist presence" structuring Melville's text?[2] That is, how does the full meaning of Billy's whiteness *depend on* the complex racializing ideologies born from new world slavery? In this chapter, I argue that Melville summarizes a figurative tradition begun with Behn and continued in the work of Equiano. He circulates the figure of the black sovereign—in Daggoo, in Atufal, in a certain "black pagod" encountered on the Liverpool docks—as part of a lifelong attempt to think through the antinomies of the modern self and its ensnarement in the mysteries of domination and subjection. Like Aphra Behn, Melville takes the problem of sovereignty as one of his basic themes. But what must be discerned around the edges of Behn's new world texts, namely, the knowledge, unhappily discovered, that in the post-absolutist modernity in which she found herself, sovereignty had become subordinated to an ideology of individualism, is for Melville the starting point: sovereignty, for this intense individualist, is first and foremost a trait, or difficult achievement, of the self. Political realities, or what he calls the "old State-secret," cannot be separated from issues of individuals in their relation to other individuals. Like Olaudah Equiano, moreover, Melville understands the black sovereign to be not merely a figure born from the African slave trade—Behn had seen that clearly enough—but also a symbol of a modern condition of dislocation or rootlessness, a condition epitomized by the sailor's life, combining as it does unusual mobility and freedom with the utmost subjection and constraint. The problem of the modern sovereign subject emerges for Melville from a matrix in which slave and sovereign, despot and pirate, trade places with confounding frequency. So pervasive is the theme of sovereignty in Melville's work that it is very difficult to get analytical purchase on it. But any account of this theme will fall short if it does not recognize the shadow of race in Melville's imaginative horizon.

We can begin by noting that Billy is, as we have already briefly seen, an insistently racialized character. His moral purity is understood as a form of racial purity: Billy is "cast in a mold peculiar to the finest physical examples of those Englishmen in whom the Saxon strain would seem not at all to partake of any Norman or any other admixture" (1360). In such a description, and in the passage about the English as angels, Melville makes use of what Reginald Horsman has analyzed as the ideology of "racial anglosaxonism." The story about the Pope to which Melville alludes, in fact, was a cherished one in this ideology: the "justly short-lived magazine *The Anglo-Saxon*, published in London in 1849 and 1850," boasted an "emblem on the front cover—Pope Gregory I looking at a group of cherubic children, accompanied by the motto *Non Angli sed Angeli*."[3] What makes this story appealing, one surmises, is that racial identity is depicted as constant, despite the fickleness of fortune: even when it manifests itself in the persons of barbarians, converts, or slaves, the essential excellence of the Anglo-Saxon racial type will shine through, visible even to a Pope. Such an idea of racial essence is easily translated into a concept of natural nobility, and thus it is not surprising that Billy's purity of "Saxon strain" is also testament that his "lineage [is] in direct contradiction to his lot," that although he is a "foundling, a presumable by-blow," he is "evidently, no ignoble one" (1360, 1361). A cluster of attributes—Billy's personal beauty, his racial purity, and his natural nobility (both a social and a moral designation)—all converge on what could be called Billy's *prehistoric* essence, the insusceptibility of his identity to complete historical analysis. This prehistoric identity could equally be called mythic, as the relentless work of allusion in the text would indicate (Billy is Adam, he is Hercules, he is Apollo, he is Christ, he is even "the 'Celtic Apollo,' known also as Beli and Budd," according to H. Bruce Franklin).[4]

But what is the figural logic underlying these mythic overdeterminations? Billy's "barbarian" essence is tied to his singularity: his status as foundling is less a matter of mere historical accident than it is an existential condition, in the sense that Ishmael has in mind when he concludes that we are all foundlings and orphans. Billy is an entire people unto himself—"His entire family was practically invested in himself" (1359). He epitomizes a race, a "lineage," a "family," while also being fundamentally separated from them. Billy is at once exemplary and exceptional. This is perhaps what it means to be *the* "Handsome Sailor" (1353)—Melville never speaks of *a* "Handsome Sailor." Even as he makes it clear that *the* "Handsome Sailor" is a type of which there can be numerous examples, what that "signal object" (1353) exemplifies is the singularity of exception—hence the definite article.

This logic of exemplary exceptionality is, as we have seen, the logic of sovereignty, and so it is not surprising that in the first paragraph of *Billy Budd* the "Handsome Sailor" is introduced to us as displaying an "offhand unaffectedness of natural regality." Melville quickly goes on in the second paragraph to offer a "remarkable instance" of such "natural regality," and I suspect that it is the imposing entrance of this "black pagod of a fellow" that, more than anything else, plants a seed of confusion in some students' minds about Billy's race:

> A somewhat remarkable instance recurs to me. In Liverpool, now half a century ago, I saw under the shadow of the great dingy street-wall of Prince's Dock (an obstruction long since removed) a common sailor so intensely black that he must needs have been a native African of the unadulterate blood of Ham—a symmetric figure much above the average height. The two ends of a gay silk handkerchief

> thrown loose about the neck danced upon the displayed ebony of his chest, in his ears were big hoops of gold, and a Highland bonnet with a tartan band set off his shapely head. It was a hot noon in July; and his face, lustrous with perspiration, beamed with barbaric good humor. In jovial sallies right and left, his white teeth flashing into view, he rollicked along, the center of a company of shipmates. These were made up of such an assortment of tribes and complexions as would have well fitted them to be marched up by Anacharsis Cloots before the bar of the first French Assembly as Representatives of the Human Race. At each spontaneous tribute rendered by the wayfarers to this black pagod of a fellow—the tribute of a pause and stare, and less frequently an exclamation—the motley retinue showed that they took that sort of pride in the evoker of it which the Assyrian priests doubtless showed for their grand sculptured Bull when the faithful prostrated themselves. (1353)

A number of the motifs later associated with Billy are here in plain view. Just as Billy is remarkably white, this first instance of the "Handsome Sailor" is "so intensely black that he must needs have been a native African of the unadulterate blood of Ham." Like Aphra Behn's Oroonoko, this "black pagod" projects his "natural regality" by being more black than anyone else, and this more intense racialization—as is the case for Billy and was the case for Oroonoko—does not limit or constrain his influence, but rather extends it: Melville's fantasy here, it bears remarking, has a black man receiving the "spontaneous tribute" of all of humanity (the Anacharsis Cloots gathering). This tribute is "barbaric," certainly, as the descriptions of the man as a "black pagod" and a "sculptured Bull" make clear (Franklin points out that the Celtic god Beli or Budd was also "represented by a sacred bull" [196]). But of course Billy, too, is essentially an "upright barbarian" (1362). A barbaric, racialized, natural regality: these seem to be essential attributes of the "Handsome Sailor." There is something preternaturally perfect, intense, exceptional about these bodies in which "comeliness and power" (1354) are conjoined, as if in their exemplification of the kinds of bodies they share with others—men's bodies, black or white bodies, laboring bodies—they accrued to themselves another more mystical, extra-historical body.

We know that *Billy Budd* underwent a particularly extensive process of revision and elaboration, with each of the main characters emerging serially in Melville's conception. Begun as a mere headnote to a poem about an old sailor named Billy Budd awaiting his execution, the story eventually generated the Handsome Sailor's nemesis and moral negation, Claggart, as it evolved in Melville's head. This primal antagonism seems to have suggested in turn the need for a witness and judge, and soon Melville introduces Captain Vere. Only after that did he interpolate this second paragraph describing the "black pagod." Although Melville went on to make further emendations in his story (mostly pertaining to Vere), the "black pagod" described in this second paragraph nevertheless stands as one of the final creations of his long writing career.[5] Melville thus places at the threshold of his most backward-glancing and testamentary fiction an African exemplar of the "natural regality" that had occupied him in many of his major works. Carolyn Karcher, many years ago, recognized the symbolic significance of this passage, describing this "epiphanic opening scene of *Billy Budd*" as Melville's "finest—and final—statement about race," an indication that he had "at last become free to dismiss the phantasm of race with complete serenity."[6] Karcher sees the "black pagod" as in a line with Daggoo, and that seems right, but the more complex antecedent would be Atufal, from *Benito Cereno*, as I will argue. Rather than constituting a dismissal of the "phantasm of race," however, it might perhaps be better to say that this late interpolation suggests Melville's abiding investment in such a phantasm. At the end of *Benito Cereno*, Captain Delano cries in frustration to the Spanish captain, "What has cast such a shadow upon you?" to which Cereno replies, "The negro" (754). By placing the "black pagod" at the beginning of the end, as it were, Melville has him cast a shadow over his entire work. This late positioning of the "black pagod" suggests Melville's intuition that the shadow or "phantasm" of race held a structural inescapability in his work as a whole.

Shadows depend on the bodies that they extend and distort—depend on them, but are never one with them. A shadow is a phantasmatic body, we might say, and one that has a fundamentally ambiguous relation to time and to history. This seems to be one implication of the way that Melville uses the metaphor of the shadow in *Benito Cereno*, where the prefigurations of the opening—"Shadows present, foreshadowing deeper shadows to come" (673)—combine with the retrospective shadow cast by "the negro" to suggest a maximal coincidence of different historical times, such that "past, present, and future seemed one" (733). But the unity of this "one" is complete and punctual only at the moment of the act—in the instant, for example, in which Cereno jumps into Delano's boat (the moment in the story in which Melville uses the phrase about past, present, and future). The superimposition of different times figured by the shadow, on the other hand, might better be understood as relation between the act and its suspension, between acting and exercising the ever-present capacity not to act. The shadow thus becomes a figure of the mutual implication of the actual with the potential, an implication realized in *Benito Cereno*, as I will argue, in the form of "suspense."[7] When asking about the shadow cast by the "black pagod," in other words, when asking in what sense we might recognize—or misrecognize—Billy as black, we will need to attend to this notion that a shadow is *always* necessarily a "shadow present," but never *merely* present: in its manner of extending and warping the body to which its presence is tied, the shadow also extends backward or forward, accompanying the body with the reminder that its present is crowded with virtual or potential other times, other bodies.

The Captive King

At the center of Melville's exploration of sovereignty stands *Moby-Dick*, and its mad captain, Ahab, a "crowned king" and a "very vile one."[8] It is actually Ahab's biblical namesake who is called "very vile" in the text, but because, like all Melville's ship captains, Ahab embodies a "dictatorship beyond which . . . there was no earthly appeal" (*BC* 681), his name appropriately links him to the Oriental despot. Indeed, for Melville the very concept of sovereignty finds its purest embodiment in the ship captain. The captain's "irresistible dictatorship" (*MD* 166) is a type of power in conformity with Hobbes's concept of the "mortal God" to whom has been given "the use of so much power and strength conferred on him that by terror thereof he is enabled to conform the wills of them all to peace at home and mutual aid against their enemies abroad."[9] *Moby-Dick* is, among other things, a story of Ahab's exercise of this "terror," a story of how the monomaniac captain "conforms the wills" of his crew, suppressing insubordination in order to orchestrate "mutual aid" against the enemy he has identified in the white whale. But of course this enemy, as a host of critics down the years have observed, is a version of himself, though perhaps a less "reverent" version, in Hobbes's sense. In Job, Hobbes tells us, God refers to that "great *Leviathan*," the monster of the deep, as "King of the Proud" (210), and it is from this reference that Hobbes takes the title for his book on the construction of the state, the "generation of that great LEVIATHAN, or rather (to speak more reverently) of that *Mortal God* to which we owe, under the Immortal God, our peace and defense" (109). Ahab is the state, and the Leviathan is the state, too—which makes a certain sense of the self-destructiveness depicted in Ahab. But how shall we understand this supplement of "reverence" that serves to distinguish the monster of the deep from the "*Mortal God*" of sovereign power who hunts him? What mediates the relation between the white whale and the white man?

Wai-Chee Dimock has offered the most sustained meditation on the metaphoric logic of empire and sovereign selfhood in Melville's work, and she discerns a racial logic in *Moby-Dick*. Ahab's sovereign status is the insignia of his barbarism and his doom: "More verdict than tribute, such allusions"—Ahab as a "Khan of the plank," as a "sultan" and a "Grand Turk," and so forth—"hardly describe Ahab: they merely brand him as a thing of the past. At once regal and barbaric, he takes his place among other candidates for extinction."[10] The main "candidate for extinction" Dimock has in mind here is the Indian. As I will discuss in the next chapter, Melville's reference to Ahab as "that wild Logan of the woods" (166) supports Dimock's argument that Ahab represents a type of "the last" Indian (though oddly enough she does not mention this passage). But we know that in the "Handsome Sailor" Melville *celebrates* "barbarian regality"—the concept has other uses than merely to mark its possessor as doomed. There is a utopian as well as melancholic dimension to the logic of sovereignty in Melville.

C. L. R. James eloquently argued a half century ago that Melville's matchless analysis, in *Moby-Dick*, of how "the society of free individualism would give birth to totalitarianism and be unable to defend itself against it" depended on his grasp of the role played by racial domination in the modern world: "The political organization of Modern Europe has been based on the creation and consolidation of national states. And the national state, every single national state, had and still has a racial doctrine."[11] The "mariners, renegades, and castaways" of his title, that colorful Anacharsis Cloots deputation manning the *Pequod*, represent the races of the world dominated by the white man, argues James. He notes how as Ahab's madness and isolation increase, Melville underscores this condition by showing Ahab's dependence on nonwhite others. When James comes to speak of Fedallah, the "Parsee" harpooner Ahab has smuggled onboard the *Pequod*, he picks up on what we have already noticed is Melville's interest in the metaphor of the shadow and its ability to convey the estranged intimacy created by racial domination: "In Fedallah Ahab sees his forethrown shadow; in Ahab Fedallah sees his abandoned substance. Sometimes Ahab seems independent of him, sometimes they seem joined together. Ahab is power, Fedallah only a shade, but the shade is always before him" (James 55). On the other side, as it were, there is Pip, the black boy from Alabama: "He begins to weaken on the side of Fedallah and he begins to weaken on the side of Pip" (54). Both Fedallah and Pip present aspects of Ahab's own identity, James suggests, aspects that he incompletely and unsuccessfully negates. "If in Fedallah, Melville has dramatized the extreme form of the return to barbarism that is dragging Ahab down on the one side, he has on the other side created an equally daring dramatization of the unattainable vision that floats in Ahab's disordered mind" (56). Both Fedallah and Pip cast shadows, in other words. Fedallah, as the "shade always before him," signifies a barbarism "before civilization" from which Ahab can never fully extricate himself, while Pip is a shadow cast into the future, a vision of an emancipation "after civilization" from which Ahab is equally barred. Pip's madness-inducing time in the middle of the ocean, in which he witnessed "God's foot upon the treadle of the loom" (*MD* 453), has left him "as indifferent and as uncompromised as God" (57), and it is this vision, James suggests, that Ahab knows is unattainable. Fedallah represents an atavistic, savage condition that can never be transcended, while Pip represents a condition of absolute emancipation that can never be attained. Ahab is shadowed by the two ideal events that sovereignty in the new world can never achieve—the extinction of the past and the emancipation of the future. In this sense, Fedallah lines up with the Indian, and all things aboriginal, while Pip's blackness renders him susceptible, as Equiano and other writers of the black Atlantic had been susceptible, to a Christian narrative of salvific reversal: "Prelusive of the eternal time," Pip "beat[s] his tambourine in glory; called a coward here, hailed a hero there" (*MD* 132).

James characterizes Ahab's relations to Fedallah and Pip as both inescapable and pathological, positions toward which Ahab "weakens" (perhaps only in his own mind). In both cases, there is an asymmetry characterizing the interdependence between Ahab and his dark other. But elsewhere James describes white interaction with the nonwhite laboring body in more purely celebratory language. The crew of the *Pequod* are doomed by Ahab's madness and exploitation, to be sure, but Melville's description of these "men associated for common labor" (28) also harbors a utopian impulse. Melville's description of Daggoo—and James's uncritical invocation of this description—is suggestive here. "The great negro" with his "broad, baronial, and superb . . . person," is, Ishmael tells us directly, a "noble savage" (165): "Daggoo retained all his barbaric virtues, and erect as a giraffe, moved about the decks in all the pomp of six feet five in his socks. There was a corporeal humility in looking up at him; and a white man standing next to him seemed a white flag come to beg truce of a fortress. Curious to tell, this imperial negro, Ahasuerus Daggoo, was the Squire of little Flask, who looked like a chess-man beside him" (131). Daggoo is supplied with a kind of epic epithet: his head is called "hearse-plumed" (165, 241) after the black feathers sported by the horses drawing the hearse, an image of deathly regalia, and certainly his "imperial," "baronial and superb . . . person" underscores the sovereign grandeur that may have brought Ahasuerus to mind. Here "person" retains something of what it means in Hobbes, namely the externalized embodiment of a power or force in itself not corporeal: thus Ishmael speaks of a "*vitality* diffused through so broad, baronial, and superb a person" (emphasis added). In the book of Esther, Ahasuerus exemplifies both the monopoly on violence granted the king—the power both to condemn to death and to grant reprieve, to make die and let live, in Foucault's pithy formulation—but interestingly he also displays a kind of subordination to his own function: having been tricked by Haman into issuing an edict against the Jews, he is unable to rescind that edict—the king's edicts cannot be countermanded even by the king—and so he must issue another edict allowing the Jews to arm and defend themselves. Likening Daggoo to Ahasuerus, Melville suggests that the African's barbarian regality is similarly bound up in the antinomies of sovereign power.

This is true not just with respect to his regal "person," but also as regards his role on board the *Pequod.* Daggoo is the third mate Flask's harpooneer, which ties him, despite his imperial grandeur, to a symbol of abjection. When Flask "enters King Ahab's presence" during mealtimes, he does so "in the character of Abjectus, or the Slave" (162). It is important to recognize that Ishmael is playing all this for laughs, as he still is when he pairs the "subaltern" (163) Flask—whose nickname is King-Post, after a ship-stanchion—with his imperial underling. With courtly politeness, Daggoo asks Flask, "Will you mount?" (240), and thereby becomes King-Post's King Post: "The sight of little Flask mounted upon gigantic Daggoo was yet more curious . . . On his broad back, flaxen-haired Flask seemed a snow-flake. The bearer looked nobler than the rider. Though, truly, vivacious, tumultuous, ostentatious little Flask would now and then stamp with impatience; but not one added heave did he thereby give to the negro's lordly chest. So have I seen Passion and Vanity stamping the living magnanimous earth, but the earth did not alter her tides and her seasons for that" (241). When James cites this passage, he does so not to interrogate the discourse of noble savagery Ishmael puts to such florid use here, nor even to explore the meaning of the ironic reversals structuring these descriptions, but rather as an instance, one among many, of Melville's heroicizing of the "skill and grace and beauty" (23) of the laboring collective, here a collective including even Flask, "mediocrity that he is" (24). To the extent that there is a "barbarian regality" that is not merely an index of Ahab's failure, then, it is this multiracial, collective, laboring body: "There is tension," James enthuses, "the tension of strenuous labor, but there is skill and grace and beauty" (23).

Cesare Casarino, in his recent moving meditation on Melville's "antinarrative of modernity in crisis," also concludes that *Moby-Dick* celebrates a utopian body.[12] Casarino pairs Melville's novel with Marx's *Grundrisse*, "two hymns to the male body as the other limit of capital" (109). Casarino's main exhibit is Queequeg, not Daggoo, but the stakes are the same: "What is certain is that the body of Queequeg as well as the interracial and cross-cultural romance between Ishmael and Queequeg constitute some of the most exemplary trajectories traced by the desires of the other limit in *Moby-Dick*" (109). The body in question is a more than merely male body—it is, Casarino writes, a "*corpus absolutus*": "a body that has broken away and freed itself—even if just for an instant—from the myriad forms of domination and exploitation, that is, that body in which life can no longer be bought or sold as it is absolutely expended in itself, in its singular and autonomous form. *Moby-Dick* and the *Grundrisse* are the living epiclesis of such a *corpus absolutus* of the other limit and of its always potentially revolutionary life: these two antinarratives of modernity in crisis are love songs to that body and to that life" (109). The *corpus absolutus* lies outside exchange, lies outside domination and exploitation, and for both James and Casarino, this limit-body appears to Melville in the form of the nonwhite laboring body. Moreover, both critics insist that the sea is the necessary site of this body's manifestation. For James, the communal life on shipboard is what cleanses the relationship of any tincture of homosexuality (always a suspect "modern" degeneracy in James): "Ishmael begins by clinging to the powerful Queequeg and, in typical modern fashion, his relationship on land has all the marks of homosexuality. But as soon as they get on board among the crew, that relationship disappears" (43).[13] In its place, there is a kind of non-aligned laboring collective: the members of the crew "are bound by the fact that they work together on a whaling-ship. They are a world-federation of modern industrial workers. They owe allegiance to no nationality. . . . Among the crew nobody is anything. They owe no allegiance to anybody or anything except the work they have to do and the relations with one another on which that work depends" (20).

Casarino's more detailed analysis both corrects and extends James's reading. For Casarino, the scenes between Ishmael and Queequeg in New Bedford are marked not by a suspicious homosexuality, but rather by Ishmael's homophobia, his panic before the idea of sharing a bed with a "drunken Christian" sailor (157). But what shows up instead is a sober cannibal—Queequeg—and this occasions a complete transformation of the topic of homosociality: "From now on, Ishmael abandons himself to Queequeg, and the affective register of their experimentation with new forms of male-male sociality" (157). What henceforth governs the relationship between Ishmael and Queequeg is indeed, as James had insisted, a swerve away from a certain homosexuality, but for Casarino the swerve is not in the mode of repudiation but rather of an "abandon" to what he calls, following Leo Bersani, a "non-psychological homosexuality." And here, too, the utopianism of this abandon is made available through the discourse of noble savagery. Casarino boldly takes the issue on directly:

> The fact that this chance encounter also constitutes the return of the cannibal-as-noble-savage from the pages of *Typee* . . . does not make such a return any less novel or unexpected in *Moby-Dick*. Unlike both the narrator of *Typee* and the South-Pacific Islanders whose captive guest he is in that novel, in fact, Ishmael and Queequeg have completely delinked from homes to which they are both painfully aware they will never be able to return. . . . As far as Queequeg is concerned, Ishmael relates that, once asked if he would ever return to his native Kokovoko so as to take the place of his father as ruler of that island, he "answered no, not yet; and added that he was fearful Christianity, or rather Christians, had unfitted him for ascending the pure and undefiled throne of thirty pagan Kings before him." Clearly, the fact that both Ishmael and Queequeg have irreparably

> quit the realm of the father-king constitutes the crucial condition of possibility of their loving each other in ways that would be unrecognizable in each of their originary realms. (157–58)

Casarino reminds us here that Melville inserts Queequeg, too, into the captive-king paradigm. But he does so with a wink: Kokovoko, we are assured, "is not down on any map; true places never are" (*MD* 61). Unlike Oroonoko, who is tricked onto the ship that forever separates him from his rightful realm, Queequeg stows away, driven by an implausible "wild desire to visit Christendom" (62). Given Melville's knowing play with the inversions of this discourse—Queequeg's "barbed iron was in lieu of a sceptre now" (62)—we might look again at the "abandon" made possible by the figure of Queequeg, and indeed by the entire captive-king, noble-savage network of tropes. It seems to me that the entire problem of the interrelation of sovereignty, race, and slavery is handled in *Moby-Dick* in a seriocomic mode, as with the description of Daggoo and Flask, or the wry observation that it is whalers that provide the oil "by which a king's head is solemnly oiled at his coronation, even as a head of salad" (*MD* 123). The rapid inversions between abjection and exaltation seem, in the final analysis, to free Ishmael up, even if that emancipation only takes place at the level of his discourse. If even sovereign Ahab can be described as suffering a "Guinea-Coast slavery of solitary command," we might well ask with Ishmael, "Who aint a slave?" (6). The captive king is useful, on this reading, as affording Ishmael, and thus the reader, a vantage from which the structure linking sovereignty and slavery can be perceived as a whole.

The dynamic into which the noble savage discourse intervenes, I would argue, a dynamic fundamentally associated for both James and Casarino with the topos of the ship, is less an "irreparable" breach from the "realm of the father-king" than it is the deterritorialization of that realm itself, a kind of intensification and volatilization of the antinomies governing the modern sovereign subject. If the magisterial, imperial, nonwhite body stands in for, grants access to, a vision of a unique *corpus absolutus* outside the circuits of exchange, we do well, I think, to recognize that such a corpus is a utopian variant of the artificial person of the state itself, a recto to its verso. The topos of the ship, precisely to the extent that it harbors utopian possibilities, presents a vision of a structure of inversion, or reversibility, between power and powerlessness, that seems to escape historical transformation. It is not until *Benito Cereno*, I would argue, that Melville confronts the moral and historical vertigo brought on by the deterritorialization of sovereignty manifested on shipboard. But before I turn to that text, and *its* circulation of the figure of the captive king, let us turn to one last passage from *Moby-Dick*, for we can see in it, I think, Melville's skepticism about the possibility of our ever being able to effect an "irreparable breach" with the "realm of the father-king."

In a famous letter to Nathaniel Hawthorne, Melville exalts the "man who, like Russia or the British Empire, declares himself a sovereign nature (in himself) amid the powers of heaven, hell, and earth. He may perish; but so long as he exists he insists upon treating with all Powers upon an equal basis. If any of those other Powers choose to withhold certain secrets, let them; that does not impair my sovereignty in myself; that does not make me tributary."[14] Melville assumes that there is an isomorphism between the self and the state, an assumption with deep historical roots in the development of international law and the rise of the European state system. "The analogy between natural persons and international persons was one of the main premises upon which the science of international law was founded in the sixteenth and seventeenth centuries," wrote Edwin DeWitt Dickinson in 1916.[15] "In one form or another," he continues, "the analogy was invoked constantly from the time when the law of nations first became a subject of juristic speculation and practical significance. The early conceptions of the nature of international society were based upon it. . . . It had an immeasurable influence upon the subsequent development of international law" (564).[16] Melville's letter to Hawthorne, I am suggesting, assumes this concept of sovereignty, and assumes its history. But Melville's literary imagination interrogates this isomorphism with great energy in all his work. Melville suggests, for example, that there are secrets harbored within the state, and within the self, secrets that are not accessible to an order in which one treats "with all Powers upon an equal basis." Such an order—the modern European state system, perhaps, or the posited "state of nature" to which that system is understood to be cognate—"withhold[s] certain secrets." In an extraordinary passage from *Moby-Dick*, Melville suggests that the "old State-secret" can best be discovered through consultation with the "captive king":

> This is much; yet, Ahab's larger, darker, deeper part remains unhinted. But vain to popularize profundities, and all truth is profound. Winding far down from

> within the very heart of the spiked Hotel de Cluny where we here stand—however grand and wonderful, now quit it;—and take your way, ye nobler, sadder souls, to those vast Roman halls of Thermes; where far beneath the fantastic towers of man's upper earth, his root of grandeur, his whole awful essence sits in bearded state; an antique buried beneath antiquities, and throned on torsoes! So with a broken throne, the great gods mock that captive king; so like a Caryatid, he patient sits, upholding on his frozen brow the piled entablatures of ages. Wind ye down there, ye prouder, sadder souls! Question that proud, sad king! A family likeness! Aye, he did beget ye, ye young exiled royalties; and from your grim sire only will the old State-secret come. (201–2)

As in so many of his writings, Melville works here with the idea that what we think of as civilization—the Hotel de Cluny and other "fantastic towers of man's upper earth"—is dependent on a "darker, deeper," and truer "root of grandeur," a foundation that, in its Roman, pagan "essence" recalls other disclosures in *Moby-Dick* of mythic, prehistorical sources of meaning, "ante-mosaic" or even "antechronical" (498). If we see the "State" as one of these "fantastic towers," then the "captive king," buried Satan-like beneath the strata of a world that he has both made possible and from which he has been exiled, becomes the keeper of the "State-secret." This "captive king," in fact, just *is* the state secret: if we are all in a sense "young, exiled royalties," if to be "prouder, sadder souls" means recognizing our own primal majesty living on exiled or alienated under civilized forms of social life, then this is because we are all, in essence, proud, sad, captive kings. This passage offers a theory of the state, in other words, in which the transition from the sovereignty of the individual—the radical human particular on which all depends—to the individuality of the sovereign—that artificial construct that "beareth the person" (Hobbes)—is a story of captivity and exile. But this "secret" does not imagine a break from the "realm of the father-king." The passage reveals the extent to which Melville was entangled in the antinomies of the modern subject, unable to extricate himself from the logic binding the state form to the subject form.

Casarino's sensitivity to Melville's utopian longings leads him to read this passage differently. For him, the passage represents Melville's treatment of the unconscious: "What is most remarkable about such a version of the unconscious . . . is that in it the unconscious is never allowed to crystallize as private and individual," but is "immediately made into a problem for history, politics, and the State." What is more, "If the unconscious manifests itself here in the mutually reinforcing patriarchal forms of a father and a king, it is also a broken, captive, mocked, and altogether pitiable father king" (124). Casarino sees this mockery as indicating a "desire to escape oedipalization altogether" (124), but the captivation of the king seems to me to offer not so much a mockery of patriarchalism as an understanding that such a secret incarceration is a constitutive feature of the "realm of the father-king" itself. The conclusion I would draw from this bizarre troping of the captive king is this: to the extent that one invests the captive king with the power to signal a utopian exit from the state subject, to that extent one misrecognizes his meaning. Whether exalted or abjected—indeed, precisely when exaltation and abjection are seen to be mutually constitutive—the captive king is an object of misrecognition.

The captive king is a foundational fiction: this is something Babo knows, and uses to his advantage when he casts Atufal in the role. *The captive king must be misrecognized*: this is the terrifying lesson of *Benito Cereno*.

The Suspense of Sovereign Power

Soon after he finds himself enslaved in Algiers, Updike Underhill, the hero of Royall Tyler's novel *The Algerine Captive* (1797), makes the following aside: "So sweet were the delusions of my own fancy, I am loth to destroy the innocent gratification, which the readers of novels and plays enjoy from the works of a Behn or a Colman; but the sober character of the historian compels me to assure my readers that . . . I never saw during my captivity, a man of any rank, family, or fortune among the menial slaves."[17] Tyler's comment suggests both the persistence of the trope of the royal slave into the era of revolutions, and the fact that it had become hackneyed. But if so, the news had not reached Melville's Captain Amasa Delano, who only two years later was treated to a little drama on shipboard off the coast of Chile:

> Captain Delano's attention was caught by the moving figure of a gigantic black, emerging from the general crowd below, and slowly advancing towards the elevated poop. An iron collar was about his neck, from which depended a chain, thrice wound round his body; the terminating links padlocked together at a broad band of iron, his girdle.
>
> "How like a mute Atufal moves," murmured the servant.

> The black mounted the steps of the poop, and, like a brave prisoner, brought up to receive sentence, stood in unquailing muteness before Don Benito, now recovered from his attack.
>
> At the first glimpse of his approach, Don Benito had started, a resentful shadow swept over his face; and, as with the sudden memory of bootless rage, his white lips glued together.
>
> This is some mulish mutineer, thought Captain Delano, surveying, not without a mixture of admiration, the colossal form of the negro. (*BC* 690–91)

This scene, as it turns out, is entirely Babo's concoction, or rather, it is entirely Melville's, because there is no such scene in the original *Narrative* on which Melville based his tale.[18] Like the famous "play of the barber" (720), during which Babo keeps up a steady stream of obsequious patter even as he presses the razor to Cereno's exposed throat, the scene with Atufal testifies to Babo's dramaturgical panache. In both cases, what Babo realizes is that a vision of the essential precariousness of the master/slave relation, its ever-present liability to reversal, is what will most call forth the energy of disavowal in the American captain, and thereby shield the actually achieved rebellion from discovery. What precisely does Delano see in the scene with Atufal? He sees a royal slave and a captive king—that is, he consumes a vision of the radical reversal of power that, by having happened to another, to an African sovereign, has *not* happened to him. Even if Delano includes himself in this scene to the extent of reflecting that such inversions and revolutions of fortune are so much the normal course of events that they could theoretically come to him as well, the captive king before him testifies that such a fate is merely potential, and not, as it is for Cereno and by extension for Delano as well, an achieved fact. What *has* happened appears only as what *could* happen.

Let us look again at the scene:

> "Excuse me, Don Benito," said Captain Delano, "but this scene surprises me; what means it, pray?"
>
> "It means that that negro alone, of all the band, has given me peculiar cause of offense. I have put him in chains; I—"
>
> Here he paused . . . but meeting his servant's kindly glance seemed reassured, and proceeded:—
>
> "I could not scourge such a form. But I told him he must ask my pardon. As yet he has not. At my command, every two hours he stands before me."
>
> "And how long has this been?"

> "Some sixty days."
>
> "And obedient in all else? And respectful?"
>
> "Yes."
>
> "Upon my conscience, then," exclaimed Captain Delano, impulsively, "he has a royal spirit in him, this fellow."
>
> "He may have some right to it," bitterly returned Don Benito, "he says he was king in his own land." (691–92)

Both captains admire Atufal: they admire the "royal spirit" made manifest by a "colossal form" that cannot be, should not be, degraded by the scourge. Oroonoko, we recall, preferred death by torture to a common flogging, and it was also to preserve an image of the perfect royal body superior to all accident of scar and wound that Equiano, as I argued in the last chapter, developed such a complexly ambiguous account of his own past and future corporeality. The "royal spirit" requires a "gigantic," "colossal," unflogged body, in the way that Daggoo's baronial "person" houses a special "vitality." Atufal shares a body, in other words, with Daggoo and the "black pagod." The symbolic power of such a body is apparently so great that Delano does not stop to wonder about details: Can it really be the case that this scene has been repeated 720 times? (Perhaps this is why Cereno looks so feeble—he never gets any sleep.) The scene encodes a further political fantasy as well: Delano consumes a vision of domination and sovereign order uncontaminated by consent and capitulation. To beg for pardon is to accede to the legitimacy of the sovereign's power to grant it: Atufal's refusal is meant to suggest that freedom is not worth having under those conditions. When Delano goes on to advise Cereno to grant Atufal his freedom, "in view of his general docility, as well as in some natural respect for his spirit" (692), we can see the way in which Babo's scene has confirmed Delano's fantasy that one can have docility and freedom at once, that the state might be populated by ostensibly "free" individuals whose "royal spirit" has insured that they have not become slaves through their total consent to the sovereign's power over them. But this fantasy that freedom and docility can coexist turns out to be the same as that *slavery* and docility can coexist, for this is what Delano believes he sees before him on board the *San Dominick*, and what Aranda learned, to his cost, was not so: "All the negroes slept upon deck . . . and none wore fetters, because the owner . . . Aranda, told him they were tractable" (740).

Ishmael's rhetorical playfulness with inversions of sovereignty and slavery relied on the perception of a structure of domination and submission more durable than any instantiation of it. This ideological perception is being put to more menacing use in *Benito Cereno.* What Babo seizes on in the brilliant drama of Atufal begging pardon is the fantasy that there is a position from which this volatility of power and submission can be observed without drawing the observer into it. It is by letting Delano think he can view the reversals of fortune from a distance, as it were, that he blinds Delano to his own peril. The central importance of Atufal within Delano's ideological tableau is made dramatically clear toward the end of the American captain's time on the *San Dominick.* Reaching once again a peak of anxiety, Delano experiences a suffocating sense of being caught between Cereno and his "shadow":

> What imported all those day-long enigmas and contradictions, except they were intended to mystify, preliminary to some stealthy blow? Atufal, the pretended rebel, but punctual shadow, that moment lurked by the threshold without. He seemed a sentry, and more. Who, by his own confession, had stationed him there? Was the negro now lying in wait?
>
> The Spaniard behind—his creature before: to rush from darkness to light was the involuntary choice. (730–31)

The scene exemplifies the way that Melville portrays moral dramas in terms of spatial tableaus, reminiscent in this regard of the picture of Cereno and Delano awkwardly clasping hands "across the body" of Babo just a few pages later, as well as the elaborate stage blocking Melville resorts to in *Billy Budd.* Cereno and Atufal form a unit here, one the "time-piece" (727) and "punctual shadow" of the other: they form, that is, a play of light and darkness that Delano can only experience as darkness itself—hence his "involuntary" dash onto deck, where he is restored to his preferred perspective, observing sun and shadow: "Glancing about the decks where he stood, [Delano] saw the oakum-pickers still gravely plying their fingers; and heard the low, buzzing whistle and industrious hum of the hatchet-polishers, still bestirring themselves over their endless occupation; and more than all, . . . he saw the benign aspect of nature, taking her innocent repose in the evening . . . as charmed eye and ear took in all these, with the chained figure of the black, [Delano's] clenched jaw and hand relaxed" (731). Atufal has gone from being a mark and measure of one's presence in a scene, the shadow cast, to being an element, albeit a crucial element, in a generalized tableau. The "benign aspect" of nature here is clearly Delano's projection of his own benignity and the "innocence" of his repose, as both nature and captain superintend an "endless" round of "industrious" labor. Far from constituting a jarring discord in this benign scene, the "chained figure of the black" secures the ideological fantasy that there is a safe position from which the "captive king"—he who, like the "proud, sad king" in *Moby-Dick* (202), lies beneath and supports the endless occupation of docile labor—can be localized, observed, and indeed moralized upon. In its juxtaposition of Delano's belief in a benignant nature, race slavery, and the play of the shadow, this scene also forms a pair with the famous conclusion to *Benito Cereno*: "The past is passed," insists Delano. "Why moralize upon it? Forget it. See, yon bright sun has forgotten it all" (754). Confronted with Cereno's deep gloom, however, Delano cries, "You are saved; what has cast such a shadow upon you?" To which Cereno replies, "The negro" (754).

Paul Downes has written of Delano's "almost unbearable vulnerability charmed by its ability to displace itself onto the body of the African other."[19] His formulation captures quite accurately the mechanism of displacement and projection that we have been looking at, but I need now to pull back from the tight focus on Atufal to explore the wider significance of his presence in the text. Delano's "vulnerability" is a condition shared, after all, in varying but never-absent measure, by both Cereno and Babo, and indeed all the players in the drama. The pardon scene with Atufal is also ideological, in other words, because even as it acknowledges a stalemate between power and its object (a stalemate hyperbolically indicated by the repetition of the scene "every two hours"), it imagines such a stalemate as populated by individuals who *know* which position they occupy and who imagine themselves to be conscious agents, even if balked ones. The scene imagines power, and its resistance, to be a property of individuals.

But the crisis aboard the *San Dominick* is a crisis in which such reassurances cannot be found. Authority and submission have entered into a generalized oscillation that no one, not even Babo, can control. I will call this state the "suspense of sovereign power," drawing from Eric Sundquist's powerful analysis: "Acting in a form of circular displacement, the three possible sources of authority are equal to the extent that they each require abdication, reserve, or suppression in order to maintain the semblance of control. Authority—like the drifting ship . . . is caught in a point of crisis and held in precarious suspension" (108). The most vivid image of this suspension is doubtless Babo's razor: "He then made a gesture as if to begin, but midway stood suspended for an instant, one hand elevating the razor, the other professionally dabbling among the bubbling suds on the Spaniard's lank neck" (717). The "bubbling suds" presage the bubbling blood that can at any moment encircle Cereno's "lank neck" (a spondee so despondent that it seems to have given up the ghost already). It is hardly surprising that in this scene Delano fantasizes an execution, that emblematic spectacle of sovereign violence: "As he saw the two thus postured," Delano cannot resist the "vagary, that in the black he saw a headsman, and in the white, a man at the block" (717–18). An apparently more minor instance of suspended violence, however, gives us an even more apt image for power's frozen condition aboard the *San Dominick*. Distributing pumpkins, Captain Delano with "good-natured authority . . . bade the blacks stand back; to enforce his words making use of a half-mirthful, half-menacing gesture. Instantly the blacks paused, just where they were, each negro and negress suspended in his or her posture, exactly as the word had found them" (711). Delano's characteristic delusion that "good nature" and authority, mirth and menace, can happily coexist here brings power and its resistance to the surface. Foucault's famous thesis that power is not a property of individuals, but rather a force differentially manifested in any given situation, is vividly realized in the frozen tableau we are shown: "Each negro and negress suspended in his or her posture," while Delano's "attention [is] fixed by this scene." This scene of suspended animation in fact presents a crystallization of power itself, a freezing or fixation of all agents by power's potentiality that, because it is never exhausted in any act or event, is most directly confronted when nothing happens and everything threatens to.

One reason that the scene with Atufal carries such symbolic power for Delano is, to repeat, that it projects a vision of suspended power, but maintains a fiction of power's containment within individuals and their wills: the individual's authority to maintain the "semblance of control" applies as much to the fiction of Atufal's refusal to beg pardon as it does to the fiction of Cereno's exercise of power. And once we grasp the logic of this reaction, we can begin to see that the anxious experience of suspended power quite consistently pushes Delano into ever-greater insistence on locating power in individuals. Even the apparent abdication of power must be so understood. The American thus perceives Cereno to be exercising a "slumbering dominion" that he associates with the "conscientious policy, more or less adopted by all commanders of large ships," a policy according to which the captain "obliterates all manifestation of sway with every trace of sociality: transforming the man into a block, or rather into a loaded cannon, which, until there is call for thunder, has nothing to say" (681). The "abdication" appears to be only in appearance here: the commander retains his power by withdrawing into the purest essence of that power, the sovereign right to kill, to "thunder." (That this exercise of sovereign power is both dehumanizing and ultimately futile is borne out by the version of this idea found in *Billy Budd*: there, at the moment in which Vere supervises the execution of Billy Budd, he too becomes a firearm, as "erectly rigid as a musket in the ship-armorer's rack" [1427]). Delano has no other way to understand Cereno's behavior than to suppose that an apparent abdication is in fact this kind of sovereign withdrawal—the retreat to the place of the sovereign exception, where there is no "trace of sociality." But the logic of reversibility applies here as well, so that the "unconditionality" of sovereign freedom becomes indistinguishable from imprisonment: "Shut up in these oaken walls, chained to one dull round of command, whose unconditionality cloyed him, like some hypochondriac abbot he moved slowly about" (679).

The "hypochondriac abbot" most on Melville's mind when he was writing *Benito Cereno* was Charles V of Spain (1500–58): Cereno's behavior reminds Delano of "his imperial countryman's, Charles V., just previous to the anchoritish retirement of that monarch from the throne" (681). Eric Sundquist has argued that this comparison, and the "compressed structure of monastic symbolism in Melville's tale" more generally, "is meant to evoke the role of the Catholic church, the Dominicans in particular, in the initiation of New World slavery" (137).[20] This is surely correct, but the significance of Charles V as a world-historical actor extends further, suggesting that the thematics of abdication and the suspense of sovereign power onboard the *San Dominick* harbor political connotations of considerably greater reach. H. Bruce Franklin showed long ago the numerous verbal parallels between Melville's descriptions of Cereno's dress, person, and environs with those offered about the Spanish monarch in *The Cloister Life of the Emperor Charles the Fifth*, by William Stirling, which had first appeared as two articles in *Fraser's* in 1851 and had been reprinted several times since then (Franklin 136–50). But Stirling was not alone in finding interesting the story of Charles's life after abdication. In 1856 the great American historian of the Spanish Empire, William H. Prescott, reissued *The History of the Reign of the Emperor Charles the Fifth*, by William Robertson, first published in 1769, to which Prescott, too, appended "An Account of the Emperor's Life After His Abdication."[21] Robertson's original study had failed to describe this post-abdication life, as it had also failed to explore Charles V's foundational role in the spread of new world slavery (an omission Robertson freely acknowledged, and subsequently addressed in his even more influential *History of America* [1777]). But what Robertson *did* argue about Charles can help us see his significance for Melville's theme. Charles is presented in the preface to Robertson's history as the figurehead of European modernity *tout court*: "It was during [Charles V's] administration that the powers of Europe were formed into one great political system, in which each took a station, wherein it has since remained with less variation than could have been expected after the shocks occasioned by so many internal revolutions, and so many foreign wars. The great events that happened then have not hitherto spent their force. The political principles and maxims, then established, still continue to operate. The ideas concerning the balance of power, then introduced or rendered general, still influence the councils of nations."[22] Charles personifies the establishment of European modernity as a "system" of sovereign entities in which "the several States of Europe having become intimately connected, the operations of one power are so felt by all, as to influence their councils, and to regulate their measures" (v). This "system" has come to be called the European state system, the legal codification of which Carl Schmitt analyzed as the *jus publicum Europeaum*. In *The* Nomos *of the Earth*, Schmitt argued in broad outlines that the medieval *nomos* governed by the concept of the *Respublica Christiana* gave way with the advent of the age of discovery to the *nomos* marked by state sovereignty and the *jus publicum Europeaum*. The spike of interest in Charles at the time Melville is writing his tale suggests that Charles connotes for Melville and his readers not only the Catholic role in new world slavery, but also the modernity of state sovereignty itself.

But if Charles connotes the modernity of sovereignty and slavery at once, the logic conjoining them seems as difficult to grasp as Delano's situation is for him aboard the *San Dominick*. Modernity—European state sovereignty—must be treated on its own, says Robertson: all that has led up to that modernity must find a different form. Mark Salber Philips has suggestively argued that Robertson availed himself of this division of labor as a solution to a problem of narrative unity:

> In the modern period, Robertson writes, which began with the reign of Charles, Europe's history stands as an interconnected whole, regulated by such principles as the balance of power. The long epoch between the fall of Rome and the emergence of the modern balance of power, on the other hand, lacked this unity, and its detailed history could only be of interest to separate nationalities. Yet taken as a whole, this history had enormous importance as the foundation of everything that followed. Accordingly Robertson came to write the long prefatory essay that is now the best-known portion of his work: "A View of the Progress of Society in Europe." For this early period a true history would not be possible since a political narrative would be too particular and a "view" sufficiently general could not be narrative. His solution, in other words, was to frame the history proper with a philosophical history quite different in its structure, scope, and lessons.[23]

The picture or "view" of modernity, with its totalizing concept of sovereignty, can only be produced through a "framing off" of all that is deemed "non-modern"—the European past, to which Robertson dedicates his prefatory essay, but also, doubtless, all those "non-modern" elements contemporaneous with Charles's reign, elements that *emerge*—for what is non-modern can always be absolutely novel—from the encounter between Europe and the new world, but find no place in his history. Because it is the modern logic of sovereignty alone that grants him the necessary distance and perspective for narrative unity, Robertson finds it impossible, just as Delano does, to truly see sovereignty and slavery together. The figure of Charles V is definitively modern for Robertson, in other words, because he emblematizes the logic of personification without which there can be no narrative unity. The seizing of such a unifying narrative perspective, and its cunning production as a lure by Babo, is what Melville is most intent on describing in *Benito Cereno*. The superimposition or co-implication of sovereignty and slavery *cannot be narrativized as a unity*: and thus we see Delano consistently re-describe the drift, suspense, or abdication of power as a story of its relocation in ambiguous bodies—the reserve of Cereno's despotism, or the dignity of Atufal's refusal to ask pardon.

How does Melville's complex historical layering, his apparent desire to present power as lingering on, bear on this logic of personification? As Sundquist, Franchot, and others have noted, Melville's descriptive language works hard to associate Cereno and the *San Dominick* with a Spanish Catholic Europe understood to have been historically surpassed, but somehow lingering on: "superannuated," yes, but "still, under a decline of masters, preserv[ing] signs of former state" (675). Such descriptions might seem to invite the language of haunting. Franklin suggests, for example, that "Benito Cereno is, in more than one sense, the ghost of Charles V—he is both his supernatural ghost and his symbolic ghost. Re-enacting Charles's abdication of the Holy Roman Empire and surrender of worldly power, he finally becomes, like Charles himself, the symbolic ghost of all power" (137). But I do not think such a figure of lingering or haunting represents an exit from the myopic logic that we have been examining. The legal documents that close Melville's tale, in the energy of their purgation, seem to imagine, in the words of Sundquist, their ability to "suppress the rebellion by legally deposing the fallen black king, Babo" (179). But such a redescription of Babo as a fallen king is finally more comforting than accurate. Babo's head on the pike at the tale's end does not represent a "haunting" of Cereno: rather, in the pictorial composition joining head, plaza, Church, and monastery, Melville gives us another frozen tableau, in which power exercised and power abdicated are always edged by the shadow they cast but can neither fully observe nor escape. The shadow is not the ghost. The logic of modern sovereignty is a logic of personification and narrativization, then, and it is a logic that literally cannot see all those elements in its scene—Atufal, Babo, new world slavery itself—unless and until they submit to its logic, become captive, fallen kings—at which point they are objects of misrecognition.

Just how powerful the grip of these logics is, and how prescient Melville's analysis of them was, can be seen in the extraordinary story of Carl Schmitt's fixation on *Benito Cereno*. "I am the last conscious representative of the *jus publicum Europeaum*," wrote Schmitt in 1950, the same year *The* Nomos *of the Earth* was published, "and experience its end as Benito Cereno experienced his voyage on the pirate ship."[24] Thomas O. Beebee tells us that Schmitt probably first read *Benito Cereno* in 1941, and was bowled over by it, writing to Ernst Jünger, "I think of *Benito Cereno* as a *Situation*-Symbol."[25] As Beebee points out, this notion of "situation" recurs in Schmitt's growing engagement with Melville, and with this story in particular. The term seems to signal a "historical situatedness" so deep and encompassing that it determines concrete action and imaginative form equally: Schmitt "saw the incident's symbolism, before it ever became a story, as a product of historical situatedness that exceeds any individual's ability to shape events and meanings, either as an actor in history or as an author. Schmitt's relationship to Melville's story equals Cereno's to his situation as a captive. The story had been forced upon Schmitt, so to speak, its relevance to the political and legal situation unasked for . . . but compelling" (116). The identification with Cereno was so intense that when Schmitt wrote, shortly after the war, a *Waschzettel* or disclaimer, to be appended to any future reprinting of his 1938 study *Leviathan*, a disclaimer that warned against reading the book, he signed it "Benito Cereno."[26]

But to understand what this "situation" was for Schmitt, and to see its relevance to our reading of Melville on race and sovereignty, we need to understand what Melville's work as a whole meant for Schmitt's understanding of history. *The* Nomos *of the Earth* begins with a mythic contrast between land and sea, between, that is, the primal act of land appropriation as an installation of "order and orientation" that grounds law as terrestrial, and the more ambiguous drift on a "sea which knows no such apparent unity of space and law, or order and orientation" (42).[27] This contrast is essential to understanding the development of modernity: "All pre-global orders were essentially terrestrial, even if they encompassed sea powers and *thalassocracies*. The originally terrestrial world was altered in the Age of Discovery, when the earth first was encompassed and measured by the global consciousness of European peoples. This resulted in the first *nomos* of the earth. It was based on a particular relation between the spatial order of firm land and the spatial order of free sea, and for 400 years it supported a Eurocentric international law: the *jus publicum Europeaum*" (49). The imperial outreach to the new world both made possible the stability—much admired by Schmitt—of the state system and its "Eurocentric international law," and initiated a definitive break from terrestrial stability altogether. At a conceptual level, the "spatial order of free sea," even when marked by amity lines or other general demarcations, corresponds to the juridically empty zone that Schmitt associates with the new world itself. As Giorgio Agamben summarizes it, "Schmitt shows how the link between localization and ordering constitutive of the *nomos* of the earth always implies a zone that is excluded from law and that takes the shape of a 'free and juridically empty space' in which sovereign power no longer knows the limits fixed by the *nomos* as the territorial order. In the classical epoch of the *ius publicum Europeaum*, this zone corresponded to the New World, which was identified with the state of nature in which everything was possible" (36). Schmitt seems thus to repeat the essential gesture of Robertson, separating out a modern, sovereign European world from its co-emergent outside ("the state of nature," the new world). But as Agamben quite correctly points out, Schmitt's very concept of sovereign power—he who decides on the exception—harbors within it the ruin of such spatial quarantining: "The state of exception is thus not so much a spatiotemporal suspension as a complex topological figure in which not only the exception and the rule but also the state of nature and law, outside and inside, pass through one another" (37). On the sea, in the new world, in the state of nature, "sovereign power no longer knows the limits fixed by the *nomos* of the terrestrial order." Sovereign power is at once suspended and generalized, stripped down to its purest form: this is as succinct a definition as one can get of "deterritorialized sovereignty."

Schmitt himself is well aware that as a matter of historical development, the relative security of the territorial order of the European state system was from its genesis being eroded by the drift overseas that made it possible. For reasons not entirely clear, Schmitt does not associate this sovereign drift with the Portuguese, Spanish, or Dutch, to name some likely candidates: it is a decidedly Anglo phenomenon. "In the 16th century," he writes, "it was England that dared to take the step from a terrestrial to a maritime existence" (Nomos 49). Schmitt also saw World War II, in Beebee's words, "as a struggle between Germany as a land power and the English and Americans as sea powers" (117).[28] It is in this context that Melville becomes all-important for Schmitt's thinking about the role of sea power in world history. As he writes to Jünger in 1941, Melville's *Moby-Dick* can only be compared to *The Odyssey* as an epic of the sea. Indeed, "it is *only* through Melville that the sea as element can be grasped," Schmitt asserts, and then adds grimly, with an eye to the war: "A most contemporary theme."[29]

So what does Schmitt mean by the "sea as element"? Of what "situation" is *Benito Cereno* the symbol? It seems to me that it can only be the crisis of sovereignty that we have been analyzing. Sundquist had noted that "authority—like the drifting ship . . . is caught in a point of crisis and held in precarious suspension" (108). If the sea is an element, it is because it is the unmarked environment in which authority drifts. From the period of the war, Schmitt increasingly turned his attention to the role of drifting authority in the constitution of the modern world. In *The* Nomos *of the Earth*, as we have seen, Schmitt sets up a primal division between land-based and sea-based *nomoi*, a division extending even to the outlaws of these respective orders:

> Just as, in other times, when a maritime empire emerged, and the pirate appeared to be the enemy of humanity for the order of the sea, so the tyrant, because he exercised power contrary to order in an otherwise autarkic and autonomous system, was both the internal enemy of this system and the enemy of the empire as the comprehensive spatial order. As long as they were consistent with historical reality, such universal and core concepts of enmity as *tyrant* and *pirate* not only obtained their meaning from, but affirmed the existence of the concrete order of the international law of an empire. (65)

One senses here the desire to secure order even in the form of its negation. As Jon Beasly-Murray points out, however, the paired concepts are not perfectly symmetrical: "Thinking tyranny enables an analytic of the exercise of state power within a given polity; thinking piracy threatens the authority of states at their geographical margins."[30]

Pirates cannot be conceptually quarantined as the negation of empire or humanity because the pirate erodes in principle and in practice the spatiality of power's exercise. At the same time, of course, as Schmitt was fully aware, piracy was an essential arm of state action throughout the age of discovery and the period of Atlantic colonization. Beebee points out that in *Land und Meer* (1954), Schmitt argues that "adventurers, whale hunters, and pirates" (128) were essential harbingers and contributors to the rise of the epoch of sea power, and indeed that "piracy [was] the foundation both of English sea power and of capitalism" (129). But then the pirate can no longer be some kind of stabilized negation or "internal" enemy of the imperial order: as Beasly-Murray puts it, "The pirate is not the colonial other: the pirate inhabits and crosses the permeable membrane that divides enemy from foe, civilization from its other" (224).

Schmitt's thinking participates in the myopic logic that we have been examining, clear-eyed about one thing and blind about another. His perception of the ways that the maritime element in the modern *nomos* affects basic ideological and experiential coordinates, while not wholly original, nevertheless anticipates influential thinking about the role of spaces and flows in the development of modernity. On the other hand, Schmitt—quite astonishingly—never discusses the slave trade in *Land und Meer*, is never tempted to add "slaver" to the list of "adventurers, whale hunters, and pirates" as foundational instances of English sea power in the rise of capitalism. When he imagines himself as Benito Cereno, recall, he stabilizes the enemy to the *jus publicum Europeaum* as the pirate, not the rebellious slave:

the *San Dominick* is a "*Piratenschiff.*" It seems that the perspective Schmitt adopts on the situation of modernity and its drifting crisis of sovereignty is not a perspective that allows him to see the slaves right before his face: as Beebee says, in both his historical studies and in his "myth" of *Benito Cereno*, "There is a kind of sublimation of slavery into piracy" (129).

Being a historian of jurisprudence, it is likely that Schmitt refers to the *San Dominick* as a "pirate ship" on legal grounds, as it were. The slave revolt, Babo's commandeering of the ship, amounts to an act of illegal seizure on the high seas. But piracy always overflows its legal definition: real or imagined, piracy seems to be everywhere onboard. When Cereno jumps into Delano's boat, he appears to confirm the American's earlier suspicions that he is a freebooter: "This plotting pirate means murder!" (733). Once the scales have fallen from his eyes, however, the attribution is switched to the insurrectionary slaves, now described as in "ferocious piratical revolt" (734). But one might say here again that Delano, "[t]rying to break one charm . . . was but becharmed anew" (705), for if the attribute of pirate seems to promise a long-delayed cognitive security, the slipperiness of its meaning elsewhere should warn us otherwise. After all, in both Delano's original *Narrative* and in Melville's retelling, the Americans' actions occur in a legal gray area, half police action and half attempt to assert the law of prize. Delano's chief mate, who directs the taking of the *San Dominick*, had been a "privateer's-man" (736). And in Delano's original *Narrative*, the historical Cereno had attempted to block Delano's claiming his prize by pressuring some Botany Bay convicts Delano had picked up on his voyages to swear that the American captain himself "was a pirate" (Delano 309). In the very promiscuousness of its attribution, the concept of piracy suggests a drive to fix agency, quarantine outlawry in ways that can be processed and placed. In this sense, the pirate's figural counterweight is, indeed, the sovereign, in whom agency is presumed ultimately to reside. More precisely, the pirate's twin is the sovereign gone bad—the tyrant.

Tyranny, piracy, slavery: that the twists and braids joining these concepts reflect a deep historical logic is suggested by a striking passage in Jefferson's draft of the Declaration of Independence, a document extraordinarily committed to locating agency in the figure of tyranny.[31] In one of the cancelled passages, Jefferson writes that George III has

> waged cruel war against human nature itself, violating it's most sacred rights of life and liberty in the persons of a distant people who never offended him, captivating & carrying them into slavery in another hemisphere, or to incur miserable

> death in their transportation thither. This piratical warfare, the opprobrium of the INFIDEL powers, is the warfare of a CHRISTIAN king of Great Britain. . . . And that this assemblage of horrors might want no fact of distinguished die, he is now exciting those very people to rise in arms among us, and to purchase that liberty of which he has deprived them, by murdering the people on whom he has obtruded them.[32]

Jefferson's notion of "piratical warfare" at once firmly tethers it to the monstrously agential tyranny of George, and proves vague and capacious enough to encompass both the slave trade and its resistance: when the slaves "rise in arms" it seems a natural consequent, enslavement and insurrection equivalent forms of (piratical) aggression. We might say that slavery is perfectly visible here in Jefferson's language, but at the same time fundamentally and defensively misrecognized. Two fictions—the pirate/tyrant, and a purely passive "human nature"—allow Jefferson to take what was, after all, a complex legal and economic *system* implicating powers and actors on three continents, and reimagine it as a starkly drawn melodramatic tableau in which villains and victims square off. These villains and victims change place as needs be, as when the slaves become piratical in turn, but the drama as a whole is only being *viewed*—in humanitarian horror no doubt—by those innocent American Delanos upon whom the scene has been "obtruded."

"And good-bye to you too, old *Rights-of-Man*!" waves Billy Budd to his previous ship after he has been impressed onto the man-of-war, the *Bellipotent* (1358). Billy's naïve cry reminds us that our apparent swerve to Jefferson's juxtaposition of piracy and humanitarianism is in keeping with Melville's own interest in the era of revolutions: *Billy Budd* is set in 1797 and Melville moves the date of Delano's story from 1805 to 1799 in order to insist that we view the "absurdly immobilized" drama as a revolutionary one (Sundquist, *To Wake*, 142).[33] Melville's last fiction discloses another actor in his maritime world—the "human," with or without his rights. *Billy Budd* is dedicated to Jack Chase, of whom Melville had made an example, in *White-Jacket; or, The World in a Man-of-War*, of the sailor's paradoxical tendency to be a "stickler for the Rights of Man, and the liberties of the world" when ashore, and yet to "bow to naval discipline afloat."[34] It is often remarked that Melville, in keeping with a widespread convention of his day, used the topos of the ship as an analogue for the state or indeed the "world," but it might more accurately be said that stepping onboard a ship was rather, for this conflicted democrat, *always* a plunge into a state of exception, *always* a farewell to the rights of man. I want to return now to Melville's last fiction to look again at its theatrical staging of power and submission, as well as to take a last look at that shadowy figure at the story's threshold, "the black pagod."

King Dick

Increasingly we are asked to see the sailor (as merchantman, as pirate, even as slave) as a quintessentially modern subject. I developed a version of this argument with respect to Olaudah Equiano in the previous chapter. The sailor's rootlessness epitomizes a transnational condition that we have come to recognize as much older and less "postmodern" than we may have thought before. The sailor's drifting condition makes visible the ligaments of the world system as a dye might help us map the branching networks of a circulatory system. This system is a trade system, and whether the sailor appears before us as the merchant vehicle of that trade or as the agent of its disruption (privateer, filibuster, pirate), whether, indeed, he who sails appears as conveyor of goods, or as the goods themselves, finally matters less than that the fluidity of this oceanic system is shown to be integral to the rise of the modern Western world order. As our treatment of Schmitt argued, the sailor makes sovereignty possible, but is excluded from it: the sailor, and better still, the sailor as pirate and as slave, is a supplement, in Derrida's sense, of the modern sovereign order.

There are at least two strands of modern thinking about this dynamic that see utopian elements therein, strands I will call the cosmopolitan and the revolutionary. Paul Gilroy's immensely influential work *The Black Atlantic* (1993) suggested that the African diaspora was a site for a kind of forced cosmopolitanism: such an interpretation allowed Gilroy to dispute Afrocentric arguments that sought to re-nationalize or re-ethnicize cultural developments that Gilroy saw as the product of "routes" as much as "roots."[35] Ian Baucom's *Specters of the Atlantic: Finance Capital, Slavery, and the Philosophy of History* (2005) could be read as an updating of Gilroy, insofar as its attempt to make available a cosmopolitan philosophy of history adequate to our age also finds its privileged site in the traumas of the slave trade.[36] Others see the sailor and the sea as the location of proletarian and subaltern resistance to the modern world order. Thus Peter Linebaugh and Marcus Rediker describe pirates, slaves, and sailors making common cause in a loosely knitted transoceanic revolutionary collective, an approach that Cesare Casarino, as we have already noted, extends and specifies when he argues that Melville makes visible a laboring and "collective body of subjectivity" that is both "*potentia*" and "*multitudo*," a kind of fugitive communism (115).[37]

In one sense these two versions of maritime modernity are versions of each other: the one realizing as a cognitive potential what the other embodies as action and praxis. Cosmopolitanism, that is, imagines a kind of transhistorical consciousness united by a collective knowledge of what lies beyond the boundaries of state or nation, while the more frankly utopian vision of a revolutionary Atlantic emphasizes an actually existing laboring collective always in excess of the determinations of state power. (The closeness of these two modalities is suggested by their intersection in C. L. R. James's pathbreaking *Mariners, Renegades, and Castaways*). In the hands of the critics mentioned above, these arguments are eloquent and inspiring, but they don't seem to get at what is going on in *Billy Budd*. Billy and his mates seem sunken in a degree of thoughtlessness that is anything but cosmopolitan. Billy especially seems nearly canine in his faithfulness and unreflective eagerness to please: "Like the animals, though no philosopher, he was, without knowing it, practically a fatalist" (1359). The most likely cosmopolitan in the story is Vere, of course, whose mind is likened to "a migratory fowl that in its flight never heeds when it crosses a frontier" (1372). But Vere's ostensibly enlarged views are no help at all when conflict arises—he is the agent of the state in executing Billy.

The question of the laboring—and potentially insurrectionary—collective on board the *Bellipotent* is also a complex and ambiguous matter. Billy is a "peace-maker" (1357), we are told: his loveliness, his loveableness, serves as a social glue—"It's the happy family here" says his previous captain of life on the *Rights-of-Man* (1357). But when that loveliness takes the form of his hanged body, the sailors do not fall apart, nor do they reaggregate as mutinous. Rather, they echo Billy's imponderable blessing: "Without volition, as it were, as if indeed the ship's populace were but the vehicles of some vocal current electric, with one voice from alow and aloft came a resonant sympathetic echo: 'God bless Captain Vere!' And yet at that instant Billy alone must have been in their hearts, even as in their eyes" (1426). Billy's collectivizing power is linked, as Eve Sedgwick pointed out some years ago, to his status as the "Handsome Sailor," his insistent display aloft as "cynosure" (1354) for every eye.[38] Looking at Billy, the sailors bless Vere. It is only once the sailors no longer have their eyes on Billy, once they have registered his transition from gallows to sea bottom, that the crew grows restive. But here again Melville stresses Billy's distracting visibility: "Upon sailors as superstitious as those of the age preceding ours, men-of-war's men too who had just beheld the prodigy of repose suspended in air, and now foundering in the deeps; to such mariners the action of the seafowl, though dictated by mere animal greed for prey, was big with no prosaic significance. An uncertain movement began among them, in which some encroachment was made. It was tolerated but for a moment. For suddenly the drum beat" (1430). My general point here is that *Billy Budd* seems to invoke certain utopian possibilities, only to close them down. The ship here serves not as a laboratory for cosmopolitanism or revolution, but rather as the site for the staged display of sovereign power.

Both the scene of Billy's execution and the one of his initial "execution" of Claggart are very carefully stage-managed in Melville's text. We see here again Melville's tendency, when approaching the mysteries of power, to offer up a tableau of suspense, as it were: a "prodigy of repose suspended in air." Like the related scenes in *Benito Cereno*, such tableaus function as sites for real or threatened inversions of place and power. Billy and Claggart, for example, trade places with respect to guilt and innocence in the scene in Vere's cabin; and the execution scene, as Sedgwick has written, describes a complex co-implication between Billy and Vere via the redistribution of masculine affect: "Vere and Billy . . . seem each to take the place of the genitalia of the other" in the hanging scene (125): "The first 'phenomenal effect, not unenhanced by the rare personal beauty of the young sailor,' is that Billy's 'unobstructed' ejaculation, 'God bless Captain Vere!' moves galvanically through the crowd . . . toward the captain whom it shocks into a visible rigor. The 'momentary paralysis' of Vere's 'erectly rigid' posture in turn comes—in the *nachträglichkeit* of the surgeon's and purser's post-mortem—to seem the supplement to a 'phenomenal' *lack* in Billy of the 'mechanical spasm in the muscular system'—i.e., to the inexplicable absence of erection or orgasm at the moment of his death" (125). The story as a whole, and this climactic scene in particular, offers an account of what the "spectacle of the scaffold" looks like in a modernity that has ostensibly left such practices behind. The general trajectory is toward the reification, indeed mortification, of whatever utopian possibilities might reside either in the laboring body of Billy or the cosmopolitan consciousness of Vere. Whatever he may be feeling, it is the case that Vere secures his power through the simultaneous exaltation and sacrifice of a part of himself. Billy's phallic beauty is both displayed and abstracted, abstracted because displayed. The detail about his lack of "spasm" is strange enough to need explanation. I suggest we see in it the manifestation of the modern sovereign subject's "second" body. And this transfixing second body is ideological through and through. The sailors look at Billy, but they bless Vere: the beautiful body of the Handsome Sailor, at once phenomenal and extra-phenomenal, mortal and transcendent, abjected and exalted, distracts the people and effects their acquiescence. Billy is an exemplar of the modern sovereign subject, as described by Agamben: "Modern democracy does not abolish sacred life but rather shatters it and disseminates it into every individual body, making it into what is at stake in political conflict. . . . He who will appear later as the bearer of rights and, according to a curious oxymoron, as the new sovereign subject (*subjectus superaneus*, in other words, what is below and, at the same time, most elevated) can only be constituted as such through the sovereign exception and the isolation of the corpus, bare life, in himself" (124). As Melville makes sure to let us see, Billy is "what is below, and, at the same time, most elevated": a "prodigy of repose suspended in air," but also an abandoned corpse around which the "oozy weeds . . . twist" (1435).

Throughout this chapter we have been interrogating the ideological implications of such a tableau. Let us look further at Agamben's version of it. Vere and Billy do seem to exemplify Agamben's thesis about the structural correlation between sovereign and *homo sacer*: "At the two extreme limits of the order, the sovereign and *homo sacer* present two symmetrical figures that have the same structure and are correlative. . . . The sovereign and *homo sacer* are joined in the figure of an action that, excepting itself from both human and divine law, from both *nomos* and *physis*, nevertheless delimits what is, in a certain sense, the first properly political space of the West distinct from both the religious and the profane sphere, from both the natural order and the juridical order" (84). The *Bellipotent* appears to "except itself from both human and divine law, from both *nomos* and *physis*." *Billy Budd* is set in 1797, shortly after the mutinies at Spithead and the Nore; Britain is at war with revolutionary France—it is, in short, a state of emergency. The "Mutiny Act, War's child" (1416) is in effect, which means, in Agamben's terms, that "chaos" has been "included in the juridical order through the creation of a zone of indistinction between outside and inside, chaos and the normal situation"; the law here exists in suspension, Agamben might say. The ship, in its isolation and its errancy, thus presents an analogue for the "essentially unlocalizable" aspect of the "state of exception" (19): thus it is that the sailor, especially perhaps "the Handsome Sailor," embodies a fundamental and "rightless" humanity. The floating exception of the ship is violently wrested from any natural order, any *physis* that might grant authority to the "feminine" in the "heart of man": "Do these buttons that we wear attest that our allegiance is to Nature?" asks Vere of his drumhead court. "No, to the King. Though the ocean, which is inviolate Nature primeval, though this be the element where we move and have our being as sailors, yet as the King's officers lies our duty in a sphere correspondingly natural?" (1414). But even as he invokes the King, Vere's situation on the *Bellipotent* is, as we have just seen, just as definitively torn free from any *nomos* understood as constituted: "The situation created in the exception," argues Agamben, "has the peculiar characteristic that it cannot be defined either as a situation of fact or as a situation of right, but instead institutes a paradoxical threshold of indistinction between the two. . . . This is the ultimate meaning of the paradox that Schmitt formulates when he writes that the sovereign decision 'proves itself not to need law to create law'" (18).

But we have seen already that Schmitt, whose theory of the sovereign exception forms one pillar of Agamben's theoretical architecture in *Homo Sacer*, adopts a perspective on these issues that we have reason to suspect.[39] "The sovereign and *homo sacer* are joined in the figure of an action": the phrase attempts to hold together the stasis of form or figure with the dynamism of an action. In this regard, Agamben's phrase seems especially attuned to what we have been analyzing as Melville's suspension of sovereign power.[40] And here again, I wish to recall the text's complex composition history as another example of how narrative and tableau come together. *Billy Budd* began as another sea ballad of the kind Melville was writing at the time, this one about an aged sailor reflecting, in a rather devil-may-care way, on his impending execution. There is no indication that this initial

Billy Budd was at all innocent of the charges of mutiny for which he was to be hanged. As the ballad morphed first into a prose headnote, and then a longer and longer tale, two new characters emerged, first Billy's moral nemesis, Claggart, and then Captain Vere, forced to take up the position as judge. The specifically moral drama, in other words, only reveals itself to Melville over time: the whole metaphysical-theological apparatus, in which Claggart's "natural depravity" tempts Billy's primal innocence, was something Melville was led into by the problem consistently present in all the various revisions—the problem of execution. The entire tale, with its strangely wrought allegorism, still bears the stamp of its genesis as schema, or tableau. It is as if Melville began with a structure, a problem, a situation—choose your own static, nonnarrative designation—that forced itself, or was purposively forced, into a narrative frame, only then to be frozen again at climactic moments, like Billy's hanging. Apparently, the situation of execution—the image of a man awaiting execution in a brig, dead to the world—held its allure for Melville relatively independently of questions of innocence and guilt, good and evil—even if these latter attributes are, as the final text shows, irresolvably present.

Let us suggest, therefore, that the moral dilemma bound up in Vere's judgment functions as something as a lure, or feint, perhaps even for Melville himself. However agonized Vere is by his execution of Billy, he nonetheless positions himself as one who watches the inversions of power and victimization, and also as the one who stage-manages this same spectacle for the crew. His humanitarianism may be balked and anguished where Delano's is complacent, but the two captains share a conviction that they have positioned themselves in such a way as to see the nature of the conflict. To the extent that we take up Vere's point of view, then, we necessarily share with him and with the crew a mesmerized consumption of Billy's exalted-abjected body—the ideological fiction that sees sovereignty and subjection as "joined in the figure of an action," as structurally correlative versions of each other.

And here, at long last, it is time to return to the "black pagod" with whom I began. I pointed out in the first pages of this chapter the ways in which the "black pagod" in his extreme racialization and his exemplification of "barbarian regality" anticipates Billy's version of this same trope. The "black pagod" casts his "shadow" over the text, confusing my students, perhaps, but also revealing how far Billy's whiteness owes its significance to a long tropological tradition putting beautiful, regal black bodies into sacrificial and captive roles. It seems to be assumed that when "I" speaks the tale's second paragraph about seeing this paragon on the docks of Liverpool some fifty years before, that it is an actual reminiscence from Melville's own time in Liverpool. A reasonable speculation, of course, although it perhaps tokens a wish for historical reality where one might just as plausibly be tempted to discern the working of convention and stereotype. Let me propose a different provenance for this "black pagod," an equally historical personage, albeit not one Melville would have seen with his own eyes, and, as the story bears out, one that lived—and manipulated—the very tropological tradition we have been examining. His name is Richard Crafus, and he was a captive king.

After the War of 1812, a number of memoirs were published by sailors who had seen action on privateers and had been imprisoned in Dartmoor prison, infamous for the incident in the days after the conclusion of the peace in which several American prisoners were fired upon and killed. In many of these memoirs, as W. Jeffrey Bolster, Reginald Horsman, and others have shown, particular attention was paid to prison no. 4, the building in which the majority of the black sailors were housed.[41] More particularly still, fascinated attention was given to a man named Richard Crafus, or "King Dick," as he was known in the prison: "Head and shoulders above the other prisoners, even without his bearskin grenadier's cap, towered a 'stout black' privateersman named Richard Crafus—known in Dartmoor as King Dick. In a world where most sailors were under 5′9″ (and the average height was 5′6″), Richard Crafus stood an imposing 6′3″, with 'a frame well proportioned' and 'strength far greater than both height and proportions together.'' . . . King Dick was the best-known man in the prison, where he played to white sailors' stereotypes for his own purposes" (Bolster 102–3).

Is Crafus an inspiration for Melville's "black pagod," towering over his retinue, topped with "bearskin grenadier's cap" where the pagod sported a "Highland bonnet with a tartan band" (1353)? The visual parallels are in themselves too slight to bear much weight—sailors were known for inventive headgear, after all. But it is the situation and the symbolic resonance of King Dick's story that seems to me irresistible. Had Melville read any of these memoirs from veterans of the War of 1812? If he read any of them, it seems most likely that he would have read the account by one Benjamin

Brown, onetime pharmacist from Salem, whose "Papers of an Old Dartmoor Prison" ran from January to September 1846 in the *U.S. and Democratic Review*, under the name of the editor of the memoir, Nathaniel Hawthorne. Here is how the memoirist introduces Richard Crafus:

> No. 4, or the negro-prison, was an exception to the democratical form of government; this was under a regal or despotic form. A tall, powerful black man, known among the prisoners as "Big Dick" or "King Dick" . . . had contrived to depose his brethren in office and to usurp the sovereign sway, and he ruled the poor blacks with as arbitrary an authority as any other despot could. . . . He was nearly seven feet tall and proportionally large, was of a muscular and athletic make, of a commanding aspect, shrewd mind, and an expert boxer. . . . Instead of a diadem, Dick usually wore a shaggy bearskin cap, and for a scepter, he carried a powerful club in his hand when he went the rounds of the prison; and many of his subjects had a *feeling* sense of his royal grace and condescension, in the love-pats with which he honored them. He dubbed his knights by a blow on the head, instead of the shoulder; and instead of rising up after the blow was inflicted, they were very apt to fall down; but this probably arose from the defective education of the monarch.[42]

There is certainly an element of racist raillery here, and in this regard Brown/Hawthorne is typical of the white memoirists discussed by Bolster: "White commentators found it impossible to imagine that African Americans, left to themselves, could create a viable social organization founded on some principle other than raw power or toadying to whites" (112). But Brown/Hawthorne's depiction of a multiracial and homoerotic dynamic in the prison may have caught Melville's attention. The veteran protests that, contrary to others' accounts, the blacks in no. 4 were at least "as orderly and correct in their deportment as their more intelligent white neighbors" (210). Indeed, as both Horsman and Bolster emphasize, no. 4 was a magnet for many prisoners. Brown/Hawthorne says that "one great means of King Dick's continuing in power was . . . the countenance he derived from the white prisoners," who "very early perceived the advantage to their own quiet which grew out of Dick's authority; for, in all cases of conflict between whites and blacks, he invariably took the part of the former" (210). This may well have been mere diplomatic policy on Crafus's part, but there are also insinuating acknowledgements that King Dick served as the organizing center for a homoerotic order:

> Like other monarchs, Dick had his parasites and flatterers; and, though as he engrossed nearly all the functions of the state in his own proper person, he had few or no offices of honour or emoluments to bestow upon them; yet, I dare say, they reaped, in some way or other, substantial fruits of his royal bounty. He kept two white lads continually about his person, whom he took care to select for their comely looks, and to keep them handsomely clad. We denominated them his secretaries, but I rather think that the office of secretary was nearly a sinecure, as I never saw or heard of any state documents within his realm. (212)

Whether Crafus's "comely" "white lads" garnered the "substantial fruits" of King Dick's "royal bounty" in physical attentions or not is left unspecified. But for Brown/Hawthorne, a world in which a gigantic Negro holds despotic sway, where kingship flowers under conditions of captivity, is already so topsy-turvy that it becomes possible to imagine King Dick's "powerful club" distributing chastisements indistinguishable from "love-pats."

As Bolster convincingly argues, there was generalized misprision of the nature of black authority and leadership structures in these memoirs: "White democrats conditioned by stereotypes of blacks as childlike and barbaric assumed that Crafus ruled by force, just as white New Englanders had long assumed Negro Election Day was nothing more than a parody of white political forms. . . . White myth-makers obsessed with Crafus's physique, command, and style shaped him into a larger-than-life figure. He played to their stereotype of the 'barbarian king'" (110–11). One gets the sense in Brown/Hawthorne's account—as indeed also in the other accounts discussed by Bolster—that the white memoirists mobilized their irony as a way of simplifying their hermeneutic task. They attempted to take up a perspective from which what was mythic and what was actual in the situation in prison no. 4 could be viewed with enough complacency that the irony of their reversals could be savored. But Crafus's instantiation of the trope of the captive, "barbarian king" is beyond the reach of such stabilizations: it is as profoundly historical and actual as it is mythic. During the War of 1812, as Bolster remarks, an inordinate number of African American sailors opted for prison in Dartmoor rather than submit to impressment into the Royal Navy. Their negotiation with the disappearance of the "rights of man" was less naïve than Billy's, and its outcome less drenched in pathos. But it was certainly as urgent. Bolster suggests that such actions bespeak a "pragmatic and calculating show of citizenship," a "desperate rear-guard action to disavow blacks' defilement in the national imagination and to defy the popular fusion of republicanism and whiteness that increasingly defined American citizenship by excluding people of color" (115). Perhaps. But maybe they just thought they might live longer by going to prison.

What if we wended—prouder, sadder souls that we are—deep down into prison no. 4, and questioned the "captive king" at its center. What "State-secret" might King Dick share with us? He might tell us that that there are prisons that are prisons, and there are prisons that are ships, and there are prisons that are nations. He might tell us that sovereignty and subjection are just as mythical as they are real and historical, and that to imagine somehow that one can untangle their ironies by projecting them onto an African, or otherwise hyper-racialized, body is to ignore the shadow you yourself cast. He might point out that while Claggart, and Billy, and Vere immolate themselves in playing out this drama of suspended sovereign violence, he lived another day, and might have been seen strolling the streets of Boston long after the war was over, and even, perhaps, along the Liverpool docks later still.

FOUR

Jefferson's Convulsions: Archiving Logan

The last man to go down with the ship in *Moby-Dick* is Tashtego, the Gay-Head Indian, whose final act is to nail a sky-hawk's wing to the mainmast: "The submerged savage beneath, in his death-grasp, kept his hammer frozen there; and so the bird of heaven, with archangelic shrieks, and his imperial beak thrust upwards . . . went down with his ship" (624). My focus in the previous chapter on the figure of the captive king led me away from what Wai-Chee Dimock has convincingly argued is the dominant racial logic of *Moby-Dick*, namely, the fate linking Ahab and his voyage with the "doomed" Indians after whom his ship is named: the Pequod, Ishmael (inaccurately) explains, were a "celebrated tribe of Massachusetts Indians" now as "extinct as the ancient Medes" (77).[1] If *Moby-Dick* tells the tale of how the "submerged savage" grips the "imperial" ship in a "death-grasp," it is because its captain is himself already both emperor and savage, a living archaism, the "last of his race," who submits everything he touches to this deathly reduction: "Though nominally included in the census of Christianity," Ishmael tells us, Ahab "was still an alien to it": "He lived in the world, as the last of the Grisly Bears lived in settled Missouri. And as when Spring and Summer had departed, that wild Logan of the woods, burying himself in the hollow of a tree, lived out the winter there, sucking his own paws; so, in his inclement, howling old age, Ahab's soul, shut up in the caved trunk of his body, there fed upon the sullen paws of its gloom!" (166). This passage has not drawn much critical attention, as far as I am aware, but it holds an important clue to Melville's conception of Ahab. In this picture of a last melancholic creature, lingering on within the precincts of the settlements and the census, it is Logan who provides the decisive reference. Logan is here "Chief" Logan, the melancholic relic of a slaughtered family, whose famous speech at the conclusion of Lord Dunmore's War had been celebrated by Thomas Jefferson in his *Notes on the State of Virginia* (1787). Logan's name, story, and closing refrain—"Who is there to mourn for Logan?—Not one"—embedded itself so deeply in the American literary archive that the speech became an oratorical exercise for schoolboys in their McGuffey *Readers* well into the nineteenth century.[2] The grisly story inspired a number of novels, poems, and plays, as well as a good bit of contentious argument among historians, starting with Jefferson himself, who tacked on to the 1800 edition of his *Notes* an "Appendix, Relative to the Murder of Logan's Family" in answer to his critics. As late as 1961, Logan was still a name to conjure with: Theodora Kroeber's own classic melancholic tale *Ishi in Two Worlds: A Biography of the Last Wild Indian in North America* includes Logan in a roll call of famed and noble Indians of the past.[3]

In the next three chapters I will elaborate what I take to be the logic of "the last of the race," a logic of melancholy that reveals new facets to the problem of sovereignty in the new world. Logan tells us that "there runs not a drop of my blood in the veins of any living creature" (*Notes* 63), and he thereby becomes a type for numerous "last men" who come after him. I will suggest that the representational logic exemplified by Logan bears fundamentally on Indians in the new world, and their prior sovereign claim to the land. But before turning to this new representational tradition, it should be emphasized that what I have up to now been analyzing as the *Oroonoko effect* of the figure of the captive king and this new logic of the last—call it the *Logan effect*—are complementary, even overlapping, phenomena. The presence of both onboard the *Pequod* signals as much, but a more compelling reminder is Oroonoko himself, who is, after all, both the exemplary captive king and "the last of his race." It is indeed in his designation by Behn as the "last of his race" that we can discern the way in which *Oroonoko* also tells a story of its hero's "becoming-Indian." I argued in Chapter 1 that it is Oroonoko's deterritorialization, his capture and transportation to Surinam, that renders him such a radically new creature in Behn's hands, a figure who both echoes older romance traditions and anticipates the sentimental tradition, but conforms finally to neither.[4] In later versions of the Oroonoko effect—in Equiano and his fellow Christian writers of the black Atlantic, in Melville's sea tales—this deterritorialization becomes something like an unsurpassable horizon, even the condition from which a utopian emancipation can be imagined. But in Behn's original text, the dislocation effected by the royal slave's captivity provokes his desperate attempts to *reterritorialize*, attempts culminating in the grotesque effort to make Surinam itself the womb/tomb of his "race" by attaching Imoinda's severed face to it. In other words, even though the middle passage irrevocably deterritorializes Oroonoko and all he stands for, the text remains a resolutely landed narrative. Midway in the narrative, Behn and Oroonoko hear of the native method for choosing their war captains, a ritual of self-mutilation on behalf of the group about which Behn comments that while it was "too brutal to be applauded by our black hero, nevertheless he expressed his esteem of them" (56). By the end of the story, it is Oroonoko himself who, Indian-like, throws a piece of his neck at his tormentors, leaving readers to adjust their own sense of what is brutal and what is estimable. Becoming "last of his race," in other words, seems to force Oroonoko willy-nilly into the subjective positions and the territorial investments of the native inhabitants of Surinam.

At this midpoint in the book, and before turning in earnest to the logic of the last, let me try to draw out the differences in these two mythic trajectories schematically. The royal slave or captive king, insofar as he is essentially African, is fundamentally deterritorialized: his mythic element is the sea, and the ideal event to which the tradition orients its confused thinking about him is an ever-postponed *emancipation*. This is why the affective ground note of this representational tradition is utopian, no matter how abjected the royal slaves are shown to be. But "the last of the race," insofar as in his purest essence he is a native, indigene, or "Indian," is a fundamentally *hyper*-territorialized creature: his mythic element is the land, or more specifically the new world territory as that must be overcoded by its European invaders. This process of getting the Indian to subside into the land, to provide the rock—to *be* the rock—on which the new territorialization can occur, is a process of reduction oriented toward an ideal event called *extinction*. If the African captive king harbors the utopian hope that one day we might all be free, though now in civilization's chains, the Indian "last of his race" presents a melancholic site for the ever-unfinished extinction of all that is savage, unmodern, or pre-civilizational in us. One presents the utopian desire (and impossibility) of ever getting *beyond* "civilization." The other represents the melancholic desire (and impossibility) of ever acceding *to* "civilization." One is thalassic, the other telluric.

In the next three chapters, I will elaborate what I take to be the Logan effect. In this chapter, I will look in detail at its matrix: Jefferson's great archival project *Notes on the State of Virginia*. Logan's translation from historical personage to mythic vehicle is best understood close to the ground, as it were, with attention to his status as symbol of frontier life, and all that life conveyed for the American political imagination and self-understanding that Jefferson is so instrumental in framing and advancing. The nature of Jefferson's project, as I understand it, suggests both why he would have been so drawn to Logan's speech and why he is unable to contain fully the ideological effects of Logan's message. Chapter 5 constitutes a fuller meditation on the register of the melancholic as that crosses and recrosses with the logic of sovereignty exemplified by the Logan effect: there I examine two early national novels written in the wake of Jefferson, Charles Brockden Brown's *Edgar Huntly* (1799) and John Neal's *Logan: A Family History* (1822), in the context of transatlantic romantic forms. And in Chapter 6 I use a contemporary act of ecoterrorism as a prism through which to view the volatile relations between territoriality, affect, and abstraction that characterize our current inhabitation of the logic of the last.

Jefferson's Convulsions

In "Archive Fever," Jacques Derrida describes a drive toward unification in the archive, what he calls the act of "consignation," or "gathering together signs": "*Consignation* aims to coordinate a single corpus, in a system or a synchrony in which all the elements articulate the unity of an ideal configuration. In an archive, there should not be any absolute dissociation, any heterogeneity or *secret* which could separate . . . or partition, in an absolute manner."[5] More than just the gathering of the corpus, "consignation" entails the *placement* of that corpus as well, an act of "assigning residence or . . . entrusting so as to put in reserve" (10). The archive refers both to origin (*arche*) and authority (*archon*); it gathers together "two orders of order," the "sequential and the jussive," "the *commencement* and the *commandment*" (9). Archives are both the actual records that conjoin history and authority, commencement and commandment, and they are the *location* of those records, the domiciliary archives that were originally the homes of the *archons*.

In 1766 Jefferson began his *Garden Book*, "on the planting, the blossoming, and where appropriate, the harvesting of flowers, fruits, and vegetables," at perhaps the most famous domiciliary archive in the United States, Monticello.[6] "With the exception of time spent away from his estate," writes Miller, "he maintained the book for fifty-eight years. . . . From 1776 until 1820 he made entries in a weather memorandum book and twice summarized portions of these, with commentary, noting how many thousands of meteorological observations contributed to his conclusions" (41). Miller goes on to say that "the collection of data was . . . the most important and at times the only step in Jefferson's studies. At this task of collection, however, he was compulsive. His formal record keeping is scarcely to be believed" (41). Jefferson suffered, we might say, from a kind of archive fever, and the same may be said of his most famous text, *Notes on the State of Virginia*. The text has a phagocytic relation to information that, for anyone who reads it cover to cover, can produce vertigo or numbing. Tables go on for pages, appendixes are piled one after another, commentaries from friends are folded into the text. The modern edition from which scholars work includes all of Jefferson's annotations subsequent to the several publications of *Notes*, some of them made nearly forty years after the initial composition. Indeed, one of the striking features of *Notes* is the way that its commitment to the presentation and unification of the "state" necessitates a prolonged encounter with heterogeneity, an unfinishable task of data collection. The *Notes* are best grasped, in other words, neither as the finished archive nor as the heterogeneity of all that is archived, but as the record of a *process* of archiving.

I will argue in what follows that it is the land itself—as site of mourning and of monument, as theater of the encounter with the Indians who have come before—that is the ultimate focus of Jefferson's archive fever. The historical horizon of Jefferson's text—what makes it continuingly relevant today—is the unresolved relation between the United States and Native Americans. Contemporary conflicts about the sovereignty of native nations—conflicts affecting everything from lawsuits seeking restitution of expropriated lands, to the rights of tribes to set up online gambling, to attempts to protect sacred sites from developers or archaeological excavation—testify to the apparent inability of American political and legal discourses to process the Indian presence within its borders. Everything about this history calls into question the very principle of the American "state," understood as the dream of a total integration of its own archive in a present synchronous totality. When Derrida writes about "consignation" as an act that involves "assigning residence or . . . entrusting so as to put in reserve," we can hear the echoes of at least two centuries' effort to archive the Native American both materially and discursively. The failure of the project of "incorporation" so central to early national efforts to deal with native peoples, for example, can be seen as repeated, rather than conceded, in the Indian Removal Act of 1830. This deadly expedient was clearly continuous with the archiving impulse behind incorporation, both in the thinking of its advocates, and in its basic desire to "assign residence" and "put in reserve" (on "reservations") a whole range of communities that had proven refractory and apparently unable to assume a stable "coordinate" in the American corpus.[7] The hoped-for "gathering of signs" has not worked. In contemporary political battles, as in the textual archives, the Indian as "sign" disturbs the "synchrony or system" to which he had ostensibly been subordinated.

In Jefferson's *Notes*, it is Logan's speech that represents the privileged location for this disturbance. Logan's example, the words he speaks, are inscribed by Jefferson as an attempt to secure his archive. But Logan fails to perform his mediating function; rather, he remains inscribed in a form never fully assimilated or processed, an archival failure legible elsewhere in Jefferson's text as certain "convulsions" traversing its surface, affective traces that, like any traumatic affect, seem at once to allude to and diverge from some primal historical violence. But to grasp this dynamic more concretely, we need to consider the economy of Jefferson's text itself.

Archiving, as Jefferson pursues it, is a process requiring the stabilization of all that is anomalous, either through explanation or, failing that, through principled refusal to offer spurious explanations not corroborated by available data. The equanimity of certitude can, however, be expressed through a profession of ignorance as effectively as through the act of explanation: the stabilizing function of doubt is one of the signal discoveries of the modern scientific posture, from Descartes to Freud.[8] One catches its accents quite often in Jefferson: "Abandoning this fact, therefore, the three hypotheses are equally unsatisfactory; and we must be contented to acknowledge, that this great phaenomenon is as yet unsolved. Ignorance is preferable to error; and he is less remote from the truth who believes nothing, than he who believes what is wrong" (33). The archive here stands at some distance from the archivist: one can, indeed one must, gather the anomalous details and phenomena, review the mutually contradictory hypotheses, but such heterogeneity need be no threat to the principle of order, because that principle resides in the *relation* between archive and archivist, between data and reason. Admissions of ignorance keep that relation visible, while overhasty conclusions made in error close the gap.

The "great phaenomenon" in the above passage refers to the presence of the fossilized remains of marine animals at the tops of mountains. Among the possible explanations, Jefferson considers some "great convulsion of nature" that could have "heaved" the "bed of the ocean" (32) to mountainous heights. But Jefferson rejects this convulsion theory, commenting that its proponents "do well to suppose the great events on which it rests to have taken place beyond all aeras of history; for within these, certainly none such are to be found" (32). This skepticism about prehistoric convulsions of the earth is more telling than it might at first seem. As Charles Miller writes, Jefferson did not "have a niche" for geology in his "cosmology of a perfected nature. Geology asked about the interior of the earth, which no naturalist could explore. It asked about time so old that no one could properly reckon it. It seemed to be a nearly imaginary science, unobservable in its processes and unverifiable as to most of its operations" (46). In the light of the scientific requirement to align space and time, visibility and reckoning, the theory of "convulsions" produces an explanation that is doubly unsettling. On the one hand, such convulsions look like an external breach, busting open the legibility of history through a violent origin that neither transcends (in some extra-temporal fiat, for example), nor is safely contained by the measurability of time. On the other hand, the convulsions presuppose a fissure *within*, a kind of spasmodic churning of the very bowels of the earth. Jefferson preferred the theory that rocks grow, primarily because "the potential of what he called a chasm in nature threatened his assumption of a perfect or near-perfect creation of the world" (Miller 48). The whole topic aggravated Jefferson. In a letter to a friend, he uncharacteristically dismissed the need for further investigation: "Why seek further the solution of this phenomenon?" (Miller 47). His defensiveness here throws an interesting light back on the earlier discussion in *Notes*, for there, at the moment he dismisses the theories about mountainous fossils, Jefferson comments ambiguously, "There is a wonder somewhere" (33). Jefferson is attempting to stabilize the "wonder" by finding it a proper place, which also means finding an appropriate vantage for the scientific eye.

The tissue of themes in the preceding discussion—great masses of earth and rock thrown up into mountains or down into chasms, confrontations with the unimaginable or the immeasurable, circuits of meaning between the objective and the subjective such that one is led to ask whether the "wonder" is outside or inside, whether the convulsion is recorded in the past or reproduced in the present beholder—recall the most enduring discursive technique for managing the relation between violence and subjectivity in Jefferson's era: the discourse of the sublime. And indeed, early on in *Notes*, we see Jefferson making use of this discourse to regulate another confrontation with the "convulsions" of nature. The description is of the passage of the Potomac through the Blue Ridge in what is now Harper's Ferry, West Virginia, "perhaps one of the most stupendous scenes in nature":

> You stand on a very high point of land. On your right comes up the Shenandoah, having ranged along the foot of the mountain an hundred miles to seek a vent. On your left approaches the Patowmac, in quest of a passage also. In the moment of their junction they rush together against the mountain, rend it asunder, and pass off to the sea. The first glance of this scene hurries our senses into the opinion, that this earth has been created in time, that the mountains were formed first, that the rivers began to flow afterwards . . . [until] continuing to rise they have at length broken over at this spot, and have torn the mountain down from its summit to its base. (19)

Here the violence of nature can be converted into a sign of power in the beholder, provided that it is processed from the requisite safe distance of a "very high point of land." Geological movements do not pose problems of measurement because their essential function is to play a part in an allegory of history in which the stasis of the mountains gives way to the dynamism of the rivers. Indeed, Jefferson's encounter with the sublime at Harper's Ferry is in the service of a species of poetic nationalism, for this natural scene is an emblem of the specifically blessed conjunction of land and vision that underwrites Jefferson's secular progressivism.[9] Garry Wills has suggested that we should hear the river rushing through its course in Jefferson's famous phrase from the Declaration, "the course of human events": the naturalizing rhetoric of this passage from *Notes* shows that he may be right. The river's motion provides a passage, literally and figuratively, from the sublime to the beautiful, from nature to the realm of humanity. This passage is provided figuratively by the way the river's "rushing" vigor communicates itself to the mind, now capable of incorporating this vast scene in thought: "The first glance of this scene hurries our senses into the opinion, that this earth has been created in time." As the rivers rush, so the senses "hurry," and the violence of both make way for a more "composed" picture, simultaneously that of land improved by human hands and the "opinion" that makes the meaning of such improvement clear:

> But the distant finishing which nature has given to the picture is of a very different character. It is a true contrast to the fore-ground. It is as placid and delightful, as that is wild and tremendous. For the mountain being cloven asunder, she presents to your eye, through the cleft, a small catch of smooth blue horizon, at an infinite distance in the plain country, inviting you, as it were, from the riot and tumult roaring around, to pass through the breach and participate of the calm below. Here the eye ultimately composes itself; and that way too the road happens actually to lead . . . to Frederic town and the fine country around that. (19)

Here the former obduracy of the mountains is converted into a kind of sexual "invitation": the sublimity of riot and tumult is also a sexual encounter, where the penetrative assault of the rushing rivers has created the very conditions for a passage "through the breach." This glimpse "through the cleft" allows for the classically sublime act of reconstructing subjective identity through a confrontation with its threatened discomposure: "Here the eye"—also the "I"—"ultimately composes itself." Jefferson is unusually in the grip of poetic conventions here, evident not merely in the anthropomorphizing of the description but also in the indication of the "infinite distance" presented to the eye. Frederic town itself, as Jefferson quickly goes on to specify, is only about twenty miles away, but the sociable, "participatory" calm it represents partakes of the "infinite horizon" of a progressive future.

This passage on the sublime proposes that one can convert the convulsive power of nature to one's own ends by adopting the proper perspective. This perspective is the product of the sublime formula, a process of self-abstraction that allows one to seize one's own cognitive, imaginative, or existential limits, and do signifying work with them. Jefferson avails himself of this technique in *Notes* when he wishes to assert a degree of epistemic control over "convulsions" that pose threats or constitute problems to his unifying archival project. If questions of natural history, of geologic convulsions, can seem to take on the significance of historical, cultural events in Jefferson's text—the Potomac's passage through Harper's Ferry calling forth a vision of Jefferson's "republican empire"—it is no less the case that political and cultural phenomena seem tied, often in disturbing ways, to nature.[10] In one of his most sustained meditations on the political future of the American "state," Jefferson appeals, as he had with regard to scientific debate earlier, to the importance of maintaining a proper perspective. The passage is his famous defense of religious freedom: "It does me no injury for my neighbor to say there are twenty gods, or no god. It neither picks my pocket nor breaks my leg. . . . Constraint may make him worse by making him a hypocrite, but it will never make him a truer man. It may fix him obstinately in his errors, but will not cure them. Reason and free enquiry are the only effectual agents against error" (159). To be fixed in error, whether that happens through the zeal of the scientist to produce explanation or is the product of "constraint," is a kind of sickness for which reason is the only "cure." The "truer man" keeps his distance from belief, and neither imposes, nor is subsumed by, some imagined uniformity. Jefferson goes on: "But is uniformity of opinion desirable? No more than of face and stature. . . . Is uniformity attainable? Millions of innocent men, women, and children, since the introduction of Christianity, have been burnt, tortured, fined, imprisoned; yet we have not advanced one inch towards uniformity" (160). Uniformity here comes under a double proscription: it is both undesirable and impossible; we should not want it and we cannot have it. The double proscription exposes uniformity as an equivocal concept, straddling the frontier between an understanding of nature, framed by notions of necessity and impossibility, and the cultural sphere, where what is possible or impossible takes on additional determination as either allowed or prohibited.

This straddling of nature and culture is, in one sense, the very essence of Jefferson's Enlightenment archival project, where the commitment to unity must account for politics and geology, natural history and belles lettres, within a single comprehensive plan. Easier said than done, however, and one sees how Jefferson, when in the process of saving the principle of unity through abstraction from, rather than false projection onto, the resistant particulars of nature, can become unsure of what counts as nature itself. Thus, for example, he argues that the republic must follow the examples of Pennsylvania and New York and enact into law guarantees of religious freedom: "It can never be too often repeated, that the time for fixing every essential right on a legal basis is while our rulers are honest and ourselves united" (161). "Essential rights," also known to Jefferson as "natural" rights, cannot be left to fend for themselves, but must be fixed at a higher, legal level. What is natural must be archived in order to be saved:

> From the conclusion of this war we shall be going down hill. It will not then be necessary to resort every moment to the people for support. They will be forgotten, therefore, and their rights disregarded. They will forget themselves, but in the sole faculty of making money, and will never think of uniting to effect a due respect for their rights. The shackles, therefore, which shall not be knocked off at the conclusion of this war, will remain on us long, will be made heavier and heavier, till our rights shall revive or expire in a convulsion. (161)

Jefferson's task here is to contain, at the level of explanation, a phenomenon whose very violence seems to be that of a contest between nature and culture. The fact of difference must be accepted—free enquiry, freedom of conscience—but it must be controlled and unified at another level—that of scientific explanation, or the legal, constitutional order. Left to itself, without this archiving supplement, natural differences will become antagonisms that produce convulsions, and such convulsions ultimately make a hash of the essential notion of the unity of nature. For inasmuch as natural rights—of an oppressed citizenry, for example—can either "revive or expire in a convulsion," such an event presents itself as simultaneously natural and against nature.[11]

When it appears as the threat of a social antagonism at once natural and unnatural, the "convulsion" poses the greatest challenge to Jefferson's archival project. Convulsion represents a fissure within the social body that imperils the ability of Jefferson to maintain a proper perspective—historical, scientific, political—on the "state."[12] As a figure for a violence at once of affect and event, convulsion names a confusion between the two, an epistemological sinkhole or traumatic eruption that threatens the very legibility of the archive. We appear to reach the most extreme edge of the threat of convulsion in Jefferson's discussion of the need both to emancipate and to expel the slaves. Just how much the prospect of a convulsive race war agitates Jefferson can be seen in his quite uncharacteristic invocation of "supernatural interference": "I tremble for my country when I reflect that God is just: that his justice cannot sleep forever: that considering numbers, nature and natural means only, a revolution of the wheel of fortune, an exchange of situation, is among possible events: that it may become probable by supernatural interference!" (163). Such an "exchange of situation" of course is nearly unimaginable, and leads Jefferson to pile up reasons for the deportation of slaves once they have been freed: "It will probably be asked, Why not retain and incorporate the blacks into the state, and thus save the expence of supplying, by importation of white settlers, the vacancies they will leave? Deep rooted prejudices entertained by the whites; ten thousand recollections, by the blacks, of the injuries they have sustained; new provocations; the real distinctions nature has made; and many other circumstances, will divide us into parties, and produce convulsions which will probably never end but in the extermination of the one or the other race" (138).

In his discussion of religious tolerance, Jefferson had proposed instituting legal protections as a way of managing difference within the state, so that it did not become a convulsion. But racial difference here—the "real distinctions nature has made"—seems beyond the power of Jefferson's imagination to manage: difference cannot be incorporated, but must be expelled lest it become some apocalyptic spasm leading to an "extermination" that is simply unthinkable for Jefferson. The terrible sublimity of this prospect is, as usual, as much epistemological as moral, for what is at stake in this unmanageable difference is a certain principle of legibility. Whereas in earlier discussions the threat of uniformity had been the danger of becoming "fixed in error," here the "difference fixed in nature" rises up as a pure opacity: "And is this difference of no importance? Is it not the foundation of a greater or lesser share of beauty in the two races? Are not the fine mixtures of red and white, the expressions of every passion by greater or less suffusions of colour in the one, preferable to that eternal monotony, which reigns in the countenances, that immoveable veil of black which covers all the emotions of the other race?" (138). Here, at an extreme edge of his attempt to archive the "state," to reconstitute at another level the unity of the heterogeneous, Jefferson encounters an unassimilable difference. This difference is unassimilable because it cannot be adequately determined. The antagonism between blacks and whites is both natural and cultural, the product at once of history and nature. The future cannot be protected from the resurgence of the past, in the form of "ten thousand recollections" or "deep rooted prejudices." This temporal confusion brings with it an affective one, for what is this "eternal monotony," this "immoveable veil of black," but a figure for an antagonism that cannot be read in the emotions of the other, that remains constitutively illegible? The "veil of black" threatens the archive because while it is a totalization—all blacks, the race itself, congeals into the "eternal monotony" of this opacity—it remains beyond sublation: it is a one in the form of an anti-one, and thus a not-one.

I have suggested that Jefferson's basic archiving operation in *Notes* proceeds via a technique of sublime conversion. As the archivist takes up his proper position vis-à-vis all that is heterogeneous, unverifiable, or convulsive in the archive, he will secure the needed formal closure of the one, not through projection onto the objective archive, but through introjection of the very limits to knowledge presented by his own finitude and particularity. One's very lack of coincidence with an immeasurably huge or heterogeneous archive ideally becomes a source of strength, because the limits brought to visibility in this encounter are suddenly revalued as that which secures the separability, and hence the productivity, of signification in its relation to empirical reality. But we have also noticed that this technique for managing difference is not always successful: the attempt to produce unity, to reduce to "one," when applied to Virginia's slave population, ends up encrypting, as it were, a pure otherness as a kind of deathless negativity, an "eternal monotony" neither in nor out of the archive. "*L'Un se garde de l'autre*. The One guards against/keeps some of the other," writes Derrida (51). The double meaning harbored within "*se garde*"—both defend against and preserve within—captures this ambivalent violence in which a drive for purity or uniformity, in its very appropriative approach to its "other," cannot but archive that otherness within.

Jefferson had notoriously different attitudes toward slaves and Indians: in *Notes*, he argues that blacks are innately inferior and cannot be incorporated, while Indians—contra Buffon—are not inferior, and they can and must be incorporated. It is all the more striking, then, how Jefferson's passage on the slaves discussed above brings forward themes and terms that would seem oddly applicable to the other great racial antagonism of his day. The "veil of black which covers all the emotions of the other race," for example, recalls that phlegmatic expressionlessness—the result of guardedness or stoicism—stereotypically attributed to Indians. And where would it be more appropriate to speak of "white settlers" "supplying . . . vacancies," or of the vicious cycle of prejudice, "recollections" of "injuries," and "new provocations," than in the context of ongoing conflict on the frontier? Moreover, the concept of "incorporation" itself was, throughout this period, much more central to Indian policy than to discussions about slavery and emancipation. The same might be said of the specter of "extinction" in Jefferson's panicked passages about race war, a term that already in his day had a more prominent and resonant place in the lexicon of Indian-white relations than in that about slavery and race: Indians provoked the thought of extinction in a way that Africans did not.

We have entered a zone here in which radical threats to the archival project, to the consignation requisite to the securing of the "state," has led Jefferson to associate blacks and Indians when otherwise he is eager to distinguish them. The two races represent complementary threats. But even if Jefferson's sublime conversion of an entire race to a single figure—an "eternal monotony"—does not finally succeed, we can recognize here a technique of reduction that Jefferson will also apply to the Indian. Even as blacks and Indians represent *real threats* to the state and the archive, in other words, they also constitute *symbolic resources* in the work of securing closure for that archive, the work of producing those meta-subjects called "Americans." As Ed White reminds us, "Both rebelling Indians and insurrectionary slaves . . . figure in Jefferson's draft of the Declaration of Independence, while 'Americans' figured themselves, in popular revolutionary culture, as independent and rebellious Indians *and* as oppressed slaves."[13] Even as we acknowledge how the slave and the Indian reveal themselves as co-implicated in Jefferson's work, however, we need now to pivot toward the latter. For Jefferson's political imagination was fundamentally landed, territorializing. Peter Onuf has argued that Jefferson turned his back on the Atlantic, ideologically speaking: "It might be better for us to abandon the ocean altogether," counsels Jefferson in his chapter on "Public Revenue and Expences," "that being the element whereon we shall be principally exposed to jostle with other nations" (175). Jefferson preferred to dream of his republican empire moving westward: "This would be an empire without a center, or dominant metropolis," writes Onuf. "Dynamic and expansive, it would spread, diffuse, and equalize benefits through the vast system of inland waterways, improved and extended by the art of man, to its farthest reaches: this would be an empire without peripheries" (68–69). *Without center and without peripheries*: Jefferson's territorial dream is also, quite evidently, an abstraction from the boundedness of territory. But he knew of course that there were bounds, that there had been considerable "jostling with other nations" as the empire grew westward, and that there would be more. This is why the very possibility of the "state" and its future was bound up in the proper management of the frontier and its indigenous inhabitants. To take real land in the name of an empire without center or periphery—to seize, abstract, and reterritorialize the frontier itself—will require ever more complex exercises of the sublime.

First One, Last One, One One, Not One

> The problem of the articulation of cultural difference is not the problem of free-wheeling pragmatist pluralism or the "diversity" of the many; it is the problem of the not-one, the minus in the origin and repetition of cultural signs in a doubling that will not be sublated into a similitude. What is *in* modernity *more* than modernity is this signifying "cut" or temporal break. . . . It opposes both cultural pluralism with its spurious egalitarianism—different cultures in the same time . . . —or cultural relativism—different cultural temporalities in the same "universal" space.
>
> —HOMI BHABHA[14]

From Jefferson's day throughout the nineteenth century, the difficulty of incorporating the Native American into the state turned on the problem of incommensurate temporal series. As Homi Bhabha remarks above, the two main strategies of pluralism and relativism are alike in attempting to sublate difference into similitude, by subordinating it to a single measure. When the *Democratic Review* writes, in 1844, that the Indian and the American represent "the alpha and omega of the ethnological chain," we can see the appeal of the series for a self-serving ethnographic imagination.[15] But the homogeneity promised by the series is only secured through the creation of a meta-subject, as it were, a vantage from which one can see the whole chain. This "extra" one, the observer both inside and outside the chain, is accompanied by the "not-one" that is the Indian, both origin and default, the "minus in the origin" of the chain. When Lewis Henry Morgan, lamenting the "nonprogressive" nature of Indian life, refers to Indians as the "zero of human society," he captures the dilemma with particular formal clarity.[16] The difficulties of incorporating the Native American into the archive, of performing the wishful sublation Bhabha refers to, might be likened to the difficulty of getting from the "zero of human society" to the "one" of the archive. The Indian as zero: that which must be incorporated into the series as what is absent from it.

The power of the series, for this kind of thinking, is based on what I have been calling sublime conversion, an exercise in representational reduction that allows the poles of a series to flip over into each other. We recall that Kant described two versions of the sublime, dynamic and mathematical, the first turning essentially on the affective disturbances created by exhibitions of power, the second on the difficulty of comprehending temporal series or magnitudes beyond human powers of apprehension. In the sublime discourse I am attempting to describe, something like these two registers appear as the axes of affect and historicity. For Euro-Americans, very little was more fascinating than the affective comportment of Indians. Ethnographic and literary discourses strove to "fix" this comportment, as is evident in the way they focused so resolutely on extremes, at the cost of subtler shades. Thus, Indians were represented, sometimes within sentences of each other, as both unimaginably violent in their affective responses (codes of vengeance were here a favorite topic), and as preternaturally controlled and stoical (here the uncomplaining endurance of physical hardship, on the hunt or under torture, were time and again described). But running parallel to this effort to fix the Native American according to schemes of affectivity was the effort to fix them in time. As many historians have noted, the mere fact of the priority of indigenous people in the new world posed a puzzle: where did these people belong in the scheme of history? And as with the predilection for representations of extreme affect, this need to inscribe the

Indian's origin is shadowed as it were with a ferocious attention to his end, the inevitable extinction to which this discourse condemned him. First and last, exploding into violence or subsiding into stony affectlessness, the Indian is submitted to a reduction where extremes meet.

Let us see how this strategy structures Jefferson's *Notes*, and his inscription of Logan, epitome of the last. There are three moments in the text that, taken together, provide a matrix for understanding Jefferson's archiving of Indians. The first is some amateur excavating Jefferson performed on an Indian burial mound, work that has led him to be characterized as having "anticipated by a century the aims and methods of modern archaeological science."[17] The context for this discussion is Jefferson's contention that the local Indians have not left monuments: "I know of no such thing existing as an Indian monument: for I would not honour with that name arrow points, stone hatchets, stone pipes, and half-shapen images" (97). Jefferson is in search of something rather grander: "Of labour on a large scale, I think there is no remain as respectable as would be a common ditch for the draining of lands: unless indeed it be the Barrows, of which many are to be found all over this country" (97). The strange about-face here, in which what has just been erased is made to appear again, and in profusion, "all over this country," is striking, as though a kind of mental weeding had proved itself just as ineffectual as the normal kind. The Indian monuments pass immediately from nonexistence to "obviousness": "That they were repositories of the dead, has been obvious to all: but on what particular occasion constructed, was matter of doubt" (97). Jefferson rehearses several such opinions, including a "tradition, said to be handed down from the Aboriginal Indians" (98). Jefferson does not rest satisfied with such opinions, but rather begins to dig, eventually making a "perpendicular cut through the body of the barrow . . . wide enough for a man to walk through and examine its sides" (99). What he discovers in this barrow, containing perhaps "a thousand skeletons," convinces him that it is neither for fallen warriors, nor the "common sepulchre of a town" (as the Indian tradition had it), but rather what he calls the "accustomary collection of bones, and deposition of them together" (100) over several disparate periods of time. The bones are, as it were, just bones, "lying in the utmost confusion" (98); this is why Jefferson does not think they rise to the status of "monument."

If the barrow is no monument, but merely an "accustomary collection of bones," this is because the "custom" involved in such a "collection . . . and deposition" seems too rudimentary and unelaborated to qualify as a truly commemorative impulse. The barrow evinces an archiving impulse, certainly, a purposeful gathering together, but the "utmost confusion" of this "collection" and "deposition" disturbs Jefferson. Moreover, the inscrutability of the impulse to collect and deposit them is merely exacerbated by the ambiguous behavior of present-day Indians, who now make an appearance, in what amounts to a second moment: "But on whatever occasion they may have been made, they are of considerable notoriety among the Indians: for a party passing, about thirty years ago, through the part of the country where this barrow is, went through the woods directly to it, without any instructions or enquiry, and . . . staid about it some time, with expressions which were construed to be those of sorrow" (100). Everything about this native archive seems ambiguous and unreliable, for even the Indians' "expressions" at the site can only be "construed" to be those of mourning. One might expect them to have been forgotten, and yet the barrows "are of a considerable notoriety," now, in the present.[18] The Indians' past, and their relation to the land itself, is, we might say, a *live issue*. Jefferson's response to this evidence of the Indians' autonomous and prior claim to the land is to attempt a deterritorialization. On the one hand the Indians must be made to subside into the land itself, become one with it. The land can then become available for reterritorialization by whites, as for instance by becoming an object of scientific study: it is in this sense that Jefferson's excavation of a burial mound on his property constitutes a response to the mourners in the woods.[19] On the other hand, the mourning of the traveling party must also be separated off from the land, and this is what, in a third moment, Logan's lament provides Jefferson: Logan's is a mourning without issue, isolated from both land and people, a mourning quarantined, or so Jefferson hopes, wholly within a poetic code.

Let us now look at the entire text of this famous speech:

> I appeal to any white man to say, if ever he entered Logan's cabin hungry and he gave him not meat; if ever he came cold and naked, and he clothed him not. During the course of the last long and bloody war, Logan remained idle in his cabin, an advocate for peace. Such was my love for the whites, that my countrymen pointed as they passed, and said, "Logan is the friend of the white men." I had even thought to have lived with you, but for the injuries of one man. Col. Cresap, the last spring, in cold blood, and unprovoked, murdered all the relations of Logan, not sparing even my women and children. There runs not a drop of

> my blood in the veins of any living creature. This called on me for revenge. I have sought it: I have killed many: I have fully glutted my vengeance. For my country, I rejoice at the beams of peace. But do not harbour a thought that mine is the joy of fear. Logan never felt fear. He will not turn on his heel to save his life. Who is there to mourn for Logan?—Not one. (*Notes* 63)

It is clear that Logan's words exemplify for Jefferson a species of archaic power no longer available to his own historical moment. This is surely part of the force of his claim that the speech equals in eloquence anything out of "the whole orations of Demosthenes and Cicero" (62). Jefferson does not mention, however, what was for him the more immediately analogous exemplar of archaic eloquence—Ossian. By 1774, when Logan's speech first made the rounds, Jefferson had already been in correspondence with Charles McPherson in an attempt to secure the "originals" of Ossian's poems, and had expressed his view that Ossian was the "greatest poet that had ever existed."[20] Like Ossian, Logan emanates that "bardic melancholy" that Katie Trumpener has shown to be so ideologically alluring for the nationalisms emerging within the framework of English imperialism. Jefferson's use of Logan participates in this tradition of bardic nationalism.[21] The speech appears in the chapter concerning "Productions Mineral, Vegetable, and Animal," that section of *Notes* containing an extended refutation of Buffon's environmentalist position that climate and other factors conspired to produce an organic degeneracy in the regions of the new world, affecting everything from the size of mammals to the "ardor" of Native Americans for each other. Such an environmentalist argument was understood, implicitly at least, to refer to the European newcomers to North American as well. To assert the genius of Logan's oratory was, then, to refute Buffon's thesis about the entire continent, and thus to advance a species of nationalism. This is perhaps clearest in the appendix of 1800, where Jefferson dismisses doubts about the authenticity of Logan's speech: "In 1797 however, for the first time, not only the whole transaction respecting Logan was affirmed in the public papers to be false, but the speech itself suggested to be a forgery, and even a forgery of mine, to aid me in proving that the man of America was equal in body and mind, to the man of Europe. But wherefore the forgery? Whether Logan's or mine, it would still have been American" (230). If Logan is a synecdoche for the land, so too must Jefferson be. If sublime oratory can be shown to emanate from the land itself, it is finally not important whether it is Logan or Jefferson who is its vehicle.

But if Jefferson and Logan share an identity as "the man of America," we have apparently already reached a level sufficiently abstract that it can allow for an identification between what are, after all, historical antagonists. Let me back up and approach this mystery with some closer attention to historical and textual detail. Some six years before he began work on his text, what Jefferson might well have termed a convulsion took place on the northwestern frontier of his state, a bloody months-long conflict between land jobbers along the Ohio and local Indians, largely Shawnee, among whom one John Logan was living, although himself by birth a displaced Cayuga, or Mingo.[22] Hostilities were apparently provoked by a series of murders supervised by Michael Cresap, or endorsed by him, actions in which members of Logan's family were killed. This conflict gained more notoriety than it might otherwise have done primarily because of the speech made by Logan at the conclusion of peace in the autumn of 1774. As Jefferson recalled, Logan's speech became the "theme of every conversation, in Williamsburgh particularly, and generally, indeed, wheresoever any of the officers resided or resorted" (227). But Logan's speech quickly went beyond mere word-of-mouth notoriety. Jefferson himself, ever the inscriber, thought enough of it to copy it in his "pocket-book" (227), and very soon the speech "flew through all the public papers of the continent, and through the magazines and other periodical publications of Great Britain" (227).[23] Even before Jefferson gave it a special prominence in *Notes*, it had penetrated the colonial culture deep enough to serve as a "school exercise for repetition" (227).[24] Moreover, some years after the first publication of *Notes*, Jefferson was drawn, quite against his inclination, into a public discussion of the historical circumstances of the speech—namely, the murders of Logan's family members and the original provocations for the frontier war. Beginning in 1797, a Maryland Federalist and political enemy of Jefferson named Luther Martin "began addressing abusive letters to Jefferson through the medium of the newspapers" (298), questioning the authenticity of the speech and charging Jefferson with having impugned Cresap's good name. It was in indirect response to these charges that Jefferson undertook a several-years-long investigation of the matter, eventually compiling a dossier of eyewitness testimony that he tacked onto the 1800 edition of *Notes* under the title "Appendix Relative to the Murder of Logan's Family."

From one point of view, of course, there is nothing new in the tale Logan tells: such attacks and reprisals, such cycles of vengeance, repeated themselves all over the frontier. Anthony F. C. Wallace points out how Logan's actions, and Lord Dunmore's War, more generally, must be understood in an historical arc that reaches back at least to the Paxton riots of 1763, during which backcountry yeomen massacred a group of Conestoga Indians under state protection (an incident to which Logan alludes in a note to Cresap that Jefferson includes in his appendix), and forward (at least) to a similar massacre at Gnaddenhütten (1782), in which Virginia militiamen killed ninety peaceful Delaware converts to Moravianism (12). What makes this barbarity special? Why does Jefferson, and subsequently the American literary tradition, subject Logan's speech to this archiving frenzy? As plangent and balanced as Logan's words are, it must also be something in the way his words convey an entire situation that makes his speech seem so unusually memorable. And here we return to the logic that is the focus of this book: it is Logan's ability to be at once representative and singular, exemplary and exceptional, that allows Jefferson to use his speech to abstract from a dynamic of historical violence. Such an abstraction elevates Logan in his typicality to a discursively constructed "historical limbo" (Wallace 11), where he lives on in a deathless and sublime solitude.

Gordon Sayre has suggested that Logan becomes "iconic" because he is both "separate from and similar to both sides in the conflict" (173). In this ability to embody separation and similarity, fusion and withdrawal, Logan seems to summarize in his person the contradictions of frontier life itself. For the frontier, as Richard White has so influentially characterized it, is a "middle ground." It is a zone of contact in which antagonists undergo a process of mutual transformation, hybridization, and imitation. Before any resemblance between Jefferson and Logan can be broached, in other words, we should acknowledge the more immediate vectors of resemblance governing frontier life, such that Logan can be seen as "a man in many ways very similar to Cresap," in White's words.[25] Rather than being a theater in which preformed identities merely clash or cooperate, then, we should think of the frontier as a zone in which a hybridizing process takes place. Such a process is visible in Logan's situation and story: he is both friend and enemy, both someone who invited whites into his cabin, who even "thought to have lived with" them, *and* someone who "glutted his vengeance." Being both friend and enemy, however, ultimately he is neither. He has stopped killing, he even accepts the peace "for [his] country," but he exempts himself from that peace. Logan's ambiguous status is, moreover, shared by other key figures in the story. General John Gibson, for example, whose wife was one of Cresap's victims and sister to Logan, worked as an envoy for Lord Dunmore to Logan himself, and is apparently the figure responsible for the "translation" of the speech.[26] William Robinson, captured in the early stages of the conflict and saved from torture by Logan's adoption of him, mirrors Gibson's mediating role by writing a letter at Logan's dictation, a declaration of war (as opposed to the acknowledgement of peace he entrusts to Gibson) that Logan subsequently "left, tied to a war club, in a house, where a family was murdered" (243). At both origin and end of Logan's story, then, stand other, hybrid, mediating figures: both Gibson and Robinson are figures of translation—within kinship structures, across linguistic and archival borders. They, too, are "not one."

If Logan can come to seem a synecdoche of the situation of the frontier, then, it will be in part because the rhetorical virtues of balance and symmetry evident in his speech are here in the service of balancing fundamental antagonisms of frontier life, seeming to contain them in rhetorical equipoise. When Logan embodies both his similarity to, and separation from, both sides of the conflict, in other words, he is quite literally personifying the dynamic field of the frontier, where mimetic violence and the mutual inscription of identities are governed by constant oscillations between the poles of separation and merger. Ed White would call these poles "seriality" and "fusion." In *The Backcountry and the City*, White adapts a Sartrean analysis of group structure to argue that "the Euro-American vernacular of seriality and fusion emerged through specific encounters with racial others, who, in the crises of colonization, were likewise developing vernacular lexicons of seriality and fusion" (169–70). In a chapter on fusion in the Paxton riots, White describes the mimetic violence at work in terms of this "vernacular lexicon":

> But as Indians began to map their situation more clearly, and adopt fusion as their response, farmers, already inclined by racism to perceive Indians as an undifferentiated collective, come to see Indians as *fused* in a life-or-death struggle to eliminate white settlers. And so *they* fuse as a counternation, as killers of Indians, in response to this perceived and actual fusion, and *in response to their own seriality*. . . . It is not that white settlers sympathized or "identified with" the surrounding Indians, but that they nonetheless modeled their response on their enemies'. And it is in this light that we must understand the outrageous massacres of Indian families as the next step after the parade. . . . The massacring yeomen see the superiority of the Indians even as they see Indian inferiority, and their

> solution is to become their enemy even as they annihilate them. They will become "white Indians" by fusing. National violence, the nation symbolically and literally massacring the other nation, is the new order of things. (112–13)

White's account has the merit of showing how events can unfold on the frontier in a highly volatile manner that is at the same time not random. And his work further suggests that the social dynamics at stake in adopting positions of seriality or fusion with respect to an enemy cannot be best understood at the psychologizing level, no matter how charged with passion such apparent "identification" is.[27] I therefore draw two lessons from White: the frontier is not a chaos, and it is not best understood in terms of individual affect. Rather, it is a dynamic field in which both individuals and groups oscillate between the poles of seriality and dispersal on one end, and fusion and agglomeration on the other.

Still following Sartre, White calls "institution" a higher-level grouping that has as one of its basic goals—at least in backcountry America—the attempt to manage and manipulate the very play of seriality and fusion: "The nexus of this colonially specific understanding of seriality and fusion in turn shaped the development of a colonial vernacular of the institution. Although European institutions and their vocabularies existed in abundance, they could not be seamlessly transferred to the New World" (170). European "institutions" undergo change in their new conditions. In White's view, the most successful "institution" to develop in colonial America was "federalism," which he sees as a very wide-ranging strategy for the suppression of group mobilization: "Federalism was constitutive of colonial modernity and the attempt to manage white agrarian settlement and Indian populations, to counter and manage seriality and fusion" (163). White concludes that the "continual interplay of seriality, fusion, and institution offers an initial sense of 'what is colonial about colonial America'" (168).

What I would like to suggest now is that Jefferson's inclusion of Logan's speech, with all that it indexes and figures so compactly, can be understood as just such an act of "institution," an attempt to "manage and counter seriality and fusion." Logan seems to promise the possibility of gathering together the entire, volatile dynamic of the frontier, and of gathering it in one place, in one person, the last. The poetic "institution" Jefferson brings to bear on Logan is a version of the sublime operation we have already seen at work elsewhere in his text. Jefferson proposes to make visible the full series of affect and historicity, as they encompass the Indian's place on the frontier, by quarantining them in the solitary figure of Logan. Thus Logan appears both as savagely violent—"he glutted his vengeance"—and as admirably stoical in the face of his isolation in historical time, with no one to mourn him. And historically speaking, Logan's marooned status as the last—"there runs not a drop of my blood in the veins of any living creature"—transforms him from being an index to the origin of the conflict, icon of the Indian obstruction to republican progress, into a distillation of its wishful and melancholy end, in the form of his people's extinction. Where does Logan belong in time? He is both here, now, in his address, and yet he is already past, he is the end of the line, there is no future for him because there is also no past, no embrace by the future of his pastness: there is no one to mourn him, "not one." Logan is not embraced by the future, but he is inscribed in an archive, and this inscription both defends against and preserves his singularity. From within the one of the archive, as it were, his "not one" points outward, to the destruction of a people that can now never be archived. But as himself one of these people under the sign of the "not one," Logan carries into the archive, in the Trojan horse of his own singularity, the "not one" itself.

In being so strangely isolated in time, Logan takes on a kind of "post mortem charisma." I borrow this apt phrase from Paul Downes, who discusses the obsession with Tamenund (or "Tammany") in revolutionary America as an example of the displacement and preservation of structures of monarchic sovereignty past their ostensible rejection by the revolution: "We are hardly predisposed to think of the most privileged of political figures (the European monarch) and the most marginalized subjects of eighteenth-century America as inhabiting any of the same political positions, and yet in the early United States there are ways in which they do" (49).[28] This helps make some sense of the insistence with which the tradition, starting with Jefferson himself, attributes "chief" status to Logan, when there seems not much evidence of it. But if Logan exerts his "post mortem charisma" by virtue of his extra-temporal exemplification of his people, we might also ask whether he is equally deathless by virtue of his self-exemption from his people's "peace." Logan is both exemplary of his people and an exception to them, and his immortality here seems to suggest both that his people are already extinct and that his enmity is nevertheless undying. The "historical limbo" in which Jefferson immures Logan is both a site for an absolute pacification and an unfinished and unfinishable race war. And it seems to me that, for deep-structural ideological reasons, Jefferson *wants* it both ways.

This ethnic sublime, this reduction to the last, turns out to be a quite successful representational strategy, and I will look in the next two chapters at some other examples of it. But as we have also seen, the production of such an extraordinary version of solitude can only be attained via a second-order accounting or formalization that leaves a "not one" harbored within. If what I suggest above about Jefferson being as invested in a concept of race war as he is in some putatively "tragic" defeat of a noble enemy is right, then this second-order account is what allows for such a maintenance of the enemy, this ability of the "one" to both defend against and *preserve within* its other. Frances Ferguson has argued that the discourse of the sublime, especially in its thematization of solitude, at bottom concerns the formal, semiotic basis of individuation: "Solitude represents the difficulties of arriving at any account of any *one* whatever outside a process of systematic formalization."[29] I take Ferguson to be commenting on how the romantic discourses of solitude and the sublime expose identity or particularity—indeed any presented oneness at all—as requiring a *re*-presentation, a second-order or doubled "account." The solitary figure is both object and subject of the sublime operation; he or she is both the presupposition and the product of a formalization. One way to read *Notes on the State of Virginia*, I have been suggesting, is as the record of this attempted formalization. In meditations 8 and 9 of *Being and Event*, Alain Badiou articulates a distinction between any given historical-social *situation* and the *state* of that situation in terms that extend Ferguson's ideas about the "aesthetics of individuation" in the direction of Jefferson's archiving project in *Notes on the State of Virginia*. Badiou is speaking of an irreducible ontological necessity for there to be a double count, as it were, of every situation. For Badiou, the world of presentation is never random, is never a mere chaos. That there is a situation at all, in other words, is due to the fact that every situation presents itself as structured, as already gathered together as a "count-as-one." But this structure does not appear on its own; as it were, it is a "pure operational result": "A structure is precisely not a term of a situation, and as such it cannot be counted. A structure exhausts itself in its effect, which is that there is oneness."[30] For this structure itself to be structured therefore requires a meta-structure, requires a count of the count: "Due to a metaphorical affinity with politics . . . I will hereinafter term *state of the situation* that by means of which the structure of a situation—of any structured presentation whatsoever—is counted as one, which is to say the one of the one-effect itself, or what Hegel calls the One-One" (95).

Let us call the frontier a situation of the kind Badiou has in mind. It is a structured presentation of what Badiou calls inconsistent multiplicity, and the beings in this presentation are marked by the most primal ontological attribute of *belonging*: Indians, settlers, missionaries, traders, Logan, Cresap—everyone engaged in their complexly structured, which is to say, both antagonistic and communal, activities—everyone is marked by a relation of belonging to the situation on the frontier. White's Sartrean analysis of the dynamics of fusion and seriality in the backcountry showed how the frontier might be both structured and non-chaotic, while nevertheless not seeming so to the individuals belonging there: the behavior of those belonging to the frontier situation manifests the structure in ways that they cannot control. The very "count-as-one" that is the structured presentation of the frontier, the "one-effect" itself of the frontier, is as it were not visible without another count, without stepping outside the situation. This other count is no longer of the order of *presentation*, argues Badiou, but of *representation*. And it is this second "count-of-the-count" that Badiou calls the "state of the situation": *Notes on the State of* (the situation in) *Virginia*. Such would be Jefferson's archival task: to produce a meta-structuring, a "One-One" of the structured presentation that is Virginia.

Badiou argues that the "state" does not treat its elements in terms of belonging, but rather in the mode of *inclusion*. This second-order collocation crucially leaves the realm of individuals behind: "The essence of the State is that of not being obliged to recognize individuals," writes Badiou (105). Two indications from Jefferson's archival labor vis-à-vis Logan and the State of (the situation in) Virginia reveal that he is operating on this level. The first we have mentioned: it is his comment that whether Logan's speech is authentic or not, whether it is by Logan the actual person or concocted by Jefferson, does not finally matter. Either way, reasons Jefferson, "it would still be American." That is to say, what Jefferson has concerned himself with here is not of the order of himself or Logan as individuals, but merely as elements *included* in the same state, namely the "American" state, as emanation from the land itself. The other indication comes from the appendix of 1800, after his initial illustrative use of Logan has snowballed into an historical argument about guilt and innocence:

"[The] material question is; was Logan's family murdered, and by whom? That it was murdered has not, I believe, been denied; that it was by one of the Cresaps, Logan affirms. This is a question which concerns the memories of Logan and Cresap; to the issue of which I am as indifferent as if I had never heard the name of either" (228). I think we must take Jefferson at his word here. He probably was, as a matter of personal investment, "indifferent" to the "memories" of either Logan or Cresap. What he was not indifferent to, however, was the position from which he might plausibly maintain that distance. This is an important point, for what is at work in the archiving of Logan is not, finally, reducible to the level of individual psychology. It bears on discursive structures, on the production and maintenance of the "one." In the sense of an actual human being, Logan quite simply *does not belong* to Jefferson's archive. But he is *included* in it.

I have been treating Jefferson's archival project in *Notes* as essentially an act of political legitimation, one that goes forward on numerous fronts. It is thus a modality of sovereign power that he is in the process of constructing. Logan's speech serves Jefferson insofar as it describes frontier conflict turning into treaty, compact, peace: "For my country I rejoice at the beams of peace," says Logan. But we must not lose sight of the fact that it is a peace won by Dunmore's force of arms, and that Logan exempts himself from full participation in such a peace: "But do not harbour a thought that mine is the joy of fear. Logan never felt fear. He will not turn on his heel to save his life. Who is there to mourn for Logan?—Not one." As Sayre reminds us, "Logan did not lead his people politically or culturally. Instead, he expressed an extreme autonomy, speaking for no one but himself. Far from presenting the demands of his tribe to a colonial adversary, he delivered his speech after *refusing* to attend a peace council with Lord Dunmore. . . . Logan's words and actions were those of a radical individualism and vigilante justice and came from a man apparently bereft of all human sympathies and obligations" (163, emphasis added). Given that Logan speaks for no one but himself, it is perhaps strange that, as Logan's tradition grows over the next decades, he becomes invested with sovereign and representative stature: he is consistently called "Chief" Logan.

But as we have already had occasion to see in this book, sovereign status and the mark of exclusion and exception can go hand in hand. The sovereign, according to the political logic developed in absolutism and expanded and refined by Carl Schmitt and Giorgio Agamben, is he who founds the law by excepting himself from it. The exception is neither within nor without the law: "The exception does not subtract itself from the rule; rather, the rule, suspending itself, gives rise to the exception, and maintaining itself in relation to the exception, first constitutes itself as a rule" (Agamben 18). From the vantage of the rule, *nomos*, or state it brings into being, the sovereign exception appears merely as a kind of included exclusion, a membrane or zone performing the essential ordering act of demarcating inside from outside. As Agamben explains, "The 'ordering of space' that is, according to Schmitt, constitutive of the sovereign *nomos* is therefore not only a 'taking of land' (*Landesnahme*)—the determination of a juridical and territorial ordering (of an *Ordnung* and an *Ortung*)—but above all a 'taking of the outside,' an exception (*Ausnahme*)" (19). By *including* Logan's words in a state to which he cannot *belong*, Jefferson effects both a "taking of land"—Logan's speech indexes the suppression of native resistance that stands in the way of such appropriation—and a "taking of the outside," of Logan himself insofar as he constitutes an exception to that peace, a figure exercising the radical autonomy of self-exemption.

The frontier becomes a version of the "state of exception" on this interpretation—included within the rule or order as that which stands outside it. But that is because the frontier exemplifies the "state of nature," as everyone had long acknowledged (Locke: "In the beginning all the world was America").[31] These two zones or conditions are homologous, according to Agamben: the "state of nature and the state of exception are nothing but two sides of a single topological process in which what was presupposed as external (the state of nature) now reappears, as in a Möbius strip or a Leyden jar, in the inside (as state of exception)" (37). The coincidence of the state of nature and the state of exception can be seen in the fact that the form of the individual must accommodate two opposed figures: if the state of exception emerges as the space of sovereignty, as the home of the sovereign—if Logan, by virtue of his location in a state of exception must attract sovereign attributes, even if the historical record does not provide them—then the state of nature harbors that sovereign's twin, the figure Agamben calls the *homo sacer*. "At the two extreme limits of the order," writes Agamben, "the sovereign and *homo sacer* present two symmetrical figures that have the same structure and are correlative: the sovereign is the one with respect to whom all men are potentially *homines sacri*, and *homo sacer* is the one to whom all men act as sovereigns" (84). *Homo sacer* is he to whom law applies only in abandonment. He does not belong to the law—he can be killed with impunity—but he is included in it, as a figure within but beyond the law, the terrible twin of the sovereign who is within and beyond the *nomos*. If Logan's autonomy and self-exemption mark his status as sovereign, then those same traits can veer toward the other side of the "symmetry" and make him *homo sacer*, absolutely exposed and abandoned, reduced to a "bare life" that, without past or future, condemns him to a mere existence as "the last."

Logan is both sovereign and *homo sacer*, both unimaginably valiant and self-exempting, and so pitiable that he stands outside the historical consolations of mourning. By archiving Logan in this way, by including him in the "state," Jefferson also includes a primal myth of sovereign selfhood, the myth that believes in a "structural analogy" (Agamben 84) between power and its object, sovereign and *homo sacer*—the myth that says that "man" in a "state of nature" can always potentially be either of these. But by projecting this myth onto the body of Logan, and by reducing him to "the last," Jefferson's inclusion makes sure that this myth will be kept forever alive by being figured as already forever past. Logan's ideological function in Jefferson's text thus anticipates a long and squalid tradition of including the Indian in a state to which he cannot belong, a tradition in which the apparent acknowledgement of Indian sovereignty was just as often an abandonment to bare life. It certainly can seem, looking at the history of U.S. treatment of these "domestic dependent nations" that have been placed "in reserve," that they have been included even as they do not belong, that they have been seized by the law of the state merely as what is abandoned by it. Jefferson's relation to Logan exemplifies a deep-seated cultural logic according to which U.S. acknowledgment and maintenance of the sovereign status of Indian peoples cannot be disentangled from a drive to forget, abject, and abandon those same peoples.

FIVE

Sovereignty, Race, and Melancholy in the Transatlantic Romantic Novel

"Who is there to mourn for Logan?—Not one." I return to these final words of Logan's lament, words at once obdurate and magnetic, fascinating and repulsive. I return to them precisely because there is nothing to be done. Logan's discursive isolation is melancholic, in the precise sense that it is not open to the consolations of mourning. Logan is himself melancholic, of course—Why would he mourn? For whom would his mourning have meaning, reduced as he is to the last?—but his more essential role is as the *object* of melancholic investment. Jefferson—or rather his text—is melancholic vis-à-vis Logan: forever defeated, Logan remains unsubsumable; he is a lost object for which another could never substitute. Logan's reduction to the last places him outside the dynamic of mourning, in the discursive location that I have characterized as the zone of lingering. In this sense, Logan's speech is a paradigmatic instance of what Anne Anlin Cheng has called the "white racial melancholia" that structures U.S. culture, an "elaborate identificatory system" "sustained by the exclusion-yet-retention of racialized others."[1]

However crucial to the political imagination of the United States this melancholic structure may be, it is hardly unique to that imagination. Jefferson understands Logan as a kind of Ossian, after all, and romantic-era texts are strewn with isolated and hopeless creatures, with physical ruins and human ruination. Indeed, the period's fixation on solitude and the sublime, its elaboration of what Frances Ferguson calls the "aesthetics of individuation," seems to have reached a saturation point by the 1820s. By that time, the theme of radical solitude had been so repetitively explored that Mary Shelley's publication of *The Last Man* in 1826 occasioned some amusement in the press. The topos of the last man had "come to seem not apocalyptic but ridiculous," according to Morton Paley: he cites a wag from *The Monthly Magazine* suggesting that "a term should be invented comprehensive enough to include those superlatively late comers that usually follow the last. But, as words are at present, last things are generally the last things in the world that are last."[2] In our own time, Barbara Johnson makes a related point: "Isn't the end precisely that which never ceases to be repeated, which one is never done with?" In this sense, "the question would not be to know how to begin speaking of the end, but how to finish speaking of it, how to narrate something other than the interminable death of the penultimate, how to be finished with the end."[3]

In 1826, across the Atlantic, there were last men too, most famously, perhaps, Uncas, Cooper's hero in *The Last of the Mohicans*, published that same year. And there were signs in America, too, that the theme of the last man was beginning to seem interminable. But this was because the last man in America was almost always an Indian, and as the representative of a people "destined" for replacement by white Americans, could only ever be "penultimate," in Johnson's sense. In early national literature, it has been often observed, Indians were perennially vanishing, and just as insistently returning, lingering, haunting.[4] In John Augustus Stone's massively popular melodrama *Metamora, The Last of the Wampanoags* (1829), for example, the point is made through some melodramatic plotting: having reduced Metamora, for poetic purposes, to the status of sole survivor, Stone has him emerge in Act V from within a tomb to exact just revenge, only then granting him a final scene in which to curse the whites and expire. Twenty years later, in his popular burlesque of Stone's melodrama, *Metamora; or, The Last of the Pollywogs* (1847), John Brougham takes it further, having his hero jump up after having been killed onstage, and shout, "I'll not die just to save your skins!"[5]

For all the raillery, however, the melancholic trope of the last had considerable staying power—the endurance of the Logan effect well into the 1820s and beyond testifies to that. Is there a way of construing this era's fascination with melancholy as something more than disavowal or mere attitudinizing? In his wide-ranging and moving study *Specters of the Atlantic: Finance Capital, Slavery, and the Philosophy of History*, Ian Baucom argues that romanticism offers a "counterdiscourse of modernity," a reaction to the speculative abstractions of finance capital. Such abstractions are epitomized for Baucom by the insurance industry that proved itself able to process within its protocols the systematic murder in 1781 of 133 slaves aboard the *Zong*, thrown overboard on the assumption that their value as insured commodities could be recuperated.[6] Against this regime of abstraction, Baucom argues, a "counterallegorical fiction making of melancholy discourse" sets itself, a discourse that "sentimentalizes, romanticizes, or encrypts the facts that wound and haunt it (and which it thus finds invaluable, beyond all value because outside all possibility of substitution, surrender, or exchange)" (225). Baucom describes this adherence to the "melancholy fact" as an "alternative vision" to the "twin ideals of consensual disinterestedness and liberal cosmopolitanism." It is an alternative, Baucom insists, that is as global in its reach as the regime of finance capital it opposes: this melancholy politics "predicate[s] itself on a frank avowal of interestedness: in the subaltern, in the hauntological, in the multitudinous scenes of global injustice, in an entire planetary array of melancholy facts, scenes, images, *and* fictions of history" (226). In the wake of Paul Gilroy, Edouard Glissant, Joseph Roach, and others, Baucom proposes an "Atlantic frame for a renovated geo-graphics or geo-optics of the modern" (227). The "global" and the "planetary" first become visible, he argues, in a "circum-Atlantic" economic and political zone: "In the figure of the slave, the Highlander, the dispossessed rural peasantry, and the Native American, the melancholy realism of eighteenth- and early-nineteenth-century sensibility discourse discovers the traumatic geopolitical facts of a hyper-capitalized, circum-Atlantic modernity" (233).

In this chapter, I offer a different understanding of the role of melancholic discourse in romanticism: whatever may be the attractions of an "interested cosmopolitanism," I do not think that the fixations of the melancholic position are likely to lead us there. In what follows, I will argue that the melancholy logic of the last produces deterritorializing effects on both sides of the Atlantic, but with a distinctively racialized cast in America. Anglophone romanticism in general was agitated by what I characterize as the political restlessness of a post-tyrannical world. My main focus will be on two American novels, Charles Brockden Brown's *Edgar Huntly* (1799) and John Neal's *Logan: A Family History* (1822). I take both novels to be examples of the Logan effect, answers of a kind to Jefferson's representation of Indians, his melancholy archiving of race war in *Notes on the State of Virginia*. But both novels are also self-consciously transatlantic, embedding their very American stories of racial conflict and frontier violence within a larger context of imperial circulation and the transatlantic displacement of people and ideas. I argue that Brown takes up and extends William Godwin's innovative investigation, in *Caleb Williams* (1794), of a post-tyrannical dispensation, a melancholy world where benevolence and ruthlessness enter into a volatile codependency, a kind of liberal or humanitarian gothic. Brown's Irish immigrant, Clithero Edny, is a cousin of sorts to Caleb: both are plucked from social obscurity through the patronage of their betters, only to find such upward mobility leading only to desperate lives led in constant motion and in flight. But while Caleb's fugitive wanderings stop at the water's edge, Clithero's peregrinations lead him to more and more peripheral locations on the Pennsylvania frontier. Neal's *Logan* also involves much Atlantic crossing: George of Salisbury, a misanthropic and disgraced Englishman, flees to America, where he marries into the Logan clan and assumes its melancholic mantle. His half-breed son, the Byronically wandering Harold, later goes back to England to plead for the rights of the Indians in America, only to return for the violent, patricidal conclusion.

We can gain an initial sense of both the essential continuities and crucial differences between the English and American variants of the logic of the last if we turn briefly to *The Last Man* (1826), Shelley's morose novel about the destruction of humankind by a global plague. Despite the mockery of her in the English press, we can assume that, having returned to England with her sole remaining child after Percy's death by drowning, Shelley was in earnest when she confided to her journal that she felt as if she were "the last relic of a beloved race."[7] Like the other novels I examine in this chapter, Shelley's links melancholy, sovereignty, and radical deterritorialization: but for her, as for her father, Godwin, thirty years earlier, the moral and political values at stake seem essentially English, bounded by the English state itself, despite the global reach of her vision. Her last man, the "savage" and yet highly literate Lionel Verney, thinks of England as a "vast and well-manned ship, which mastered the winds and rode proudly over the waves. In my boyish days she was the universe to me" (7). The fact that England's sovereign, territorial autonomy is figured as a ship adrift finds grim confirmation at the novel's close: Verney, the last (English)man on earth, climbs into a boat, but he is going nowhere. "A solitary being is by instinct a wanderer" (365), he observes, summarizing the coincidence of radical isolation and fundamental deterritorialization. If there ever were a novel not of mourning, but of melancholy, it is *The Last Man*: it is as though Shelley seals off her terrible personal losses by rendering them commensurate with global history itself. The "melancholy politics" Baucom discerns as one of romanticism's bequests to the future is not so much negated in this novel as exposed, in the way that a rejected child might be exposed on a hillside. *The Last Man* turns to various romantic ideals, one after another, ideals both personal and political, only to demonstrate their pathetic inadequacy in the face of the global plague. The political force of Baucom's melancholy "encrypting" is altogether lost when the earth itself "become[s] a wide, wide, tomb," "vaulted over by the omnipotent present" (196, 282). Let "vaulted" have both its temporal and architectural connotations here: when the present is omnipotent, it has vaulted over its place in the successions of time, and this temporal dislocation is also a kind of absolute immurement, as though all the world has become a "vaulted" tomb. There are hints that the plague might be a racialized figure for Shelley—it appears to emanate originally from the Near East—but in the final analysis it is an extra-human antagonist; the only real relation the plague has to the world's various cultures is to end them.[8] The contrast with Neal's Logan, for example, is striking. Whereas Shelley's apocalypse is more or less bloodless, a wasting away, the American novel is steeped in gore: Neal's melancholic world begins and ends in the zone in which cross-racial identification coincides with genocidal violence.

What if we substitute the "Logan incident" for the *Zong* incident as our touchstone trauma, if our central "melancholy fact" concerns territorial violence rather than the slave trade? In early national America, the cultural projects of mourning and melancholy are decisively conditioned by conflict over the land itself. In the previous chapter, we noted Peter Onuf's characterization of Jefferson's vision of a republican empire "without a center" and "without peripheries" (68, 69). Such an extreme territorial vision seems more the rule than the exception. Attitudes toward the legal "soil status" of the continent were notable for their rejection of all prior precedent (even as the United States insisted, somewhat contradictorily, that it remained a part of the European family of nations). "American soil would not belong to any soil status that European international law had recognized in the 19th century," argues Carl Schmitt: "neither soil with no master (and thus open for occupation in the former sense), nor colonial soil, nor European soil as the territory of European states, nor a battlefield in the sense of the old amity lines, nor a European sphere of extraterritoriality with consular jurisdiction, as in Asian countries" (Nomos 289). The "soil status" of the American periphery, in other words, was self-consciously up for grabs, in legal and symbolic terms. A space of fluidity and the negation of previous codes, the American "periphery" becomes the setting for a dream of radical individuation: the "demarcation line of the Western Hemisphere is a line of isolation in a very specific sense. By contrast with the distributive *rayas* and the agonal amity lines"—these are earlier legal apportionments discussed by Schmitt—"it represents a completely different, third type, namely a line of self-isolation" (287). The American periphery becomes a site for the indulgence of a fantasy of "self-isolation." Such "self-isolation," at once territorial and subjective, can never be successful, however, because it must contend with prior native habitation of the land: it is for this reason that settler and Indian, Creole and native, Jefferson and Logan, become bound together in a dynamic of identification that does not obtain between Thomas Clarkson, say, and the slaves whom Clarkson honors, according to Baucom, in his melancholic memory. For Baucom, the melancholic position, in its refusal to exchange or substitute, its refusal to transmute the particularity of the horrors of the past into types or exempla, constitutes a resistance to the deterritorializing effects of finance capital and its techniques of abstraction. But in American romanticism, national identity is fundamentally linked to a dynamic of deterritorialization, and the individual in his irreducible particularity is not the last redoubt against abstraction, but the very engine of a deterritorialization affecting land, memory, genealogy, and the semiotic register itself.

Before turning to my analysis of Brown and Neal, let me develop a last introductory argument. I suggested above that the political environment explored in both *Caleb Williams* and *Edgar Huntly* could be called "post-tyrannical." I mean something fairly simple by this: both novels unfold in the aftermath of the death of a tyrant—Tyrrel and Wiatte, respectively. Godwin and Brown are writing anatomies of political subjectivity after the death of the father. This is also true, in even more extreme ways, of Shelley and Neal: *Logan* is a veritable orgy of oedipal violence, while the thoroughness with which Shelley takes up various political arrangements in order to expose their futility suggests an animus against her father's own political imagination (indeed, a minor character in *The Last Man* seems to caricature Godwin himself).[9] "We are all little colonies and it is Oedipus that colonizes us," write Deleuze and Guattari.[10] In recent years, much excellent scholarship analyzing colonial and imperial logics in British North America and early national America has provided a powerful sense of how political and economic transatlantic contexts impinged on the cultural imagination of the period: restricting myself only to some of those whose research has renovated our sense of Charles Brockden Brown's responsiveness to transatlantic realities like immigration anxieties or the Caribbean trade, I would mention Jared Gardner, Philip Gould, Sean Goudie, Bryan Waterman, Luke Gibbons, David Kazanjian, and Andy Doolen.[11] These critics have largely, though certainly not exclusively, left behind the psychological dimension implicit in the idea that it is "Oedipus that colonizes us" in favor of rich and detailed historical contextualization. I consider my framing of this chapter's exploration as building on this work, but while I will not offer a sustained psychoanalytic interpretation, I contend nevertheless that without some attention to the oedipal dynamic at work in these novels' literary logics, we risk misunderstanding what it means that in the (post)colonial configuration of early national America the fusion of melancholy and sovereignty is so decisively inflected by race, and so insusceptible to reduction to rational, contextual coordinates.

Paul Downes has argued cogently that postrevolutionary America, in the very energy of its "monarchophobia," harbors forms of sovereign selfhood within the newly democratic person; indeed, the appeal of the mythic Indian sovereign—Tammany, or Logan—is due precisely to that figure's ability to invite identification with his sovereign autonomy even as his racial otherness allows for the disavowal of any suspiciously aristocratic vestiges.[12] The logic underpinning Downes's argument—that the overthrow of the father, king, or patriarch in no way spells the eclipse of the *figure* of sovereignty—is familiar from another source as well. "The dead father" is "stronger than the living one had been," writes Freud in *Totem and Taboo* (1913), his investigation into "some points of agreement between the mental lives of savages and neurotics."[13] In Freud's myth the primal father's posthumous power is expressed in the form of guilt over his murder, and these guilt-ridden compensations, which both memorialize and obscure the historical crime, are nothing less than the basic features of civilization itself—"social organization," "moral restrictions," and "religion" (142). Wherever there is a putative "passage to civilization," Freud suggests, we can expect to see repetitions of the original sons' ambivalent efforts to compensate for the crime. The very story that "civilization" tells itself, about the surpassing of the original despot, implies its guilt. The myth of the "dead father" indexes a primal violence that no amount of subsequent moral justification can excuse or expunge. One powerful implication of Freud's theory is that any humanitarian and "civilizing" mission is self-deluding whenever it imagines itself as untainted by violence, greed, and guilt.

It's easy enough to make fun of Freud's primal horde theory, or the tenacity with which he clung to it his whole career—he is still elaborating perhaps its most scandalous version in *Moses and Monotheism* (1939). But it's worth remarking that the readiness to see the professions of altruism or humanitarianism as disguises for aggression and exploitation, or at the very least in some form of structural complicity with such aggression, is alive and well in cultural critique of most political persuasions. Freud merely provided a just-so story for a condition that we continue to believe is ours. It's also true that Freud's just-so story is not purely his invention, but rather stands in a venerable line of speculation on the origins of society going back to the seventeenth century at least. F. R. Ankersmit recently dubbed Freud the "last natural law theorist," while Philippe Lacoue-Labarthe and Jean-Luc Nancy describe a "Freudian repetition of political philosophy," according to which Freud's insistent focus on the figure of Narcissus amounts to a "canonical" rereading "of Hobbes and of Hegel."[14] We don't need to go far in Freud's texts to see the influences of this tradition. Consider the following—one passage among many—from Freud's essay on "emotional ambivalence" in *Totem and Taboo*. Having drawn attention to the fact that primitive taboo punishments are directed against the self, while obsessional neurotics characteristically describe their behavior as designed to protect *others* from misfortune, Freud wonders how to account for the "unexpected nobility of mind of the neurotic" (72). The answer of course is that this "attitude is not primary." Originally the neurotic, like the "savage," fears for himself, because he harbors a wish that the loved one "should die." To defend against this wish the neurotic transforms it into a fear, "so that when the neurosis appears to be so tenderly altruistic, it is merely *compensating* for an underlying contrary attitude of brutal egoism" (72). This is how what appears to be a structural ambivalence is resolved, as it were, into one side of the conflict. In the beginning, there is "brutal egoism." Hobbes would have approved.[15]

Freud diagnoses *restlessness* as the symptom following the "great event" of the passage to civilization: "All later religions are seen to be attempts at solving the same problem. . . . All have the same end in view and are reactions to the same great event with which civilization began and which, since it occurred, has not allowed mankind a moment's rest" (145). Let us take this restlessness as both psychological and geopolitical in nature, a matter at once of the circulation of thoughts and desires through *psyche* and *socius*, and of whole peoples across the globe. Indeed, when Freud theorizes the matrix of civilization he often assumes a preexisting variety of peoples. In *Totem and Taboo*, he cites with characteristic deference Frazer's "view that the earliest kings of the Latin tribes were foreigners who played the part of a god and were executed at a particular festival" (151). The idea that the coincidence of the political form and the subject form in the person of the father/king/god—the sovereign self—might have originally been "a great stranger" fascinates Freud.[16] It is the essence of his argument in *Moses and Monotheism* that it was an Egyptian Moses who was the murdered father of the Jews (and thus of "the West"). More mysterious still is the notion Freud advances that Ikhnaton, the "inventor" of monotheism in Egypt, "derived the idea from his foreign wife: some of the king's wives were Asiatic princesses, and possibly even direct encouragement of monotheism had penetrated from Syria" (23). Lacoue-Labarthe and Nancy, approaching Freud's theses from a more theoretical perspective, have identified this motif of a preexisting, maternal, and foreign ground out of which the primal father erects himself: they refer to an "originary sociality" that would consist in an identification "not with the mother, but *beyond* the mother, with what could be called the *outre-mère*"—a pun on *outre-mer*, "overseas"

("Unconscious" 203). Lacoue-Labarthe and Nancy argue that psychoanalysis overflows its own borders, as it were, in the direction of a "no man's land": "The psychoanalysis of identification necessarily led to the analysis of the 'wider stage,' of the *no man's land*" ("Panique" 18). This other/mother, this "overseas" no man's land, evokes the volatile zone of sovereign fusion that we have been tracking in this book, as, for instance, in Behn's Surinam, where sovereigns and victims merge in a twilit region beyond life and death. This "*outre-mère*" is another name for the place of lingering and being last. We will see its personifications in two relatively minor characters that rise up like dream figures in the nightmare texts of Brown and Neal.

All four novels that I have invoked above display the restlessness Freud ascribes to civilization. These novels depict characters on the run—uprooted, displaced, oscillatory, in flight. The peregrinations of Caleb Williams or Edgar Huntly, the displacements of Lionel Verney or George of Salisbury, are not episodic or touristic, however: their plots are not shaped by the conventions of the picaresque or the travel narrative. If anything, these romantic novels have a claustral feel, as if the violence of the movements described served only to emphasize the capacity of social space to imprison. We could call them "open-air" gothic. In this sense, these novels respond quite directly to Freud's diagnosis of restlessness as a condition *internal* to a social world in which the sovereign is at once past and gone, even as he is resurgent in more virulent and uncontrollable forms. This world is one in which the postures of care, humanity, and civility that are ostensibly the achievement of a post-despotic world are gripped by a melancholy that renders benevolence and ruthlessness versions of each other. The mixture of solicitude and aggression at work here, I would argue, is of a piece with Jefferson's ambivalence vis-à-vis Logan, a version of Jefferson's attitude that betrays "the ruthlessness of a benevolent zealot," in Anthony F. C. Wallace's words (19). By keeping a close eye on the relations between the motifs of movement and flight and this structure of emotional ambivalence we will see how Brown and Neal explored, long before Freud, an oedipalized world essentially defined by the many "points of agreement between the mental lives of savages and neurotics."

The Humanitarian Gothic

"You wandered in a world of your own creation," wrote Elihu Hubbard Smith to his friend Charles Brockden Brown in May 1796. "Now and then a ray of truth broke in upon you, but with an influence too feeble to dissipate the phantoms which errors had conjured up around you. *Godwin came, and all was light!*"[17] Brown had read with fascinated attention Godwin's novel *Caleb Williams; or Things as They Are*, and probably the *Enquiry Concerning Political Justice* (1793) as well, and it seems clear that the main direction of Brown's fictional inventions was laid out for him by his exposure to Godwin. What exactly had Brown learned from Godwin? Pamela Clemit proposes Brown's first novel, *Wieland* (1798), as the best place to see the two authors' shared commitment to "rational fictions," but I think *Edgar Huntly; Or, Memoirs of a Sleep-Walker* is a more direct response to Godwin's innovations. Smith's letter weirdly anticipates the very themes of Brown's novel: like his titular hero, Brown is in the dark, a somnambulist in his own nightmares, until Godwin's enlightening example appears. Smith's tone is lightly ironic, but enlightenment was pretty serious stuff for both Godwin and Brown. In the *Enquiry*, Godwin rather stridently insists that we "trust" to the "omnipotence" of truth, "to its congeniality with the nature of intellect, to its direct and irresistible tendency to produce liberty, and happiness, and virtue."[18] But Caleb Williams is markedly unable to derive any benefit from the truths he controls. Brown's relation to enlightenment ideals was, if anything, even more vexed: the hero of Brown's first novel, *Wieland*, might be said to have received his "enlightenment" in the form of the fireball created by the spontaneous combustion of his father. And in *Edgar Huntly*, Brown plots a narrative of regression to "savagery" and return to "civilization" that seems to undermine rather than underscore any distinction of enlightenment between the two.

In the preface to *Edgar Huntly*, Brown describes his novel as "series of adventures, growing out of the condition of our country."[19] These words have been often invoked as a signal moment in the development of a self-consciously American literary project, but the story within the story, of Clithero Edny's rise and fall, is set in Ireland, and two other characters (one of them, Weymouth, seemingly brought in solely for the purpose) describe their adventures in a world linked by trade and empire. Rather than seeing the novel as a defiant American riposte to the "exploded manners, Gothic castles and chimeras" (3) of the old world, then, I would suggest that Brown saw how Godwin had already transformed castles into open space as the setting for unbearable isolation. Brown's translation of Godwin across the "salt seas" that mark the limit of *Caleb Williams* reveals a geopolitical dimension to what I call the humanitarian gothic through its focus on ambivalence and the catastrophes of benevolence. When these motifs emerge in the peripheral locales of Ireland and Pennsylvania, the lingering reduction of the sovereign self becomes exacerbated by race.

The immediate political context for Godwin's novel is the anti-Jacobin crackdown leading to the Treason Trials of 1794. Although these trials took place after the publication of *Caleb Williams*, the Home Office had for some time been ramping up its spying on the radical Correspondence Societies, and the preface to the first edition was dated May 12, 1794, the very day that Pitt suspended habeas corpus, by which date Godwin had already visited radical Joseph Gerrald in jail.[20] "Terror was the order of the day" (4), Godwin wrote from the vantage of his preface to the second edition in 1795, a terror of surveillance. "I had my eye upon you in all your wanderings," Falkland informs Caleb. "You have taken no material step through their whole course with which I have not been acquainted. I meditated to do you good" (326). The slippage between menace and benevolence in this announcement is a consistent feature of Godwin's novel, and I believe an inspiration for Edgar's sympathetic harassment of Clithero in Brown's novel. Consider the unnerving moment in *Caleb Williams* when Falkland reveals that he considers his persecutions of Caleb—imprisonment, slander, hounding across the country—as extensions of his patronage, dedicated not to Caleb's destruction but to his preservation: "Were you so stupid and undistinguishing as not to know that the preservation of your life was the uniform object of my exertions?" (326). Caleb might be excused for not recognizing the benevolent hand of Falkland during his travails, because earlier Falkland had menaced his protégé in no uncertain terms: "You write me here, that you are desirous to quit my service. To that I have a short answer, You shall never quit it with life. . . . That is my will; and I will not have it resisted. The very next time you disobey me in that or any other article, there is an end to your vagaries for ever" (177). "That is my will; and I will not have it resisted": this is the voice of what Godwin and his contemporaries would call arbitrary tyranny, projecting a power that brooks no resistance.

Falkland exemplifies a tyranny of surveillance and benevolence, then, a tyranny dedicated to maintaining and preserving his enemy, rather than destroying him. In this regard, Falkland embodies the mutual implication, or terrible proximity, of the tyrant and the humanitarian liberal hegemon, the kind of twinship that Foucault had in mind when he paired the classic sovereign's power to make die or let live with biopower's inverted drive to make live or let die.[21] The aggression involved in the desire to make live also characterizes the perverse solicitude Falkland directs toward the odious Tyrrel: "I am accused of having committed murder upon the body of Barnabas Tyrrel. I would most joyfully have given every farthing I possess, and devoted myself to perpetual beggary, to have preserved his life. His life was precious to me, beyond that of all mankind" (116). Falkland is being disingenuous here, but only partly. He knows that he did in fact kill Tyrrel, but he wishes that he hadn't, because he would have preferred to kill him under different circumstances: "I confess that I would have called him out to the field, and that our encounter should not have terminated but by the death of one or both of us" (116). As it happened, he killed Tyrrel in a rage, and thereby deprived himself of the honor of the duel, a procedure that would have confirmed his equality of status with Tyrrel. But it is just such aristocratic egalitarianism that Tyrrel so flagrantly rejects. "I am no tyrant," protests Mr. Tyrrel. "I know very well that tyranny is a bad thing" (88). Despite this nearly charming example of bad faith, however, Tyrrel cannot escape his own name, which encrypts the tyrannical temper everywhere remarked: he is a "wild beast," an "untamed, though not undiscerning brute," a particularly disagreeable combination of "sullenness and tyranny" (21, 42). Every inch the "rustic tyrant" (41), Tyrrel exercises his sovereignty in the classic form of absolute control over territory and population, displacing the Hawkins family, and opposing the presence of any rival "equal" within his domain. Falkland understands perfectly the nature of the conflict: "Mr. Tyrrel, be reasonable! Might not I as well desire you to leave the county, as you desire me? I come to you, not as a master, but an equal. In the society of men we must have something to endure, as well as to enjoy. No man must think that the world was made for him" (34). But for Tyrell, there can be no "equal" within the limits of his territory. Tyrrel is, finally, a figure of fantasy, an avatar of Freud's primal father, exercising power without law, commandeering all the women to himself (namely, Emmy Melville), the terrifying autocrat who thinks that "the world was made for him." Tyrrel does not, in fact, live in the "society of men"—he antedates it.

It is Falkland's murder of Tyrrel, and then Caleb's discovery of that murder, that constitutes the trauma of the novel. As Freud would have predicted, Tyrrel's "bad father" is stronger in death than he had been in life, a recrudescence that takes the form of fastening tyrannical isolation and deathlessness onto the liberal individual who has disavowed tyranny in the first place. When he berates Tyrrel for his crimes, Falkland predicts for him an extremity of isolation—"Society casts you out; man abominates you. No wealth, no rank, can buy out your stain. You will live deserted in the midst of your species; you will go into crowded societies, and no one will deign so much as to salute you. . . . You have the stamp of misery, incessant, undivided, unpitied misery!" (89)—but it is really Falkland, and then Caleb, who endure the fate of living deserted in the midst of society. Here is Falkland describing his death-in-life: "Your decision can never have the efficacy to prevent the miserable remains of my existence from being the most intolerable of all burthens. . . . I am compelled to drag for ever the intolerable load of existence, upon penalty, if, at any period however remote, I shake it off, of having that impatience regarded as confirming a charge of murder. . . . The man who now stands before you is devoted to perpetual barrenness and blast" (116–17). Falkland's position here, and throughout the novel, is melancholic in the sense that the requirement to deny his murder of Tyrrel means that he can never "get over it," never exchange the lost object of Tyrrel for another by means of the (social) consolations of mourning. The disavowal of the murder of the tyrant ends up reproducing tyranny in the liberal sovereign self, now isolated in a deathless agony of "perpetual barrenness and blast." And that liberal self, in turn, now reproduces its own isolated condition in those toward whom it directs the terroristic benevolence that constitutes the other face of its ambivalence. So it is that Falkland's requirement to keep Caleb in the circuit of his disavowal both preserves his life—against Caleb's will—and condemns him to "solitude, separation, banishment!" Caleb muses on this banishment, "The pride of philosophy has taught us to treat man as an individual. He is no such thing. He holds necessarily, indispensably, to his species. He is like those twin-births that have two heads indeed, and four hands, but if you attempt to detach them from each other, they are inevitably subjected to miserable and lingering destruction" (351–52).

"Perpetual barrenness and blast." "Miserable and lingering destruction." Such is the fate of those who are last—from Ossian and Logan, to Manfred and Chingachgook. What Godwin has perceived is how the logic of the last is tied to the disavowal of tyranny that begets the liberal sovereign self. And it is this analysis that makes Godwin's imagination outrun his progressive politics. Pamela Clemit describes succinctly the political schema apparently at work in the novel: "Tyrrel, the rural despot, is superseded by the aristocratic Falkland, who is challenged in turn by Caleb's egalitarian views" (52). But there is no progression, no evolution toward greater freedom, implied in Godwin's novel: instead, *Caleb Williams* describes the infection of all parties by the structure and effects of tyranny. An "emphasis on typical qualities" actually "underlines the breakdown of a progressive view of history," observes Clemit, and "all three phases collapse into violent conflict, as tyranny begets tyranny" (52). Godwin's narrative imagination is not progressive, in this novel at least, but structural: his main goal is to "enrich and destabilize the symbolic opposition of master and servant" (Clemit 45).

At the end of the book, when Caleb's horror at Falkland's behavior is at its apogee, he compares him to Nero and Caligula, exclaiming, "Falkland! Art thou the offspring in whom the lineaments of these tyrants are faithfully preserved?" (364). But what begins as a description of Caleb's condition—the inability of the "unoffending victim" to escape the global reach and "power of the tyrant" (364)—flips over into a description of the social isolation of the sovereign himself: "Tyrants have trembled surrounded with whole armies of their Janissaries. What should make thee inaccessible to my fury? No, I will use no daggers! I will unfold a tale—!" (364). Caleb and Falkland—victim and persecutor—pass into one another in this analysis. We have a series of analogies that all focus on the way in which the sovereign and his victim share a "trembling" isolation in the midst of society. In the passage just quoted, the point at which the tyrant becomes vulnerable, where power and protection become threat ("surrounded by whole armies of . . . Janissaries"), is marked by a single word, set off and centered on the page: "Tremble!" (364). This trembling characterizes a vulnerability that affects all alike, and thus makes possible the transition from sovereign to victim.

When Caleb asks the crucial question, "What was the nature of this power from which I was to apprehend so much, yet which seemed to leave me at perfect liberty?" (330), it seems clear that Godwin understands his dilemma as having to do with the compromised liberty of the English subject. Falkland's regime is a version of the English state, which sets clear bounds on a putatively "perfect liberty" that is in fact an imprisonment. Falkland's agent Gines informs Caleb:

> Beware the salt seas! They are out of my orders. You are a prisoner at present, and I believe all your life will remain so. Thanks to the milk-and-water softness of your former master! If I had the ordering of these things, it should go with you in another fashion. As long as you think proper, you are a prisoner within the rules; and the rules with which the soft-hearted squire indulges you, are all England, Scotland and Wales. But you are not to go out of these climates. The squire is determined that you shall never pass the reach of his disposal. He has therefore given orders that, whenever you attempt to do so, you shall be converted from a prisoner at large, to a prisoner in good earnest. (363)

The power that seems to leave Caleb at "perfect liberty" is, evidently, the power of the sovereign state, bounded by the territorial limits of the "salt seas." Within this space, notably described in the terminology of system and law ("the rules . . . are all England, Scotland and Wales"), one can be a "prisoner" with "perfect liberty." The superb innovation in Godwin's novel over the gothic tradition he is revising is to have shown that such isolation, such "miserable and lingering destruction," did not require dungeons or monastic incarceration, but could be more effectively presented when set against the background of open spaces and the crush of humanity, "the corrupt wilderness of human society" (377). Caleb calls Falkland's tragic flaw his obsession with the "poison of chivalry" (377), but it seems to the modern eye more like the poison of liberalism, the conviction that a formal equality and an actual inequality are both ineluctable features of social life. Godwin's novel shows how this structural contradiction according to which the individual trembles between the position of sovereign and that of victim becomes experienced as a temporal disturbance. The dead other (Tyrrel) can never be revived, and one's own death can never come soon enough. The putting to death and the power to preserve are equally undermined by this twilit zone of lingering, and it is this confusion that makes "benevolence" indistinguishable from persecution.

But why should the "corrupt wilderness" of human society stop at the water's edge? Why should it be bounded by the "salt seas"? Brown takes up the main features of Godwin's project—the death of the tyrant, the destabilized relation between master and servant, the misdirection of attachment and sympathy, the reduction of the sovereign self to an isolation that simultaneously aggrandizes and abjects it—and he sets it adrift beyond the salt seas. In *Edgar Huntly*, the American disaster is linked to an Irish one, where the original trauma is, once again, the death of a tyrant. The primal father corresponding to Tyrrel is the fiendish Arthur Wiatte, whose monstrous egotism is characterized, according to the hyperbole so basic to the concept of sovereignty, as an absolute anomaly: Clithero calls him "an exception to all the rules which govern us in our judgments of human nature" (43). Wiatte also exhibits the ambiguous existential status of the sovereign exception, such that a character can say in all seriousness that "this is the man, *whether once dead or not*, he is, at present, alive and in this city" (61, emphasis added). Having been previously transported for his crimes, Wiatte returns to Dublin, and thereby literalizes the notion, so dear to Freud, that the archaic sovereign is simultaneously the most intimate and the most strange, always an other. Wiatte is in one sense a traditional blocking agent, preventing the marriage between his twin sister, Euphemia, and Sarsefield, a surgeon of common birth, but this link to Sarsefield is underscored by their both being onetime denizens of colonial peripheries. In the expanded geopolitical imagination of Brown, the primal father takes shape as a transported felon on the lam, while the subjugated son becomes an agent of the colonial apparatus. At one point, Sarsefield describes his imprisonment in Bengal, and his subsequent wanderings feel self-consciously recapitulative, a kind of *translatio studii* from India to Turkey to Greece, thence to Venice and Tuscany, northward to the Alpine countries, and eventually America, from where finally he returns to Dublin, as if drawn magnetically to his "Archfoe," Wiatte.

Just as Brown's plot of wandering and peregrination is an exacerbated form of Godwin's, so too is the oedipalism of Clithero's Irish backstory more pronounced than anything in Godwin. Clithero refers to himself as the "son" (78) of Mrs. Lorimer, and to Arthur Wiatte—by virtue of his having fathered Clithero's beloved, Clarice—as the "father of my love" (70). "What were the limits of his power? How may he exert the parental prerogatives?" (64), asks Clithero, as if Filmer's *Patriarcha* were still required reading. Oedipal violence is, however, the order of the day: Wiatte, the primal father, bars access to both the mother and her substitute, and the plot demands his removal. Brown stages the confrontation as a matter of both narrative and psychological necessity, as a system running by itself. Upon his return, Wiatte attempts the life of Clithero and is destroyed. Clithero remarks: "I had meditated nothing. I was impelled by an unconscious necessity. Had the assailant been my father the consequence would have been the same. My understanding had been neutral" (70). That Brown has the phenomenon of tyrannicide in mind is suggested by the echo of Antony's great speech foretelling the destruction that will succeed the murder of another famous tyrant ("Cry 'Havoc!' and let slip the dogs of war!") in Clithero's exclamation: "Havock and despair, that were restrained during his life, were let loose by his last sigh. Now only is destruction made sure" (73).[22]

Recall that Falkland had asserted a panoptical efficiency: "I had my eye upon you in all your wanderings. You have taken no material step through their whole course with which I have not been acquainted. I meditated to do you good" (326). Here the meditation and the ability to observe the material step are versions of one another. In Brown's colonial theater, by contrast, such sovereign control is nowhere to be found, and the catastrophes of benevolence accordingly spin out of control in a process of displacement and infection. Clithero "had meditated nothing":

> Previously to [the killing of Wiatte] I was calm, considerate, and self-collected. I marked the way that I was going. Passing objects were observed. If I adverted to the series of my own reflections, my attention was not seized and fastened by them. I could disengage myself at pleasure, and could pass, without difficulty, from attention to the world within, to the contemplation of that without. Now my liberty, in this respect was at an end. I was fettered, confounded, smitten with excess of thought, and laid prostrate with wonder! I no longer attended to my steps. (70)

Liberty here is figured as an ability to "mark the way" as well as control "the series of . . . reflections." Prior to this catastrophic event, Clithero could correlate walking and thinking: his physical steps and his mental steps could both be attended to. But now the inability to access the "meditation" Falkland commands has led to an excess of thought cognate to, but destructively disarticulated from, a furious peregrinating. The sovereign control of Falkland allowed for Caleb's "perfect liberty" to be exercised within the limits imposed by the imprisoning "salt seas"; Gines had warned that should he cross that limit, Caleb would find himself a "prisoner in good earnest" (363). Such appears to be Clithero's post-tyrannicidal fate: "Now my liberty . . . was at an end" (70). More even than Caleb, Clithero exemplifies the impossibility of attaining a fury of movement, an intensity of "restlessness," that would be sufficient to allow him to escape the prison constituted by the liberal subject's melancholia—not even if he runs all the way to the Pennsylvania frontier.

Falkland had both cared for, and persecuted, Caleb: this is the way in which Godwin's novel destabilizes the opposition between master and servant. In *Edgar Huntly*, this ambivalence born from the disavowal of the persistence of despotic forms in a liberal regime is distributed across the terrible twinship of Wiatte and Mrs. Lorimer. If the brother presents unbridled aggression, the sister's humanitarian project of uplift produces effects of equivalent intensity. Mrs. Lorimer's goodness is a terrible, an inexpiable, burden to Clithero. It was she who plucked him from peasant obscurity and elevated him to a near-equal status with her. He becomes an ersatz landlord: "My personal ease and independence were less infringed than that of those who are accounted the freest members of society. I derived a sort of authority and dignity from the receipt and disbursement of money. The tenants and debtors of the lady were, in some respects, mine. It was, for the most part, on my justice and lenity that they depended for their treatment" (39). It was this initial elevation that Clithero "for a long time [had] regarded as the most fortunate of my life: but which now I regard as the scheme of some infernal agent and as the primary source of all my calamities" (36).

This apparent promotion to the status of small-scale landlord—calling in debts, dispensing justice—turns out to be a more pernicious form of servitude, the kind of infinitization of debt that Deleuze and Guattari describe as one effect of the arrival of the state—and its money form—over the horizon of despotism.[23] Clithero is gripped by mounting panic: "No time would suffice to discharge the debt of gratitude that was due to her. Yet it was continually accumulating. If an anxious thought ever invaded my bosom it arose from this source" (42). Much as Falkland had refused to release Caleb from the grip of his "benevolence," so too does Mrs. Lorimer upbraid her protégé: "She had arraigned my impatience of obligation as criminal, and condemned every scheme I had projected for freeing myself from the burthen which her beneficence had laid upon me" (72). With the death of Wiatte, this inherently unstable dynamic spirals out of control, to the point that Clithero decides that his only possible act of gratitude to Mrs. Lorimer is to kill her:

> How have I discharged the measureless debt of gratitude to which she is entitled? Cannot my guilt be extenuated? Is there not a good that I can do thee? Must I perpetrate unmitigated evil? Is the province assigned to me that of an infernal emissary, whose efforts are concentrated in a single purpose and that purpose a malignant one? I am the author of thy calamities. Whatever misery is reserved

> for thee, I am the source whence it flows. Can I not set bounds to the stream? Cannot I prevent thee from returning to a consciousness which, till it ceases to exist, will not cease to be rent and mangled? (78)

Here Clithero's only expedient is to humanely put Mrs. Lorimer out of a misery that she has not even entered yet! But Brown pours yet more catastrophic benevolence on poor Clithero's head. Arriving just in time to keep him from murdering his beloved Clarice (who was asleep in her mother's bed), Mrs. Lorimer then keeps Clithero from killing himself. Never has the power of preserving life seemed so merciless: "Every new moment added to the sum of my inexpiable guilt. Murder was succeeded, in an instant, by the more detestable enormity of suicide. She to whom my ingratitude was flagrant in proportion to the benefits of which she was the author, had now added to her former acts, that of rescuing me from the last of mischiefs" (81).

Clithero's existence, as well as Mrs. Lorimer's, takes on the lingering status we have come to know: "To shake off the ills that fasten on us by shaking off existence, is a lot which the system of nature has denied to man" (81). His next comment on the subject is equally unusual: "The torments that grow out of [the 'dismal spectacle' of his crimes], can terminate only with the thread of my existence, but that I know full well *will never end.* Death is but a shifting of the scene, and the progress of eternity, which, to the good, is merely the perfection of felicity, is, to the wicked, an accumulation of woe" (82, emphasis added). At this point, Clithero is fairly clearly mad, but the novel need not be. Clithero articulates the condition of the last man, at once reduced and exalted, unimaginably solitary but by that fact also able to transcend the finitude of the human. His excruciating experience is human, in other words, while his status as immortal is wholly symbolic. Clithero's melancholia has become strictly speaking infinite, but his sufferings from the sympathy of others are not yet over. There is one more "shifting of the scene" for this dead-alive creature: he strikes out for Pennsylvania, where he falsely imagines that he might attain an absolute solitude.

Brown's humanitarian gothic is, in the end, more extreme even than Godwin's: there is no frontier beyond which one might wander and thereby escape the harassments of the good intentions of others. The "wilderness" nourishes fantasies of escape (for Clithero) or priority (for Edgar), but Brown seems insistent on proving that solitude is always peopled, that there is always at least one to appear before and beyond you, that the logic of the last is interminable. In a scene that recalls Jefferson's "sublime" description of the Natural Bridge, Brown describes Edgar admiring a chasm from an elevated point: "My delight was enhanced by the contrast which this lightsome and serene element bore to the glooms from which I had lately emerged" (98). He continues à la Jefferson: "A stream, rushing from above, fell into a cavity, which its own force seemed gradually to have made. The noise and the motion equally attracted my attention. There was a desolate and solitary grandeur in the scene" (99). Edgar draws the properly romantic fantasy of priority from this vision of the sublime: "A sort of sanctity and awe environed it, owing to the consciousness of absolute and utter loneliness. It was probable that human feet had never gained this recess, that human eyes had never been fixed upon these rushing waters" (99). He is destined to be disappointed, however, for Clithero is already there. I would draw the allegorical point in this way: because the last man never ceases, the first man never emerges without antecedent. It is Clithero that embodies this condition of mankind—always first and last, suspended in a dislocated zone in which temporal series collapse. Edgar hails the suffering maniac with what we should probably understand by now as a tautology: "*Man! Clithero!*" (100).

The Road to Nowhere

The opening scene of *Edgar Huntly* is remarkable for its cinematic sharpness:

> You know the situation of the Elm, in the midst of a private road. . . . I proceeded in this . . . direction with speed. . . . I was familiar with the way, though trackless and intricate, and I climbed the steeps, crept through the brambles, leapt the rivulets and fences with undeviating aim, till at length I reached the craggy and obscure path . . . The shape of a man, tall and robust, was now distinguished. Repeated and close scrutiny enabled me to perceive that he was digging in the earth. . . . A figure, robust and strange, and half naked, to be thus employed, at this hour and place, was calculated to rouse up my whole soul. His occupation was mysterious and obscure. Was it a grave that he was digging? Was his purpose to explore or to hide? Was it proper to observe him at a distance, unobserved and in silence? . . . He seemed wrapt in meditation; but the pause was short, and

> succeeded by sobs, at first low, and at wide intervals, but presently louder and more vehement. . . . Never did I witness a scene of such mighty anguish, such heart-bursting grief. (9–10)

This "Elm," so mysteriously situated in "the midst of a private road," is where the body of Edgar's friend Waldegrave was found murdered before the novel begins. We will eventually learn at the end of the story that Waldegrave was a victim of arbitrary vengeance by an exasperated Delaware Indian, but at this point Edgar has some reasonable doubts as to the innocence of this "robust and strange" figure digging under the tree. It turns out that the figure is a somnambulating Clithero, burying Mrs. Lorimer's memoirs and venting a grief that seems inconsolable—and surely is, given the neurotic, solitary, and unconscious nature of it. But for Edgar, the figure is "connected to the fate of Waldegrave," perhaps the murderer himself. All the more remarkable, then, the effect this scene of lamentation has on him: "I was suspended in astonishment. Every sentiment, at length, yielded to my sympathy. . . . My caution had forsaken me, and instead of one whom it was my duty to persecute, I beheld, in this man, nothing but an object of compassion. . . . I was prompted to advance nearer and hold his hand" (10–11). Clithero's trauma coincides with Edgar's, and the result is the mysterious transformation of a "duty to persecute" into an occasion for hand-holding.

Sydney Krause has argued that this "fatal Elm" is a deliberate revision, or inversion, of the famous "Treaty Elm" in Shackamaxon underneath which William Penn and the Delaware Indians first expressed their mutual amity.[24] I will return to the implications of this argument, and the trope of the tree more generally, in the next chapter, but consider first some other evidence that this scene between two Europeans encrypts an encounter between Americans and Indians. This entire opening scene is a kind of revision of the scene in Jefferson's *Notes* in which he describes the traveling Indians, like Edgar and Clithero, able to find their way through a wilderness "with undeviating aim," arriving at the barrow in the woods where they give vent to "expressions construed to be those of sorrow" (*Notes* 100). Jefferson decidedly keeps his distance from this scene; he defends himself, as it were, by projecting an ambiguity on the Indians' behavior. Jefferson's archival project, I suggested, depends in its entirety on the keeping of distance, but Brown's project is to investigate the transfer of affect, not its containment. Thus, Edgar is unable to keep the ambiguities of the lamenting figure's behavior from infecting his own response: in a flash, his "duty to persecute" is transformed into an overmastering sympathy. Melancholy presents itself as viral in this scene, a transmission of affect that creates in its victim a near coincidence or superimposition of aggression and care.

Edgar spends considerable energy over the next several chapters marveling at the convertibility of these emotions. "I had no need to provide against the possible suggestions of revenge. I felt nothing but the tenderness of compassion" (30), Edgar remarks with self-satisfaction, and then goes on to philosophize about the inherent instability of our feelings toward others: "Were futurity laid open to my view, and events, with the consequences unfolded, I might see reason to embrace the assassin of my best friend" (31). He characterizes his emotional state as "sublime," and here we see the dilation of ego characteristic of the sovereign subject:

> The suggestions of sorrow and malice had, for a time, taken their flight, and yielded place to a generous sympathy, which filled my eyes with tears, but had more in it of pleasure than of pain. That Clithero was instrumental to the death of Waldegrave, that he could furnish the clue, explanatory of every bloody and mysterious event that had hitherto occurred, there was no longer the possibility of doubting. He, indeed, said I, is the murderer of excellence, and yet it shall be my province to emulate a father's clemency, and restore this unhappy man to purity, and to peace. (32)

We are once again reminded how a narrative of clemency and rehabilitation—the liberal, humanitarian project of forgiveness and preservation—can also harbor fantasies of power and self-aggrandizement.

What logic dictates the superimposition of Clithero's and Edgar's traumas? What prompts Brown to have Clithero, "robust and strange, and half naked" (9), indulge his melancholy beneath this tree? Edgar does not know yet that the murderer of Waldegrave was an Indian, but we can already notice how this site—the tree in the road, the environing dreamscape of Norwalk—initiates a process of "becoming-Indian" in both Clithero and Edgar, as they tear off through the wilderness, displaying their survivalist bona fides. Jared Gardner influentially argued some years ago that what conjoins Clithero, the Irishman, with the Indian for whom he here substitutes in Edgar's private history of trauma (recall that Edgar's family had *also* been slaughtered by Indians, long before Waldegrave's assassination) is the figure of the "alien": early national paranoia about the Jacobin tendencies of all "aliens" being what it was in John Adams's America, Edgar's murderous identification with Clithero represents a kind of purgation of dangerous (Godwinian) tendencies within Brown himself.[25] This makes sense to me, but as with Godwin's relation to the time of the Treason Trials, the political imagination of Brown overflows the immediate context of the Alien and Sedition Acts. I want to consider the possibility that in the juxtaposition of European, American, and Indian trauma that makes up the scene of lamentation beneath the Elm Tree, we are witnessing how the American scene provides "points of connection between the mental lives of neurotics and savages."

One such connection is suggested by an exhibition of waxworks mounted in New York in 1789. As described by Eric Slauter, the exhibition "featured a life-size figure of 'An Old Hermit' in the company of the President of the United States, members of the British royal family, and an 'Indian Chief . . . holding a real scalp.'"[26] Waxworks, being a kind of effigy, participate in the political magical thinking at work in the production and projection of transcendental selves and second bodies. Such traditions reach back, as Giorgio Agamben reminds us, to the colossi of the ancient world, and were alive and well in revolutionary America, when effigies of George III were put to a range of colorful uses.[27] George is notably absent from the description above, however: in his place, there are merely assorted "royals," their very multiplicity suggesting that we are in a post-tyrannical world, albeit one from which sovereignty is not absent. Perhaps the plural royals are to be understood as sublated by Washington's monumental singularity, as if the very principle of legitimate sovereign power had been first negated and then reconstructed on the American shore.

But the pairing of the other two figures interests me even more, for the Indian chief and the hermit present complementary and analogous forms of individual isolation, the one presocial and the other postsocial. Slauter argues that the early national period "was marked by a fascination with sociability and solitude, by narratives of entering into and exiting from civil society" (36). *Edgar Huntly* is no exception: various characters enter and exit civil society, usually after traveling through the wilderness zone of Norwalk. The thinness of social description in Brown's novel is also consistent with what Slauter sees as a pervasive tendency in the era to conflate "written constitutions and social compacts, as if society was not itself a distinct mediator between government and the mythical state of nature described by political philosophers" (31): thus it is that Clithero's strange obsequies with Mrs. Lorimer's manuscript can provoke in Edgar the kind of Pavlovian encounter typical of accounts of the state of nature, where all responses to the other seem reduced to vectors of alliance (Locke) or of aggression (Hobbes). Slauter suggests that the era's fascination with hermits like Clithero "confused presocial beings with postsocial beings," and caused Americans to base their fantasies about the state of nature on "those individuals who left, rather than those who entered society" (44). But Brown's novel and the exhibition Slauter describes both suggest the collapse of any meaningful distinction between presocial and postsocial. The manifest content of the dream of legitimate sovereign power—the details of which are played out in the juxtaposition of the plural royals and the solitary Washington—is subtended by a latent dream logic according to which the sovereign self is simultaneously presocial and postsocial, savage and neurotic, Indian and hermit. If you turn your fascinated gaze away from the waxwork of Clithero as hermit, you'll notice that the Indian chief with the scalp is really Edgar Huntly, the face paint merely gore. Sarsefield makes the same mistake when he shoots at Edgar, who is trying to make his way back home from the cave.

Sarsefield's mistake is worth pondering, for ostensibly he knows his way around Norwalk, having given open-air tutorials to Edgar in his youth. What it suggests, I would like now to argue, is that Norwalk represents a new world setting that escapes even Sarsefield's considerable abilities to map. "When Sarsefield came among us, I became his favorite scholar and the companion of all his pedestrian excursions," Edgar tells us. "He was fond of penetrating into these recesses, partly from the love of picturesque scenes, and partly to carry on more effectually that species of instruction which he had adopted with regard to me, and which chiefly consisted of moralizing narratives and synthetical reasonings" (92). Pennsylvania, we recall, is Sarsefield's last stop on his tour of the empire, before returning to Ireland and all the woe unleashed there by Clithero. Sarsefield's lessons concerning how to conjoin synthetical reasoning, moralizing narrative, and an ambulatory appreciation of the picturesque seem clearly connected to his ability to negotiate the newly complex environments of the empire. (Again, think of Jefferson at the Natural Bridge or Harper's Ferry.) Does Brown approve of Sarsefield? He does at times seem the lone voice of reason, and the novel rewards him, after a fashion, with the hand of Euphemia Lorimer. Similar rewards are not in the cards for Sarsefield's two disappointing students, however. As Elizabeth Dillon has pointed out, the entire novel is framed by Edgar's failure to marry Mary Waldegrave, and as for Clithero's love life, the less said the better.[28]

In striking contrast to Sarsefield's picturesquely synthesizing travels, both Clithero and Edgar suffer from somnambulism, an affliction in which thinking and walking are maximally disjoined. In the beginning of the novel, Edgar tries to apply Sarsefield's lessons: "My steps partook, as usual, of the vehemence of my thoughts. . . . I could not endure that my reflections should be so speedily interrupted. I, therefore, passed the gate, and stopped not till I had reached a neighboring summit" (13). This is Edgar's initial attempt to compose himself after his unnerving encounter with the lamenting Clithero at the elm tree. Over the next several chapters, Edgar tries to keep up with this strange new half-clad tutor as they tear around Norwalk, and Edgar moralizes and synthesizes in Clithero's wake. But the effort fails; something fundamental has happened at the tree, and all Edgar's efforts to understand Clithero and corral his own emotion merely accelerate the aberrant drift, leading to the perversely persecutory sympathies that we have already noted. When Edgar starts to mimic Clithero even in his bouts of somnambulism, and wakes up in the bottom of a pit miles from the bed he lay down in, *his* return itinerary has none of the satisfying civilizational assurances of Sarsefield's. Edgar's trip, composing a good portion of the second half of the book, is less *translatio studii* than ontogeny recapitulating phylogeny, as he moves from mere sensorium to beast to savage to borderer to settler and finally back home, bloodied and bedraggled.[29] How does he get there? One is tempted to say, "Dead reckoning," because Sarsefield's lessons are no help at all: "The road could not but have some origin as well as end" (195), he begins by reasoning, but on the next page acknowledges that "the circuity of the path had frequently been noticed, and I began to suspect that though I had traveled long, I had not moved far from the spot where I had commenced my pilgrimage" (196). In exasperation, Edgar finally exclaims, "The road was intricate and long. It seemed designed to pervade the forest in every possible direction" (223).

This last image should give us pause. A road that pervades the forest in every direction is a road that one can neither follow nor avoid. Something deeply unusual is going on here in Norwalk, some bending of historical space-time. I will examine at some length in the next chapter what is implied by Brown's interest in clearing, roads, and trees, but here I want only to remark that a road that "pervade[s] the forest in every possible direction" puts to rout the assumptions underlying Sarsefield's lessons. In fact, Norwalk represents the destruction of *method* itself, and its attempt to conjoin movement, vision, and synthetic reasoning. In *Ramus, Method, and the Decay of Dialogue*, Walter Ong argues that there is a general drift over the medieval and early modern periods away from understanding knowledge as something concretely enunciated and toward viewing it as an atomized, external, objective thing.[30] "The decay of dialogue" in his title refers to the transformation of dialectic from aural/communicational argument to an abstracted, spatialized "method." He cites Melanchthon: "The Greeks thus define the term: Method (*methodos*) is an acquired habit establishing a way by means of reason, a habit, that is . . . which finds and opens a way through impenetrable and overgrown places (*loci*), through the confusion of things" (158). Method is a road or path. Ong observes that "Agricola and other Renaissance rhetoricians show the influence of the Greek concept—(*hyle*, Latin. *Silva*—woods, bush, forest)—insofar as they tend to think of the 'matter' of discourse in the terms of a woods to be dealt with by a process of 'sorting out' or 'cutting out' or 'arranging.' Ben Jonson calls his commonplace book *Timber*, or *Discoveries upon Man and Matter* . . . and Francis Bacon styles his collection of miscellaneous or random remarks on natural history *Sylva Sylvarum*; that is *A Forest of Trees*" (119). Thinking in this tradition is a species of clear-cutting, or road building; memory and method are habitual headings, local motion, across these clearings, observing the things that have been cleared and arranged.[31] And from Melanchthon to Freud is less of a leap than one might at first think, as Derrida's observations on Freud's spatialized concept of memory suggest:

> We ought to examine closely . . . all that Freud invites us to think concerning writing as "breaching" in the *psychical* repetition of this previously *neurological* notion: opening up of its own space, effraction, breaking of a path against resistances, rupture and irruption becoming a route (*rupta*, *via rupta*), violent inscription of a form, tracing of a difference in a nature or a matter which are conceivable as such only in their *opposition* to writing. The route is opened in nature or matter, forest or wood (*hyle*), and in it acquires a reversibility of time and space. We should have to study together, genetically and structurally, the history of the road and the history of writing.[32]

I bring in such references because the question of "reversibility of time and space" is, it seems to me, at the very heart of *Edgar Huntly*: it is a question that bears fundamentally on the melancholia that grips this novel. What Ong and Derrida can help us see is that when Brown offers us a territorial vision that defies methodical management, he is also offering us a vision of time and history. *Edgar Huntly* is a Ramist's nightmare: instead of binary forks in the road that one can follow and retrace, there is a full disconnect between walking and thinking (Brown's conceit of somnambulism), and there are "roads that pervade in every direction." Edgar keeps imagining that one can travel a road into the past and return unscathed. He opens Clithero's special box looking for clues, only to find that he cannot close it again. He thinks he can rectify the errors of the past, but when he tells Clithero that Mrs. Lorimer is still alive, Clithero rushes off to finish the history that he has only begun. The lesson seems to be that one cannot go back to the past from some starting place in the present and then return to that starting place. Each action is an irreversible new notation, a swerve in the path that can never be retraced.

Norwalk thus represents the space of melancholia in *Edgar Huntly*, a palimpsest in which traumas are superimposed without any of them being submitted to the substitutive logic of mourning. Every trauma resonates with the others, but is not thereby relieved of its particular painful lingering. Norwalk is the very location of melancholy restlessness, which is what makes it a peculiarly fitting zone for the dramatization of the postlude to the European catastrophe of the death of the tyrant. When the restless figures caught up in this catastrophe arrive, however, they enter a racialized zone not visible in Godwin's England or even in Clithero's Ireland: the zone of Norwalk draws all its inhabitants into an identificatory vortex that overflows but does not undo the racial antagonism at its heart. For above all, Norwalk indexes Indian removal. Edgar's uncle's home was once the "village inhabited by [a] clan" of Delaware that "abandoned their ancient seats and retired to the banks of the Wabash and Muskingum" (198). One ancient female "declared her resolution to remain behind, and maintain possession of the land which her countrymen should impiously abandon" (198): this lingering figure is "Old Deb," or "Queen Mab" as Edgar whimsically names her, after the fairy said to preside over dreams. With its roads pervading everywhere and going nowhere, Norwalk is therefore the contested frontier presented as dreamscape, a kind of "sterile" umbilicus connecting American present and Indian past: "the termination of a sterile and narrow tract, which begins in Indian country" (165). Old Deb is Norwalk's genius loci. Lacoue-Labarthe and Nancy had spoken of an alien, female matrix of the sovereign Narcissus: the *outre-mère* toward which psychoanalysis and political philosophy overflow their borders. While anything but maternal, Queen Mab had been something of an ersatz mother for Edgar in his childhood: "She seemed to contract an affection for me," he remarks, and the fact that Edgar "had taken some pains to study her jargon" also "wonderfully prepossessed her in my favour" (200). But it seems that Edgar has misunderstood Old Deb. He treats her pretensions to sovereign power as risible, describing her "absolute sway" as exercised only over her obedient dogs. In Edgar's view, Deb is a charity case, and in this regard she returns us once again to the proximity between sovereign power and the structures of care, preservation, and benevolence that would seem to replace the rigors of sovereign power in a liberal regime:

> She seldom left the hut but to visit the neighboring inhabitants, and demand from them food and clothing, or whatever her necessities required. These were exacted as her due: to have her wants supplied was her prerogative, and to withhold what she claimed was rebellion. She conceived that by remaining behind her countrymen she succeeded to the government, and retained possession of all this region. The English were aliens and sojourners, who occupied the land merely by her connivance and permission, and whom she allowed to remain on no terms but those of supplying her wants. (199)

In her own instantiation of the logic of the last, in her insistence—apparently flying in the face of historical reality—that she "retained possession of all this region," Old Deb manifests a melancholy refusal to forgive and forget that marks the very territory over which she symbolically presides. Edgar blindly thinks that her claims can be humanely humored. But his own story indicates how a posture of sympathy and care is but an alternate modality of aggression. It is pathetic Old Deb who organizes the Indian reprisals that ignite the frontier and pull Edgar's world around his head.

Abandoned Dominion

> O signifier, terrible archaism of the despot where they still look for the empty tomb, the dead father, and the mystery of the name!
>
> —DELEUZE AND GUATTARI, *Anti-Oedipus*, 208–9

In 1824 John Neal traveled to England and soon thereafter was allowed to publish a series of articles on "American Writers" for *Blackwood's*, for which he adopted the persona of an Englishman. He singles out Charles Brockden Brown as a "hearty specimen of Trans-Atlantic stuff" (57), by which he apparently means both that Brown was "an imitator of Godwin, whose Caleb Williams made him," and that it was the English who first recognized Brown's value: "Some years ago, WE took up CHARLES BROCKDEN BROWN; disinterred him; embalmed him; did him up, decently; and put him back again . . . Since then, poor Brown has had no peace, for his countrymen."[33] Given the nearly plagiaristic relation that Neal's *Logan* maintains to Brown's romances, we might say that it is Neal who disinters Brown and gives him no peace. Long known for his early and strident calls for a distinctively American literature, Neal is self-consciously transatlantic in ways that go beyond the assumption of an English persona or his cracks about Brown. Neal was one of the first American writers to celebrate Byron's poetry, in a series of reviews in *The Portico* in 1816, for example, and his *Logan* exemplifies a strain of melancholic Byronism that eventually lost out, in America, to the modulated mournfulness that Cooper copied from Sir Walter Scott. *Logan* is, in fact, something of a summa of Anglophone romantic melancholy: he names his brooding, violent, half-breed hero Harold, while Harold's older brother, Oscar, seems meant to recall the son of Ossian in Macpherson's *Fingal.* The strategy of asserting an American identity through its differentiation from both British and Indian fathers is here focused on the talismanic name Logan, which applies both to the famous Mingo warrior immortalized by Jefferson *and* to a misanthropic British nobleman named George of Salisbury, who has emigrated to America and married into the remnant of the Logan clan, and who proves to be the biological father to both Oscar and Harold. Even this minimal sketch suggests that Neal's plotting is excessive, and his prose is even more notoriously over the top, "a fermented syrup of romanticism."[34]

The very extremity of Neal's manner reveals, however, aspects of the melancholic project in America that are less visible in more restrained efforts. As Teresa Goddu has remarked, "It is through the book's incoherent plotting and gothic excesses that the ideological maneuvers of the frontier novel are made apparent. *Logan*'s disjunctive and repetitious form registers its culture's contradictions" (62). In its plotting, in its ironic—at times well-nigh plagiaristic—relation to prior texts, in the rhythm of its prose, with its tendency to spastic iteration, we find exposed in Neal's novel crucial contradictions inherent in the American "melancholy fact" exemplified by

Logan. From one perspective, of course, the substitution of a white "Logan" for the historical one might seem like the greatest scandal of all, an instance of what Baucom has identified as Scott's strategy of making a feint in the direction of a "politics of resentment or revenge" only to convert such melancholy into fuel for a romantic liberalism.[35] This would seem to be Dana Nelson's view, when she argues that Neal "extends and amplifies as a narrative of national origins Jefferson's adoption of the Mingo chief and orator, making his male descendants (and his namesake in the novel) white Americans, not just analogically, as does Jefferson, but *genealogically*. Thus Neal effects, through family romance, the consolidation of national manhood—and a model for national literature—in (yet another) symbolic appropriation of Indian manhood. This arrogated identity, at once territorial and affective, legalizes its claims (yet again) through characterologically inconsequential, symbolically idealized Indian women."[36] But this makes Neal sound more like Cooper than I think is warranted. As mournful as Cooper's novels are, their endings are also always beginnings, which is what makes them self-consciously national narratives. At the end of *Logan*, on the other hand, everyone is dead. Incest, rape, madness, parricide, and infanticide are all well and good, but if there's no one left to assert "territorial and affective" claim to the national narrative, then what purpose do they serve? Rather than the extension of a national narrative, I would argue, Neal is describing its implosion.

Neal invested considerable energy, in fact, in imagining the destruction of the American republic. Here he is in July 1830, offering a thought experiment to the alumni of Waterville College:

> Suppose a man should appear before us tomorrow in the character of a prophet—or a soothsayer, and throwing up his arms to the sky, suppose he should pretend to see a new wilderness rolling forward from the unvisited depths of our country, and taking the place of our cities—growing louder and louder and more and more powerful every moment—our palaces vanishing—our monuments overwhelmed with the frightful vegetation of the desert—our navies dropping away—our very churches begirt with a new forest, and disappearing flash after flash in the darkness thereof—what should we say to such prophecy?[37]

Such a prophet in previous empires, he answers himself, would "have been pitied, or scoffed at, or peradventure put to death for the outrage upon [the] magnificent destiny" (8) of his people. Neal's address self-consciously opposes an ideology of America's expansionist "destiny" that he understands as dominant. He would remind his countrymen about the inevitability of a "*Retrocession of Empire*": "Nations like men are mortal" (3, 5). However critical Neal is of the religious justification for the great Protestant American empire ("One class of believers . . . *are* a preponderating power in the State, a hierarchy of wealth and perpetual accumulation—a state hierarchy—a political antichrist" [23]), he is not immune to the racialist thinking that forms a basic plank of that platform. Territorial overreaching looks like racial amalgamation to Neal: "Let it be remembered that a grain of dust dropped into the heart of the unfathomable ocean may have—and probably must have—some influence upon every drop thereof; causing a pulsation it may be, in the furthest tide upon the furthest shore—and then say whether with such neighbors as we have—with the British—the Mexicans—the Blacks—the native Indians—we have nothing to fear; with the sister commonwealths that may spring up hereafter beyond the reach of representation—we have nothing to fear" (13). How exactly Neal proposes to get clear of such "neighbors" as "the Blacks" and "the native Indians" is not explained. But he knows that we cannot assimilate any more such "neighbors": our "magnificent system . . . cannot keep together contradictory, and essentially-different elements—it could not . . . embrace within its proud orbit, the republics that have lately appeared and disappeared in the South—the unprepared, the unestablished governments of our other America. It could not govern a people beyond its reach—it cannot—be their fathers whom they may" (13). Neal evinces here a characteristic Anglo revulsion at the perceived pervasiveness of racial mixture in the former Spanish dominions. "Our other America" is "beyond the reach of representation," and this is because it is peopled by "essentially-different elements." And white fatherhood is no guarantee of assimilation, or of representation: *be their fathers whom they may*.

Eight years earlier, in his sanguinary *Logan: A Family History*, Neal had also indulged in fantasies of dominion and destruction, and in that novel too the importance of fatherhood is both wildly aggrandized and strangely suspended. Harold is given to visions of the destruction of the whites and the restoration to the Indians of their land, about which Neal has this to say: "What think ye of his dreaming? And is it dreaming? May not—are ye sure that the inheritance of the Indian may not, even yet, be plucked from the spoiler? May not, oh ye that blaspheme the Great Spirit, may not the thunders of the everlasting God lay waste your habitations . . . This he has done to many a nation. This he may do to yours. Look ye for Babylon? Whither is Jerusalem? Ye are but as one Babylon; and one who measureth the sins of Jerusalem against yours."[38] Oddly enough, however, the race war that such thundering might seem to be endorsing turns out to be a purely white affair in the novel. After all, it is Harold's father, the white Logan, who instructs him to "pursue the whites to extermination" (34), and it is he who returns at the end to kill off his own sons: the apocalypse that closes this novel is restricted to the Salisbury/"Logan" clan. This confusion about the source and target of Harold's project of "extermination" is, in fact, already present in his initial fantasies:

> Lo, she is there!—her naked feet upon a brazen chariot, a whirlwind of smoke and dust rolling about her; her head encumbered with stars; her locks streaming, like a rent banner in the wind, her chariot wheels rolling over, and grinding to dust, the shattered and glittering fragments of an empire—an eagle with thunderbolts upon her right hand—her garments rolled in blood! There—there—for ever there! stands she, the object of his idolatry.
>
> Hark! hear ye not the far-off barbarian gong? The isles of the ocean are in arms. The daughters of the blue Pacific are in battle. Look, look, the temple totters in the blue flame of its ascending altar. It dissolves—the firmament reddens—it rains fire! and the smoke drifts like a hurricane by us. A shout—the clouds are rolling away. A continent breaks upon our view—the shores, the islands are peopled, and joyous with the wild music of many nations—feathers in their hair—their idolatrous temples vanishing—their bows unstrung—their quivers untenanted, and the green wilderness rising behind them. (45)

The context suggests that Harold is having a vision of leading the Indians in a war to reclaim their lost empire. But this war seems to destroy the Indians as much as the whites: it is *their* temples that are vanishing, *their* bows that are unstrung, and yet they are unaccountably happy. The object of Harold's "idolatry" would appear to be a version of America herself, with her eagle and arrows, but this anti-imperial American juggernaut destroys everything in its wake, "grinding to dust" white and Indian alike in its blood-soaked drive to return to the land itself: a "green wilderness rising behind them." Apocalypse and discovery converge here: "A continent breaks upon our view."

I present these visions of the retrocession of empire to suggest that Neal's relation to the "national narrative" is more complex than Nelson suggests. It is perhaps not fair to ask for coherence of vision from Neal. (He does not even ask it of himself. In his *Blackwood's* series, he describes *Logan* as, precisely, "incoherent—so evidently without aim, or object, worthy of a good or a wise man—so outrageously overdone, that nobody *can* read it through" [169]). But the very extravagance of Neal's idiom is revelatory: what Neal's vision in his speech of 1830 and Harold's of the "far-off barbarian gong" have in common is their eager erasure of political structures—imperial or national, "barbarian" or "civilized"—in favor of a seizure of the land itself as a kind of deterritorialized space. If apocalypse and discovery become indistinguishable, the land can be understood as simultaneously pre- and post-historical, unfixed by temporal codes altogether. And as with the land, so with the prophet or visionary left alone in it: the dilations of time and space that affect the one also affect the other. Harold's sovereign isolation is equally intense: "Never before had he walked so fearlessly over the dominions of his God. . . . Never, never, had he felt such a melancholy and awful solitude of the spirit: it was as if he has suddenly been enthroned and sceptred within the illimitable dominions of space, and there left alone in his sovereignty" (39). To be "alone in one's sovereignty" is the deepest fantasy of the novel, and it is a fantasy of a fully deterritorialized power, where both time and space become "illimitable."

What does this fantasy of a "melancholy . . . solitude of the spirit" have to do with the Logan that Jefferson inscribes in the American archive? In the beginning of the novel, we are told that the historical Logan—"Who has not heard of Logan? Who cannot recount the deeds of his generation?"—did not finish his days childless, as Jefferson's version of his speech would suggest, but rather "abandoned his dominion, that his dominion might not abandon him" (4). It is a strange phrase, a strange idea. What does it mean? After his family had been killed—"The shot rang, and many generations mingled their blood at his feet" (3)—Logan decides to start a new family, this time dedicating his child to race war:

> He made his boy a warrior. He was born a chief. That done, the old man called a council of his nation, pronounced an awful malediction upon the whites, and disappeared for ever. . . . But Logan—he went alone . . . to the wilderness. He devoted himself with the solemnity of one about to meet in convocation the builders of his race. . . . He knelt—he laid down his child at the foot of an oak, that instant shattered and riven with the midnight thunderbolt, and prayed that the cloud might not pass over his head, unless it were to confirm his destiny, and

> render the hands of the babe that had dabbled in blood yet more and more familiar with it, as they waxed older and stronger. (3)

Neal, like Brown before him, invokes here the tree as symbol of social compact—the place for "convocation" with the "builders of his race," the "Treaty Elm" that Krause argued was encrypted in Brown's "fatal Elm"—while also insisting that it is a site of trauma, a mnemonic for ceaseless vengeance. To abandon dominion here means to abandon territorial control: Logan disappears. But this abdication is also, Neal tells us, a way of concentrating dominion, as if sovereign power were best exercised, most terribly exercised, from a radical isolation and abandonment. In a sense, Logan withdraws into his name, becomes a genealogical principle unbound by genealogy: the name of the father. The "Logan" of the rest of the novel is not this historical Logan, as we have noted, but the hero's father, George of Salisbury, who takes the name of Logan after he has married into the remnant of the Logan line, now a "family neither Indian nor white—neither savage nor civilized" (4). This white Logan, however, also might be said to have abandoned his dominion. Having epitomized old-world corruption—scion of a "noble family," George had "rioted through every excess of indulgence" (4)—the white Logan also represents the misanthropic repudiation of that world, an antisocial individualism associated with new world heroism: "Such was the father; a savage before he left the palaces of the white men. But he was a great savage. He had a desperate but sublime ambition. He was full of the fiery element, that rises in the arteries like mercury in a thermometer, at the approach of greatness. His whole nature was heroic—but it was the nature of him who thundered at the battlements of heaven" (5). The last clause confirms what the epigraph to the first chapter—"Evil!—be thou my good"—had already implied: Logan is one of the romantic "metamorphoses of Satan."[39] In Book IV of *Paradise Lost*, Satan rails: "Evil be thou my Good; by thee at least/Divided empire with Heav'n's King I hold/ By thee, and more than half perhaps will reign" (ll. 110–12). Satan's unbending opposition articulates the principle that unites the historical Logan and his white avatar: sovereign power is all the more implacable when it ceases to be attached to territorial control, but becomes the insignia of deterritorialized individualism. Abandoned dominion is the condition in which Indian and settler—Logan and "Logan"—endlessly battle each other in America: race war.

A world defined by such abandoned dominion, by such a deterritorialization of sovereignty, is one in which the signifier reigns supreme. The strangely abstract, citational quality of fatherhood in Neal's novel comes out in the narrator's first description of the white Logan. He has just described the mother of a family, "the nearest blood descendant of the great Logan" (4), whose "wild sovereignty" does not prevent her from being in "perpetual travail for her people":

> The father—I feel my heart growing warm again as I recall the dear, dear spot to my remembrance, and if I do not soon take my eyes from the picture that is, at this instant, assembling itself before me, limb by limb, and feature by feature, I shall grow sick at heart, weary of my appointed trial, and throw aside my pen for ever, fainting in very wretchedness of spirit. But there is a cure for this—the father!—at his name I revive; my faculties arouse themselves. Let us talk of the father then—of him that never forgot nor forgave. What sublime constancy! I will imitate him—I—well then "the father." (4)

The father intercedes here as a figure of melancholic memory—he "never forgot nor forgave"—that prevents a "picture" from "assembling itself." What is this picture? To what scene, to what wretchedness, is the father "the cure"? We have just had the description of the "Indian queen" turning her "fine eyes toward her naked children, that lay basking about in the sunshine" (4), and we will learn shortly that what the father "never forgot nor forgave" was the massacre of this family: "What became of this family? What! they were slaughtered—butchered, and profaned" (5). There is a temporal collapse at work in the narrator's description, in which a scene of basking children and a scene of carnage are superimposed: if the narrator is "sick at heart" at the "picture . . . assembling itself . . . limb by limb," it is because the disassembled body parts (as in the phrase, "limb *from* limb") already lie about in the mind's eye. Like some kind of Lacanian "mirror phase" in which the unity of the family scene can only be projected from, and undermined by, the disaggregation of the scene of massacre—the *corps morcelés* of the American cultural imaginary—the "family history" collapsed in this disturbing tableau can only be "cured" by the intervention of "the father," whose scare quotes indicate as succinctly as we could wish his status as agent of the symbolic register: "But there is a cure for this—the father!—at his name I revive; my faculties arouse themselves. Let us talk of the father then—of him that never forgot nor forgave. What sublime constancy! I will imitate him—I—well then 'the father'" (4).

Well might the narrator falter at the prospect of imitating the father: the oedipal delirium that Neal has tapped into here is characterized by a well-known double bind of imitation. As Freud argues in *The Ego and the Id*, the superego's "relation to the ego is not exhausted by the precept, 'You *ought to be* like this (like your father).' It also comprises the prohibition: 'You *may not be* like this (like your father).'"[40] The intricacies of the psychoanalytic apparatus are legion, of course, and I do not wish to become too tangled in them here. Let us rather take the tack of Deleuze and Guattari, for whom the floridly oedipal psychodynamics on show in this passage from Neal's novel would be understood as epiphenomena of social relations, rather than the source or truth of those relations.[41] Let us return, in other words, to the social and historical matrix to which this text constitutes a melancholic response. Jefferson's Logan, we remember, simultaneously acknowledges the "beams of peace" and exempts himself from them, invokes a scene of compact and treaty even as he embodies its suspension. Logan would thus seem to present a historical instance of the double bind described theoretically above, in which identification with paternal law is both required and interdicted, both installed and suspended. This double bind expresses itself in our present context as a disturbing superimposition of massacre and compact: thus, the tree that Logan was said to deliver his speech to Gibson beneath might be the iconic treaty tree, as some traditions have it, or it might be the oak beneath which Neal's Logan dedicates his son to slaughter. The narrator above seems to imagine that "the father" is the cure for this unsettling convergence, the inability to keep separated the picture of interracial family peace from that of massacre.

But the novel itself knows better. Although it is not made explicit, we can assume, I think, that the oak tree of the opening scene is the "blasted tree" beneath which Harold and Logan later battle, and beneath which Logan, apparently dying, reveals himself as Harold's father. This tree is essentially a plagiarism of the "fatal Elm" in Brown's *Edgar Huntly*; it also serves to mark a space in which massacre and treaty making become inextricable. Harold, like Edgar and Clithero, finds that he has unconsciously engaged in violent business beneath this tree: "The circumstances of his dream are all before him now! here had he been! here—in that very spot, in his delirium! By that shattered and blasted tree it was done!" (47). But when a party returns to recover Logan's body, it is gone: the blasted tree is in fact a dream space, just as it is in Brown, and it is the empty tomb of the father who, because he is always already dead, can never really disappear for good: "The father too—the adopted Logan—the fell George of Salisbury—even he was buried among the bones, . . . under the very tree which he had haunted with a spirit so deadly . . . —a place, which had at last become a terror to the very red men, and was overgrown and tangled so, that the whites were fain to choose another route. . . . No one ever knew how he had been preserved, or by whom; but he haunted the place, and made it a desert" (174–75).

The gothic motifs so flamboyantly displayed in Neal's novel are silly enough, to be sure: but they also reveal the deep structure of a melancholia that, by setting aside at least one—"the father," or "Logan"—as "outside all possibility of substitution, surrender, or exchange" (Baucom 225), puts in place a self-consuming regime of semiotic deterritorialization, a regime whose relation to the past looks more like traumatized repetition than the kind of ethical adherence to the "melancholy fact" that Baucom admires. Deleuze and Guattari, with their affinity for American literature, bring us closer to the dynamic revealed by Neal's response to Logan. America represents for them, conventionally enough, the surge of energy that accompanies the modern uprooting of tradition, which they encapsulate with their notion of deterritorialization. But this unleashing of desire is also always an occasion for more and more distributed and small-scale re-territorializations. Hence the odd double movement of American literature: "Isn't the destiny of American literature that of crossing limits and frontiers, causing deterritorialized flows of desire to circulate but also always making these flows transport fascisizing, moralizing, Puritan, and familializing territorialities?" (*Thousand Plateaus* 277–78).

What Neal demonstrates is that the melancholic project in American romanticism is highly unstable, at once a critique of the pieties of official mournfulness and a vehicle for more and more volatile territorialities. To identify with "the father" and his melancholia does not resolve the oedipal contradiction between law and its suspension. In fact, this identification exacerbates the contradiction by subjecting it to a regime of the signifier. What surges forth in this oddly weightless world is the figure of an archaic despotism: "O signifier, terrible archaism of the despot where they still look for the empty tomb, the dead father, and the mystery of the name!" (208–9). At every level of its structure, Neal's novel is marked by violent repetition, as if the adherence to the absolutely singular and sovereign individual—

Logan as unmournable—is precisely superimposed by the "not one" that perforates that closure, initiating a generalized confusion of all those values—race, identity, paternity, history—from the grip of which the novel nevertheless cannot be released. The deterritorialization of its central values is present at both macro and micro levels. Even at the level of the sentence, such violent repetition results in what can only be called spastic iteration, as if the semiotic engine attempting to speak the value of "one" were failing to turn over: "Yes, I saw him . . . alone, alone! all, all alone!" The bed shook under him; "Not dead!—no, no, not dead!—not dead!" (14). Or consider an aspect of the text's plotting: why does George of Salisbury need to marry into the Logan clan? His first family, we recall, is destroyed (save Harold). But subsequently, Logan menaces the governor with the threat of annihilation—"Another moon, ye are exterminated, extinct, forgotten" (28)—unless the governor takes action that will allow him to "marry a Logan" (28). The object of his desire is his son's beloved, Loena, "the only true Logan left" (19). Loena is, as Nelson says, "characterologically inconsequential," but the oedipal rivalry for Loena is not, finally, about her character, or even her lineage, her blood. We are in the deterritorializing regime of the signifier, where "blood" can be what you marry into or what you welter in. What Loena signifies for these American melancholics is, rather, the purity of individuation: according to the logic of sovereign exemption, Loena has the most precious resource, the letters "a-l-o-n-e." Loena, like Old Deb in *Edgar Huntly*, serves as the matrix, the *outre-mère*, for the fantasy of sovereign dominion.

The American melancholic that is at the semiotic heart of Neal's novel is, then, neither Indian nor white, but rather both at once. Let me conclude by considering the implications of Neal's fixation on the "mystery of the name" Logan. We do not know with complete certainty who Jefferson's Logan was, but there is little doubt that he was one of the sons of Shickellamy, an Oneida leader who became a key negotiator on the Pennsylvania frontier in the 1730s. Shickellamy had a long-term relationship with James Logan, agent for the Penn family in Pennsylvania during the mid-eighteenth century. In *The American Empire: Its Historical Pattern and Evolution*, Richard W. Van Alstyne singles out James Logan as an important figure in early Anglo-American imperial expansion in North America. A "good example of colonial influence on the Board of Trade," Logan was "instrumental in inducing the Board to commit itself" to such ventures.[42] James Logan was a classically powerful go-between, an important transit point for the economic, political, and ethnic interfusion that marked North American colonial history. Shickellamy, for his part, was also a go-between (and indeed some contemporaries claimed that he was by birth a Frenchman who had been taken captive by Indians as a child). It might be said, then, that Shickellamy and Logan shared a status as liminal figures who necessarily found themselves straddling the line separating law from lawlessness, with one foot in a realm of treaty, legitimation, and peace, while the other remained in a zone of violence, conflict, and expropriation.[43] Jefferson's Logan, as his speech tells us, also lived in such a mixed world, or had tried to: "Such was my love for the whites, that my countrymen pointed as they passed, and said, 'Logan is the friend of the white man.' I had even thought to have lived with you, but for the injuries of one man." By naming his son Logan, Shickellamy encrypted an entire history of ambiguous contact between white and native: Logan as "name of the father" is a symbolic miscegenation.

To be fixated on such an untraceable source is to remain gripped by that which you have repudiated. The same might be said for Neal's entire attitude toward the historical record itself: the clearest sign of his obsession with the "melancholy facts" of history is his repudiation of their veracity. For it turns out that on at least two occasions after the publication of *Logan*, Neal expressed his conviction that the original Logan speech was inauthentic. "Mr. Jefferson knows very little of the Indian character," he writes in 1826 in his attack on John Dunn Hunter, another "impostor" in Neal's eyes. "There can be no better proof than the speech of Logan, which is repeated here on his authority, Logan the Mingo chief. It was altogether a humbug, that speech, and Mr. Jefferson is now aware of it; nay, I am not sure that he may not be charged with a part of it."[44] *Be their fathers whom they may*, indeed. The "mystery of the name" Logan, then is that it points to a purity and particularity of identity, a sovereign individualism, that cannot be mourned—*because it never existed*. The mystery of the name Logan is that despite the multiplicities to which its history attests, it can still encrypt a dream of some fact, event, or identity that lies outside surrender and exchange, a dream that must be placed into an inaccessible past to be sustained.

SIX

Treaties, Trauma, Trees: The Dream of Hadwin

> If a text always gives itself a certain representation of its own roots, those roots live only by that representation, by never touching the soil, so to speak. Which undoubtedly destroys their *radical essence*, but not the necessity of their *racinating function*.
>
> —JACQUES DERRIDA[1]

The Golden Spruce and the Logan Elm

Here is a parable from "west of everything."

In 1997 a man named Grant Hadwin swam the frozen Yakoun River with his chainsaw in tow and cut down an extremely rare golden spruce in the Queen Charlotte Islands of British Columbia. The tree was both ancient—it had stood for more than three hundred years—and a genuine scientific puzzle, and its symbolic importance was recognized both by the timber company MacMillan Bloedel, which had, under pressure, set aside the land on which the tree stood, and by the local Haida nation, into whose oral history the tree had been incorporated and revered as an ancestor. Hadwin had worked for MacMillan Bloedel and had evidently concluded that his counsel on forest management was not being heeded, but in the statement he sent to the Vancouver *Sun*, MacMillan Bloedel, the Haida nation, and Greenpeace, Hadwin's motivations seem more obscure: "I didn't enjoy butchering, this magnificent old plant, but you apparently need a message and wake-up call, that even a university-trained professional, should be able to understand. . . . I mean this action, to be an expression, of my rage and hatred, towards university trained professionals and their extremist supporters, whose ideas, ethics, denials, part truths, attitudes, etc., appear to be responsible for most of the abominations, towards amateur life on this planet."[2] The distinction between professional and "amateur life" is an elusive one, admittedly, but as a university-trained professional who has been trained to train others, I take myself to be an addressee of this message and act. From what, and to what, does Hadwin wish me to "wake up"? And what is the status of this act that wakens?

Hadwin apparently thought of his act as a kind of terrorism: "He advocated terrorism as the most effective means of bringing about change, and he talked a great deal about trees" (126). In addition to his fierce opposition to clear-cutting, Hadwin had aligned himself with Native American grievances. In a letter to CNN, he wrote: "Your focus appears to be on Bosnia and O.J. Simpson. Your Native American problem, however, parallels our own and yet your coverage, appears to be non-existent" (109). It turns out that the golden spruce and its surrounding forest had, through the sustained lobbying of the Haida and other environmental groups, already been protected from further logging, a fact that makes Hadwin's violence look rather self-defeating, directed at the very compromise between economic, native, and environmental interests that he would presumably have sought. Such self-destructiveness may make his act seem more authentically "terrorist," of course, insofar as one interpretation of terrorism understands it as a practice in which sending a "message" ultimately trumps the achievement of any more limited political goal. Such terrorism, Roland Barthes suggests, "remains within the signifier."[3] But as far as Hadwin was concerned, it was not he, but the powers that be that absurdly remained within the signifier in their overestimation of a single symbolic tree: "When society places so much value on one mutant tree and ignores what happens to the rest of the forest, it's not the person who points this out who should be labeled" (139). Perhaps Hadwin was not so much attacking a symbol as he was attacking a mode and practice of symbolization. The very process of compromise, with its demarcation of a preserve or sanctuary, and its elevation of one tree over all the others, was apparently too much for Hadwin to bear.

Here now is another parable, apparently more peaceful, but just as bound up with the symbolism of trees, land, and Indians as the story of Hadwin and the golden spruce. In January 1842 the inaugural issue of *The American Pioneer*, the short-lived organ of the Logan Historical Society published out of Chillicothe, Ohio, described the dedication ceremony of their society: "We were on the very spot where Logan, the Mingo chief, the Indian philanthropist and friend of the white man, delivered his celebrated speech, sent to Lord Dunmore, creditable to mankind and honorable to him and his nation."[4] The scene is imagined in the issue's title page (Figure 1): seated on a felled log and beneath what tradition refers to as the Logan elm, the great "chief" delivers his lament to Gibson, who will convey it to Dunmore. Symbols of peace abound: Logan's weapons are laid on the ground, Gibson holds a calumet, a dove perches above them on a branch of the elm. But the dedication described in *The American Pioneer* replaces the tree with a monument, and the oral scene depicted in the engraving is now decisively textualized: Logan's "speech, as given by Thomas Jefferson, shall be fully engraved in gilt letters on said monument, which shall also bear the name of that great patriot who preserved that speech for us.—In the base of the monument shall be deposited a copy of Jefferson's Notes on Virginia, and the Declaration of Independence, and the Constitutions of the States and the United States, the previous proceedings of the society, and the name of every member thereof" (5). It's an astonishing vision of legitimation through archiving, the collection and deposition of the texts implying a descent from the "philanthropist" Logan to "every member" of the society founded in his name, a genealogy transmitted via the sacred texts of the nation. *The American Pioneer* vows to keep faith with this vision of a racially shared history, announcing its intention to "safely keep all that is or can be well authenticated of aboriginal history," as well as to "secure from oblivion the unpublished history of our early and successive western settlements" (5). But a glance through its volumes suggests that for every article dealing with "aboriginal history" there are five recounting western campaigns against those aborigines, with nicely reproduced engravings of encampment locations and fort designs. There's a powerful moment in Cormac McCarthy's *Blood Meridian* that suggests a darker interpretation of the Logan Historical Society's archival work. Having come across the relics of an older cliff-dwelling culture, McCarthy's Mephistophelean "judge" makes careful

THE

AMERICAN PIONEER,

A

Monthly Periodical,

DEVOTED TO THE OBJECTS OF THE

LOGAN HISTORICAL SOCIETY.

CHILLICOTHE, O.:

EDITED AND PUBLISHED BY JNO. S. WILLIAMS.

1842

Entered according to Act of Congress, in the year 1841, by JNO. S. WILLIAMS, in the Clerk's Office for the District Court of Ohio.

Figure 1. Title page from *The American Pioneer*, a publication of the Logan Historical Society. (Courtesy of the Lilly Library, Indiana University, Bloomington, Indiana.)

sketches of the various artifacts he finds, after which he systematically destroys them. Asked what he "aimed to do with those notes and sketches . . . the judge smiled and said that it was his intention to expunge them from the memory of man."[5]

Two parables, then, each in its way knotting together questions of white/ Indian relations, historical memory, and a relation to the land that is at once powerfully concrete—"on the very spot," marvels *The American Pioneer*— and subject to the most extravagant symbolizing violence. The one scene celebrates peace and shared history, the other is an assault on just such compromise. But both scenes emerge from the matrix of the Logan effect, and its unfolding of the logic of the last. In Chapter 4 I argued that Jefferson's legitimating project of archiving the "state" led him to mobilize a discursive technique—the sublime—in an attempt to wrest unity from the violence and heterogeneity with which he was confronted. Logan's lament recommended itself to Jefferson as precisely an emblem of such salvaged singularity. At the same time, the melancholic self-exemption of Logan from the peace he otherwise acknowledged prevents Jefferson from entirely closing off his text, and this signifying ambiguity in what I called the ethnic sublime means that Jefferson's effort to produce the American "one" by controlled encounters with the limit presented by the Indian never quite gets clear of Logan's "not one," which itself gets folded in, offered sanctuary—like the golden spruce—in Jefferson's text. In the melancholic novels of Charles Brockden Brown and John Neal, as Chapter 5 demonstrated, the ambiguities lingering in Jefferson's ethnic sublime take a gothic turn. The logic of the last no longer applies exclusively to Indians, but rather all who find themselves within the ambit of the oneiric territory typified by Brown's Norwalk, a zone in which cross-racial identification and murderous violence are the order of the day. These two expressions of the logic of the last, the sublime and the gothic, are intimately related. For all the complacent Jeffersonian archiving at work in the Logan dedication ceremony, the members of the society are, after all, busily engaged in the peculiar activity of burying texts—Jefferson's texts, no less—at the base of a monument symbolizing a tree. As Edgar Huntly and Clithero Edny might tell them, what is buried while awake can be disinterred while asleep, and vice versa. "Was it a grave that he was digging?" Edgar wonders as he watches Clithero scrabbling in the dirt beneath the Elm. "Was his purpose to explore or to hide?" (10). We can pose the same questions to the Logan Historical Society: they proclaim that they are "Dedicated to the Truth and Justice of History" (3), but are they exploring history or hiding it, digging up the past or burying it?

Using Grant Hadwin as my guide and provocation, then, I retrace in this last chapter some of the ground covered in the previous two. Taking a more surveying and speculative approach, I will draw more sharply the distinction between the sublime and the gothic manifestations of the logic of the last. The central figure here will be the tree itself—the golden spruce, the Logan elm, and so many more—as that figure attracts the multiple and contradictory meanings of the historical field. In addition, I want to keep in view a methodological conundrum that it seems to me affects all research aiming to put the typical and the anomalous, the exemplary and the exceptional, into dialogue with each other. That conundrum is, How does the single case, the unique text or figure, ever attain through the pressure of interpretation the status of the exemplary? Is Grant Hadwin, for example, an example or an exception, an illustrative case or an aberration? The same question can be approached via reflection on the nature of his violence. Terrorism is sometimes called "senseless" violence, implying that it is a mistake to try to come to rational terms with its meaning. One could reply to this view that such a willful embrace of a failure to comprehend is actually a species of historical amnesia—or repression—and that to confront the phenomenon of terrorism requires the often painful work of tracing its historical roots. The first approach sees the violence as an exception, irreducible to causal explanation; the second seeks to reduce the act's anomalousness to mere exemplarity. I am not sure either approach will prove very satisfying in this case. Far from being "senseless," each element in Hadwin's story seems saturated with sense, seems "overdetermined" in the sense Freud gives that word in his dream analyses. And as for the historical approach, how far back do we need to go? How will we know where to stop in tracing a network of historical determinations?

In the epigraph to this chapter, Jacques Derrida suggests that a text can represent its own rootedness, can perform its "*racinating function*," only at the cost of those roots never actually touching the ground. Something like this paradoxically deracinated root system structures Hadwin's act, I will argue. Because such a structure is not susceptible to an analysis that is either consistently historicist or consistently formalist, I offer something closer to

Freudian dream interpretation, with its attentiveness to how what is historically given and contingent (call it the "day residue" of history) becomes transformed and deformed in accordance with interpretable circuits of desire and meaning. In his famous comment about the "navel of the dream," Freud writes that there is in principle no end to the filaments and associations netted together in the dream: "The dream-thoughts, to which interpretation leads one, are necessarily interminable and branch out into the netlike entanglement of our world of thought." A certain density in this infinite net, Freud argues, both reveals the dream wish itself and bars access to any complete interpretation of it: "Even in the best-interpreted dreams, there is often a place that must be left in the dark, because in the process of interpreting one notices a tangle of dream-thoughts arising which resists unraveling . . . This, then, is the navel of the dream, the place where it straddles the unknown. . . . Out of one of the denser places in this meshwork, the dream-wish rises like a mushroom out of its mycelium."[6] In the navel of the dream before us, what rises up is in fact a golden spruce with a "peculiar radiance, as if it were actually generating light from deep within its branches" (Vaillant 120), illuminating the forest primeval, that other "place that must be left in the dark." But I am getting ahead of myself. Before we advance further into the mystery of the tree, we need to ask about the hero of this dream.

The Xtreme Individual

There is a remarkable man living in North Carolina named Eustace Conway, an American cousin of sorts to Grant Hadwin. "By the time Eustace Conway was seven years old, he could throw a knife accurately enough to nail a chipmunk to a tree," writes Elizabeth Gilbert in her biography of Conway, to which she gives the significant title *The Last American Man*.[7] What makes Conway last? Gilbert evidently thinks that Conway embodies a masculine ideal that is no longer generally available: his lastness means that he embodies a type no longer with us. At one point, Conway compares himself to Ishi, "the last wild Indian in America," and I would suggest that it is the combination of Conway's hypermasculinity and the identification with Indians—those paragons of lastness—that qualifies him to be the "last American man." Is Grant Hadwin last in this sense? Like Conway, Hadwin was notorious for his survival skills and imperviousness to the elements, a man who sought and found "total immersion in the environment where he felt most at home, and most himself" (209).[8] A self-described "extreme swimmer," Hadwin had once alarmed local police in Whitehorse, Yukon, by spending a quarter of an hour in the Yukon River when the air temperature was thirty-five degrees below zero—an example of "total immersion" if there ever was one (124). Taking our cue from Hadwin's self-descriptions, then, with their ESPN2 flavor, let us call Hadwin's manifestation of the logic of the last the "Xtreme individual."

At the risk of tautology, we could say that the Xtreme individual is an individual in extremis, on the furthest edge of a condition of experiential solitude, whether that condition is registered in terms of the powers and limits of the individual body, or of some more social or metaphysical isolation. Like Conway seeing himself as Ishi, or like Huntly's "becoming-Indian" in the wilds of Norwalk, Hadwin's status as Xtreme is fundamentally connected to an ambiguous, ultimately aggressive, identification with Indians. Toward the end of his life, Hadwin formed a close relationship with Cora Gray, an elder of the Gitxsan tribe of British Columbia. Driving her home one night, Hadwin's car hit a pickup truck head-on, seriously injuring Gray. In a strange and profound observation, Gray remarked, "I've always wondered if Grant was trying to kill us both so he wouldn't have to be alone" (126). Such a phrase suggests a desire for union or merger so intense that it amounts to a violence against identity itself, against the unbearable solitude identity represents. We have seen before—in the frontier convulsions that Jefferson tries to manage, in the narrative delirium of the novels of Brown and Neal—how such cross-racial identification can become indistinguishable from murderousness. Perhaps the native identity that forms the target of this identification is what Hadwin means by "amateur" life, a mode of being not yet mortified or abstracted to the level of the "university-trained professional." But if so, this identification with the aboriginal and autochthonous—with the land, and its original inhabitants—seems to impel Hadwin toward murder-suicide. And so he nearly kills his sole (Indian) friend, and he cuts down the tree revered and protected by the Haida. He can only unite with his roots by ripping them up.

In one sense, this murderous identification is old hat, just a particularly violent version of what Philip J. Deloria has called "playing Indian."[9] The inevitable comparison here is Natty Bumppo. Like Natty inveighing against the "wasty ways" of the white settlers whose interests he nonetheless serves, Hadwin's militant commitment to a vision of ecological balance was both provoked, and compromised, by his employment as a "forest technician" laying out roads to facilitate the logging of old-growth forest. Natty had his Chingachgook, Hadwin his Cora Gray. Hadwin's physical prowess and formidable survival skills led many to see him as indestructible; there's a story of him outwitting a couple of charging grizzlies that in its excessiveness might have been used by Twain in his burlesque of Bumppoesque woodcraft.[10] In Cooper's *The Pioneers* (1823), Natty has a run-in with the law and ultimately evades it by moving further west. Five days before *his* trial for criminal mischief, Hadwin took off in his kayak, which was found four months later seventy miles up the coast, broken apart but with his provisions and equipment in a suspiciously undamaged condition. Vaillant describes all the good reasons to assume that Hadwin drowned, but he also spends a good bit of time discussing "Hadwin sightings" and the convictions of some that he is alive. All this suggests the kind of deathlessness that characterizes the mythic individual: like both Bumppo and Chingachgook who, despite their recorded deaths in early installments of the Leatherstocking cycle, come back to life, Hadwin's combination of hardiness, isolation, and opposition to established powers qualify him as, indeed, indestructible. Vaillant is quite taken with this mythic dimension: "Whether he is alive or dead, he has, for all practical purposes, become what the Haida call a *gagiid*. The word *gagiid* (ga-GEET) translates, literally, to 'one carried away,' and it refers to a human being who has been driven mad by the experience of capsizing and nearly drowning during the wintertime. . . . With the right equipment, and proper observance of ritual, the *gagiid* can be captured and restored to his human state, much as Europeans might treat a traumatized or mentally ill person with love, therapy, and/or medication" (235). This notion of Hadwin as a *gagiid* is Vaillant's fantasy, however; the Haida have no interest in Hadwin as a *gagiid*: "If they catch him, he will pay. As far as many Haida are concerned, Hadwin is one more white guy who came to their islands in order to take something away only to leave behind yet another imported illness: this time, a new strain of terrorism" (235).

For all their similarities, however, Natty and Hadwin exemplify different modulations of the logic of the last. The best-known "last" person in America is still the "last of the Mohicans." But who exactly is this person? The novel names Uncas as the "last of the Mohicans," but Uncas dies in the course of the story, leaving Chingachgook as last, mourning the extinction of his family, lineage, race—like Logan before him. What's more, Chingachgook is not at all alone when he attains lastness: he is described—in a phrase to which I'll return—as a "blazed pine, in a clearing of the pale-faces."[11] "I am alone—" Chingachgook announces to the thronging crowd observing his funeral rites, to which Natty cries, "No, no . . . God has so placed us as to journey in the same path. I have no kin, and I may also say, like you, no people" (349). Here we witness the Cooperesque management of lastness. Natty and Chingachgook might share the isolation of having "no kin," "no people," but Cooper never really believes that there is a "same path" for white and Indian—Cora and Uncas are even segregated in the afterlife. What Cooper is effecting here through the intimacy between Natty and Chingachgook, through the identification across racial difference, is a *transfer* of properties: Natty's singularity, his epitomization of American individualism, is borrowed, as it were, from Chingachgook, for whom singularity, by contrast, is all limit, absolute extinction. This is what I have called the strategy of the ethnic sublime, in which the problems of the "one," the way in which the one always seems shadowed by its negation or its repetition, is "solved," as it were, by being distributed across a racial divide: first Chingachgook, then Natty; first Logan, then Jefferson; and so on. Cooper's ethnic sublime is sequential and segregationist. It is hard to deny the durability of this strategy, even if D. H. Lawrence, for one, was not convinced by Cooper's ideological legerdemain. In *Studies in Classic American Literature* (1923), Lawrence writes, "The American landscape has never been at one with the white man. Never. And white men have probably never felt so bitter anywhere, as here in America, where the very landscape [is] opposed to us. Cooper, however, glosses over this resistance, which in actuality can never be quite glossed over. He *wants* the landscape to be at one with him."[12] Lawrence suggests that Cooper's attempt to archive the land itself—archive it by getting the Indian to subside into it—will prove in the long run no more successful than Jefferson's. And yet, Lawrence also goes on to predict that "the oneing will surely take place—some day" (61). It is hard to know how to take Lawrence here. I like to think that he's ventriloquizing the wishfulness he elsewhere exposes, and that his coinage of "oneing" is meant as a backhand swipe at Teddy Roosevelt and all those who promote a spurious vision of the "oneing" of the West.

Although Hadwin and Natty share a genealogy, then, Hadwin's way of exemplifying the logic of the last is governed not by sublime sequencing but by gothic merger. In this regard, he is closer to Samuel Monson, the "Indian Hater" of James Hall's 1829 story of the same name, another Xtreme individual and legatee of Logan. "The Indian Hater" concludes with Monson's cold-blooded murder of the narrator's Indian guide, which Monson justifies by describing the murder of his own family by Indians: "Go!" he continued, "pursue your own way, and leave me to mine. If you have a parent that prays for you, a wife and children that love you, they will receive you with joy, and you will be happy. I am alone;—there is none to mourn with me, no one to rejoice at my coming."[13] "None to mourn with me, no one": Monson is a white Logan and, like Logan, exempts himself from the consolations of mourning. By giving the Indian Hater the last words in the story, Hall structures his ideological address in such a way as to puncture the complacency of the narrator, whose East Coast pieties are suspended: "When all that you cherish is torn from you in one moment, condemn me, if you can" (73). The challenge remains unanswered. Both formally and ideologically, Hall's story repudiates the closures of mourning, exposing instead the Xtreme individual as gripped by the melancholy of race war, forever facing off with his Indian double and negation.

How far have we wandered from Hadwin and his golden spruce? Not very far, I think. It turns out that according to Haida legend, the spruce is itself an Xtreme individual, subject to the same doublings and undoings as the other solitaries we have looked at:

> The first tree was a woman and the second tree—the one Hadwin cut down—was a man: the woman's nephew. They were the sole survivors of a smallpox epidemic; it was clear to them that their clan was doomed and that the magic . . . was finished. Because of this, they requested that the spirits leave a sign that this magic had once existed so that future generations, whoever they might be, would understand who had lived there and the power they had once wielded. The aunt died first and the nephew buried her on the banks of the Yakoun; it grew for "about three hundred years" before being struck by lightning. The nephew, by this time, was very old and not feeling well, so he went to his aunt's grave to wait for death to come. When he died, a second golden spruce grew. This was the sterile male—the last golden spruce. (Vaillant 200)

As a solitary remnant of a people whose "magic" has passed, a remnant whose mournful testament is both inescapable and unassimilable by those who come after, the "last golden spruce" is appropriately a "sterile male." Perhaps this is why Hadwin hated it: this bizarrely blanched Xtreme individual may have seemed a mirror image of himself—cut asunder from the cycles of life and generation, mortified into symbol, epitome of a past that is neither absent nor present, a fold in time and space testifying to the fact that the West is not yet "one." But how does a tree, in legend or in fact, come to hold such varied and charged associations? I turn now to the remarkably complex dream history of trees in the West. If I have called the story of the golden spruce "the dream of Hadwin," we should now take that to be an objective genitive: Hadwin is less the dreamer than the dreamed.

The Blazed Pine and the Fatal Elm

Let us return, a last time, to Jefferson's *Notes on the State of Virginia*. I argued in Chapter 4 that there are three moments in that text that, taken together, provide a matrix for the development of the ethnic sublime over the next several decades. This matrix brings together the topics of mourning, the land, and the monument. The crucial scene is that of the party of Indians mourning in the woods: "But on whatever occasion [these barrows] may have been made, they are of considerable notoriety among the Indians: for a party passing, about thirty years ago, through the part of the country where this barrow is, went through the woods directly to it, without any instructions or enquiry, and having staid about it some time, with expressions which were construed to be those of sorrow, they returned to the high road . . . and pursued their journey" (100). Jefferson's treatment of Logan's lament, and his excavation of the burial mound, represent paired responses to the challenge posed by the inscrutable conjunction of mourning, monument, and land provided by the party of Indians in the woods.

Following Jefferson, the ethnic sublime follows a similar reductive strategy, converting the many into the one, the party of nomadic mourners into the fixed and solitary individual, the multiplicity of the forest into the exemplary tree. The basic strategy will be to make the Indian subside into the land, become his own gravestone or monument, so that nature itself seems to do the mourning. Mark Twain abused Cooper for not making it clear which characters were alive and which were dead, but when it comes to this sublime Indian, there's a certain grim logic to the confusion: "Seated, as in life, with his form and limbs arranged in grave and decent composure, Uncas appeared. . . . Directly in front of the corpse, Chingachgook was placed. . . . So riveted and intense had been that gaze, and so changeless his attitude, that a stranger might not have told the living from the dead. . . . The lips of the sagamore closed, and he remained silent in his seat, looking, with his riveted and motionless form, like some creature that had been turned from the Almighty hand with the form, but without the spirit of a man" (340, 345). The ambiguity we noted earlier as to who is rightly designated the last Mohican, Uncas or Chingachgook, is expressed here as an uncertainty about who's alive and who's dead. True to his essential vigor, Uncas remains an active agent: he "appeared" "as in life." His father, meanwhile, "was placed" like a piece of divine statuary, "with the form, but without the spirit of a man," "riveted and motionless." And like Jefferson's Indians giving vent to expressions only dubiously "construed to be those of sorrow" (100), Chingachgook's "monody" is not fully intelligible: "But they listened in vain. The strains rose just so loud, as to become intelligible and then grew fainter and more trembling, until finally they sunk on the ear, as if borne away by a passing breath of wind" (345).

It is in the context of this funeral scene that Chingachgook calls himself a "blazed pine in a clearing of the pale-faces." Conventional as it is, Cooper's figure of the blazed pine bears some scrutiny. To blaze a tree is to cut into its bark enough for the pale wood to show through, for the purposes of marking a trail through uncleared forest. You blaze trees to blaze a trail. But if your blazed tree stands in a clearing, then it has a belated aspect. It stands, that is, as a testament to an initial act of clearing—the breaching of a path, road, or trail—that has now been superseded. What is condensed in the figure, in other words, is Chingachgook's status as an enabler of a pattern of white settlement that then renders him archaic: he is neither the wilderness, nor the clearing, but the index of the passage between the two. The blazed pine is a sign of civilization in excess and in default at one and the same time: in excess because its trace of the act of civilizing seems superfluous when the clearing itself so amply embodies it; but the tree is also is in default of the clearing, inasmuch as it embodies what has been cleared. A blazed pine in a clearing is an image of a reserve or sanctuary in which what exceeds and precedes the civilization of the clearing is folded in, made to linger.

We thus approach once again the signifying ambiguity inherent in the discourse of the ethnic sublime, a disturbance in its effort to produce the American one by controlled encounters with the limit presented by the Indian. It's as though this discourse never quite gets clear of Logan's "not one," itself folded in, offered sanctuary, in Jefferson's text. Or it's as if the ethnic sublime never quite manages to reduce the indefinite multitude of mourners in the wilderness to the single blazed pine. There's always less than one and more than one. Consider in this regard Catherine Sedgwick, who, writing under the strong influence of Cooper, would initially seem to invoke the conventions confidently:

> The old chief fixed his melancholy eye on a solitary pine, scathed and blasted by tempests, that rooted in the ground where he stood, lifted its topmost branches to the bare rock, where they seemed, in their wild desolation, to brave the elemental fury that had stripped them of beauty and life.
>
> The leafless tree was truly, as it appeared to the eye of Mononotto, a fit emblem of the chieftain of a ruined tribe. "See you, child," he said, addressing Magawisca, "those unearthed roots? the tree must fall—hear you the death-song that wails through those blasted branches?"[14]

Both William Hubbard (Sedgwick's primary source) and John Winthrop mention Mononotto as a "noted" leader of the Pequots, who by the nineteenth century were the veritable type and instance of a "ruined tribe," as Melville knew when he named Ahab's doomed ship the *Pequod* after the "celebrated tribe of Massachusetts Indians, now as extinct as the ancient Medes" (164).[15] But Sedgwick's Pequot chief indexes extinction while inhabiting an ambiguous limbo: the pine is still standing but "stripped of beauty and life"; it is somehow both "rooted" and "unearthed." We find again a strange equivocation in the effort of the ethnic sublime to produce a "last one," a kind of repetition effect that proliferates "emblems" of extinction. Sedgwick's passage is a case, quite literally, of rhetorical overkill. Lastness here is evoked by Mononotto's tribal status, by the solitary tree itself, and even by the tree's anthropomorphic "death-song," a native practice invariably linked, in European descriptions, to the immolation of the torture victim. (When Ishmael announces *his* status as sole survivor of the *Pequod*, we can see the repetition effect in the doubling of his solitariness: "And I *only* am escaped *alone* to tell thee" (625).[16]) This repetition effect, in turn, issues from a complex and prior negation, as though putting lastness in the form of negation ensured its timelessness: "I will fight no more forever," announced Chief Joseph, in a phrase that equals Ishmael's verse from Job for pleonastic poignancy.[17] Such a negation effect is paradigmatically present in the conclusion to Logan's famous speech: "Who is there to mourn for Logan?—Not one." The limbo in which the last one finds himself is marked by a negation of the one. It is because Mononotto is "not one" (mono/not) that his solitariness is in need of proliferating emblems.

Perhaps the most complex attempt to untie the Jeffersonian knot of mourning, monument, and land is presented in Cooper's *The Prairie* (1827). In one scene Natty argues with the ludicrous naturalist, Dr. Obed Bat, about the Jeffersonian problem of monuments. To Bat's skeptical request to be shown the "columns, catacombs, and Pyramids" that would testify to the prairie's prior inhabitation, Natty replies:

> They are gone. . . . This very spot of reeds and grass on which you now sit, may once have been the garden of some mighty King. It is the fate of all things, to ripen, and then to decay. The tree blossoms, and bears its fruit, which falls, rots, withers, and even the seed is lost. . . . From that moment its beauty begins to perish. It lies another hundred years, a mouldering log, and then a mound of moss and 'arth, a sad effigy of a human grave. This is one of your genuine monuments, though made by a very different power than such as belongs to your chiselling masons; and after all the cunningest scout of the whole Dahcotah nation might pass his life in searching for the spot where it fell, and be no wiser when his eyes grew dim, than when they were first opened. (240–41)

Here the "mighty King" slides easily into the fated tree, which becomes the "mouldering log . . . a mound of moss and 'arth," a figure echoing both Jefferson's "barrows" and the considerably larger burial mounds that provoked so much speculation in the early republic. But what makes this monument "genuine" for Cooper is its decisive disarticulation from actual Indian inhabitants. It is merely an "effigy of a human grave," and in a brutally efficient revision of Jefferson's account of the party of Indians making their way to the burial mound in the forest, Cooper emphasizes the absolute erasure of this "effigy," its immemorial status: "The cunningest scout of the whole Dahcotah nation might pass his life in searching for the spot." By converting the king to a tree and then to a decayed log that cannot be found, Cooper neatly transfers Indian sovereignty to nature itself, which now becomes a kind of generalized memorial available to everyone and no one.

This network of themes finds a different configuration in the treatment of the text's other last man, the settler patriarch Ishmael Bush. Like Logan or his many avatars (Cooper's Chingachgook, for example), Bush is bereft of a son, and thus in a sense marooned in history. And like these Indian models, Bush is drawn mysteriously to a dead tree, the symbol of his lost fertility:

> A solitary willow had taken root in the alluvion, and profiting by its exclusive possession of the soil, the tree had sent up its stem far above the crest of the adjacent rock, whose peaked summit had once been shadowed by its branches. But its loveliness had gone with the mysterious principle of life. As if in mockery of the meagre show of verdure that the spot exhibited, it remained a noble and solemn monument of former fertility. . . . The meeting of the pair [Ishmael and Esther Bush], in this naked spot was like an interview held above the grave of their murdered son. (356)

Unlike the "mouldering log" that simply subsides into the land unnoticed, the tree here serves as a monument of sorts; it marks the land with loss: it was "like . . . the grave of their murdered son." Bush confronts on this site his own inevitable extinction, just as countless Indians had done before him, and for the same reasons: he must serve as the vanishing mediator between the lawless prairie, home for both the wandering "Ishmaelite" Indians and Ishmael's settler clan, and the law of the settlements. But Bush is not merely a superseded sovereign figure whose "exclusive possession of the soil" can only be memorialized. He retains as well a sovereign power to exact justice: for what Bush has seen in this dead tree is an excellent gallows, and he will use this spot for the execution of his summary judgment on his murderous brother-in-law, Abiram. This elemental act of justice, supplemented with minimal gestures of mercy, is meant by Cooper to stand as a passage to civilization. But the passage to civilization is also an act of vengeance. The murdered son and the executioner father inhabit a zone, marked and enabled by the solitary willow, that is neither law, nor pure lawlessness. In this respect Bush's willow condenses in a single figure the contradictions that the ethnic sublime struggles to resolve, and he accordingly falls under its singularizing force at this moment of his erasure: "*For the first time* . . . Ishmael felt a keen sense of solitude" (362, emphasis added). Once this sublime solitude is achieved there is no more need for him in the national narrative, and he and his wife quickly vanish into the "blending" settlements and are "never heard of more" (364).[18] Cooper tries valiantly to manage the contradictions of the ethnic sublime, primarily through a strategy of racial segregation, as I have already remarked: sovereignty is both assigned to the land, as the immemorial legacy of a definitively lost people, and reestablished as the property of white settlement, through an act simultaneously of mourning and of summary vengeance. But the fact remains that Cooper tells a story of the passage to civilization via the law of the talon. Bush's frontier justice ultimately resembles Logan's revenge: it stands to one side of a narrative of peacemaking and legitimacy (the treaty ending Lord Dunmore's War, the settlement of the west) that it both enables and escapes.

A generation before Cooper, Brown had more directly confronted the problem. In place of Jefferson's party of Indians engaged in lamentations "construed to be those of sorrow" in the woods, the opening scene in *Edgar Huntly* finds Edgar confronted with a half-clad figure uttering doleful cries and suspiciously scratching at the base of the elm tree beneath which Edgar's significantly named friend Waldegrave had been murdered before the novel begins. Like Chingachgook's "blazed pine," moreover, what Edgar calls "the fatal Elm" is anomalously situated: "You know the situation of the Elm in the midst of a private road" (8). Who leaves trees in the midst of roads, or who builds roads that lead to trees?

In the previous chapter, I investigated what might be called the Brownian motion of *Edgar Huntly*, the ceaseless wandering of its characters in a space that cannot be adequately mapped. I noted Edgar's frustration at finding himself in a place where the road "pervade[d] the forest in every possible direction" (223), in which, that is, clearing and wilderness are strictly indistinguishable. The location of the "fatal Elm" in the middle of a road shares this nonstandard topography. We know that the idea fascinated Brown. His short story "Somnambulism: A Fragment," published in 1805 but possibly drafted before *Edgar Huntly*, also features a narrator hero, young Althorpe, conducting unusual and violent business in his sleep around a tree in the road.[19] In both *Edgar Huntly* and "Somnambulism" the tree operates as a kind of magnet and switch point in which sympathy, solicitude, and protectiveness merge unconsciously with violence and vengeance. In "Somnambulism," Althorpe's concern that his beloved, who is betrothed to another, will carelessly crash into the tree in the road is the cover for an underlying aggression of the "If I can't have her, no one can" variety, as the denouement makes clear when Althorpe shoots her (in his sleep) while she perches on a natural seat formed in the trunk of the tree. In *Edgar Huntly*, rather than love turning into aggression, it's the other way around. As far as Edgar is concerned, the elm is originally merely a dark landmark of murder, and yet faced with Clithero's lamentation, "every sentiment, at length, yielded to my sympathy. . . . My caution had forsaken me, and instead of one whom it was my duty to persecute, I beheld, in this man, nothing but an object of compassion" (10–11). In both cases, the tree in the road marks the peculiar space of Brown's humanitarian gothic, where love and aggression, compassion and persecution, enter into terrifying proximity. We need now to look more closely at this tree in the road, for Brown's gothic version of the "blazed pine in a clearing of the pale-faces" takes us closer than Cooper can to the deregulated identificatory energies at work in the dream of Hadwin.

For a Philadelphian like Brown, the Delaware must have seemed *the* treaty Indians. It was with the Delaware that the new United States, in 1778, concluded their first formal treaty with any Indian nation.[20] Sydney Krause is surely right when he suggests that by having Waldegrave, whose "piety was rapturous" (7), murdered beneath this elm by an exasperated Delaware, Brown has encrypted a reference to the entire history of relations between the Pennsylvanians and the Delaware, or Lenni-Lenape. For it was the pious William Penn himself, as legend has it, who made the exemplary compact of peace beneath the "Treaty Elm" in Shackamaxon in the late seventeenth century. In the Penn legend, the tree stands not so much for the last sovereign—Chingachgook or Mononotto—as it stands for a myth of sovereignty itself, an index of the primal compact ushering in peace and legitimacy, ushering in, indeed, society itself from the edge of the state of nature. Benjamin West's famous painting (Figure 2) is a touchstone here. *Penn's Treaty with the Indians* (1771–72) places the famous umbrageous elm back right, where it stands as a kind of leading edge for the work of civilization: to its left, Penn standing with open arms, his fellow Quakers fronting their busy ships and the sturdy buildings still being erected; to its right, the masses of the Indians, some gathered still in the gloom of the base of the tree, a nursing mother—here, as in the eyes of Amasa Delano, a vision of "naked nature"—being directed by a boy's hand to the momentous proceedings between Penn and the native negotiators. It is hard to underestimate how beloved this story of amity and agreement was in colonial and

Figure 2. Benjamin West, *Penn's Treaty with the Indians* (1771–72). (Courtesy of the Pennsylvania Academy of Fine Arts, Philadelphia. Gift of Mrs. Sarah Harrison [The Joseph Harrison, Jr. Collection].)

early national America. It is regularly referred to throughout the eighteenth-century treaty negotiations with the Indians of the northeast. Some measure of its staying power is suggested by the fact that Edward Hicks is thought to have painted *Peaceable Kingdom*, his amazing visualization of Isaiah 11:6—"The wolf shall also dwell with the lamb . . ."—as many as a hundred times. In many of these, Hicks has placed a version of West's composition in the back left—the elm, the cluster of Delaware Indians, portly Penn still with his arms open in amity and acceptance. Hicks has elevated Penn's treaty to a theological significance. And in a grouping from early in the series, Hicks places the Penn scene both beneath the elm *and* in the embrasure of the Natural Bridge, that emblem of sublimity and the prospect for rising American glory celebrated by Jefferson in *Notes* (Figures 3 and 4).

Edgar Huntly is a novel that has disputed Indian land claims as a motivating conflict, and Krause, Chad Luck, and others have suggested that Brown

Figure 3. Edward Hicks, *The Peaceable Kingdom* (1845–56). (The Phillips Collection, Washington, D.C.)

is actively calling into question the myth of accord honored by West and Hicks. It has proved notoriously difficult, however, to decide whether Brown is urging historical memory or demonstrating amnesia in this novel. The very inextricability of the two may, in fact, be part of the wider associative reach of the "fatal Elm." For this tree, I would argue, alludes quite generally to what could be called the "treaty form." Eighteenth-century treaties between Euro-Americans and Indian nations enfolded into their protocols a scene of enunciation. The very space of the treaty was part of its rhetorical structure, a space understood as liminal between wilderness and civilization, just as the treaty itself would be understood as liminal between conflict and resolution. "The clearing to the woods-edge contrasts with the forest," observes William N. Fenton of Iroquois treaty protocol, "as community and polity contrast with anarchy, as 'talk in the bushes' v. 'deliberation in council.'"[21] Negotiations would begin by announcements that the wear and tear of travel needed to be ameliorated, wounds treated, and tears dried. "Peace, like a road, required constant upkeep," writes historian James Merrell. Quoting from recorded treaties, Merrell observes that

Figure 4. Edward Hicks, *The Peaceable Kingdom of the Branch* (1822–25). Note the tiny figures of William Penn and his Delaware auditors beneath the required tree, the whole party nestled beneath Jefferson's Natural Bridge. (Abby Aldrich Rockefeller Folk Art Museum, The Colonial Williamsburg Foundation, Williamsburg, VA.)

is was important to "'clear . . . every Grub, Stump & Log,' in the road between peoples, 'that it may be straight, smooth & free for us and for you.'"[22] The relation between place and language, land and symbol, is very intimate here, as they entwine in a complex topology in which the road that accesses the clearing, and the clearing that enfolds the participants, are themselves enfolded by the symbolic space that both assumes them and calls into being their continued existence.

We are familiar with many of the topoi of treaty protocol—the buried hatchet, the polished covenant chain—but it is the convention of the "Tree of Peace" that sends us most directly back to Huntly and Hadwin. It was part of the language extensively deployed in the "condolence ceremonies" that addressed head-on the difficulties of memory and forgetting. Here is Thomas King, an Oneida spokesmen, during negotiations at Lancaster in the mid-eighteenth century:

> There is a large Pine Tree in the *Oneida* Country, which I take and pull up by the Roots, and then it makes a great Hole; when I look down the Hole, I see a great River, running very strong at the Bottom. By this Belt I gather all your Bones, wherever I can find them, and bury them in that Hole, and the Hatchet with them; when I put them down the Hole, they fall into that strong Stream, and float down it, I know not where. I stick that Pine Tree down again in the same Hole, and then no Body can discover that there has been a Hole; so that neither you nor I, nor our nor your Grandchildren, shall ever be able to know where your Bones are laid. This is the Custom of our Forefathers, that when any Difference arose between them and their Brethren, they buried it in this Manner.[23]

The tree here is both rooted and uprooted, both a memorial of violence and an index of its forgetting. It is a reminder to forget. Brown's elm, too, symbolically marks the zone in which memory and forgetting cannot be separated: what Clithero busies himself with beneath the tree is a "monument" (115), a text taken as a body; he may be burying something or disinterring it; and he is neither awake, nor, precisely, asleep. Everything in the environs of this tree is, as Edgar comments with an adjective that resonates to the furthest historical horizon of this novel, "unsettled" (114). Brown's "fatal Elm . . . situated in the midst of a private road," like the pine tree in Oneida country and the blazed tree in the clearing, inhabits, and defines, an anomalous, contradictory space, a zone of indiscernibility between fundamental antagonisms that can neither be resolved nor ignored, and that cannot be sublated dialectically.

Does the golden spruce work on Hadwin the way that the fatal elm does for Clithero and Huntly—as a magnet for the unconscious enactment of the very contradictions it demarcates? Why *is* the golden spruce an unbearable provocation for Hadwin? It apparently incensed Hadwin that the Haida, Greenpeace, local government, and the logging company had all conspired, as it were, in refusing to see the forest for the tree. It seemed to him to represent a lie about the past, about the relation between the white world and the land and its inhabitants, a lie taking the form of a symbolic resolution. The golden spruce must have seemed too terribly perfect a vehicle: as an anomalously albino tree it could stand as at once an exception and an example. An *exception*, in that it had been set aside, exempted, offered asylum, saved from a general destruction. But like Pennsylvania's Treaty Elm, it could also serve as an *example* of compact, of peace and amity and agreement across divisive political and racial lines. What else does Hadwin see when he looks at the golden spruce? Does he see a white symbol, a symbol of whiteness, a symbol of white sovereignty, the white sovereignty of the symbol? It is not the West alone that makes trees serve as symbols of sovereignty or other notions of originary legitimacy; the Oneida Thomas King just demonstrated otherwise. But Hadwin's story, and its entanglement in the dream work that I have been tracking this chapter, suggests that the deployment of this network of tropes in the West has a distinctive violence to it. Let me try to specify this violence by pulling out the focus once more for a long shot.

Ilex and Rhizome

The relationship between trees and sovereignty goes back a long way in the West, it turns out. Robert Pogue Harrison, in his wonderful book on the real and symbolic battle between forests and civilization, from *Gilgamesh* to Calvino, points out that "the Latin word—*foresta*—does not come into existence until the Merovingian period. In Roman documents, as well as in the earlier acts of the Middle Ages, the standard word for woods and woodlands was *nemus*. The word *foresta* appears for the first time in the laws of the Longobards and the capitularies of Charlemagne, referring not to woodlands in general but only to the royal game preserves." The original forest is *already* a preserve or sanctuary, which leads Harrison to quip that "an ecologist today cannot help but be a monarchist of sorts."[24] The *foresta* enfolds within the precincts of civilization a wilderness that indexes sovereign power and exceptionality; or stated otherwise, the monarch founds the civilized state by embodying and incorporating the state's savage antithesis. If the environmentalist's commitment to such set-asides makes him a "monarchist," Hadwin's assault on such symbolic preservation makes him seem more and more like a regicide.

Perhaps it was such a logic that suggested to Charles II that he hide *himself* in an oak tree after the battle of Worcester in 1651. This same monarch plays a key role in the story of what may well have been the only tree better known than Penn's elm in colonial America. Charles had granted the colonists in Connecticut an especially liberal charter. When James II succeeded Charles, he sought to revoke it, and sent Sir Edward Andros to Connecticut to retrieve the offending text, but before he could do so a wily Captain Wadsworth hid it in the hollow trunk of a large oak tree. Andros left empty-handed and when, two years later, William and Mary ascended to the throne, Connecticut was in the clear. It is this legendary tree whose likeness presently graces the verso side of the Connecticut quarter coin, and whose toppling in 1856 called forth a "flag-draped . . . hero's funeral."[25] Gayle Brandow Samuels puzzles about the logic of this legend in ways that seem familiar: "Was their action"—hiding the charter in the tree—"symbolic of a wish to survive hostile Indians and a sometimes equally hostile environment? If the tree was outside the wilderness, the pejoratively native world, was it inside the ordered and rational community or did it inhabit some halfway house of its own?" (20). If indeed the tree is a symbolic "halfway house," part of what it symbolizes is the historical palimpsest that superimposes violent land appropriation, treaty agreement, and sovereign legitimacy, the palimpsest that makes up Connecticut's history. (This history is fundamentally similar to Pennsylvania's, as Brown's *Edgar Huntly* shows.) The Dutch were the first Europeans to settle Connecticut, having "bought the land for their Hartford settlement from the Pequot, who claimed to have acquired it in conquest" (18). As their enemies give way to the Pequot, and the Pequot to the Dutch, so the Dutch eventually abandon their trading post to English settlers from Massachusetts. Hereafter the absorption becomes more textual: in 1662 Charles II issued the Connecticut Charter, "a liberal document, which superseded but endorsed the limited self-government the colonists had already set up under their Fundamental Orders" (18). The manner in which textual legitimation and appropriative conquest alternately "supersede but endorse" each other is at the heart of the semiotic puzzle I am exploring.[26] As in the dream of Hadwin, real territory and symbolic spaces are intimately braided together here.

The cumulative effect of these stories is to suggest that something fundamental about the relation between politics and the manipulation of symbols is at work in this arborescent tropology. Once one begins to look for them, trees are everywhere in modern political philosophy. For John Locke, the tree is the site of a primal appropriation, nature lending itself to transformation into property: "He that is nourished by the acorns he picked up under an oak, or the apples he gathered from the trees in the wood, has certainly appropriated them to himself. Nobody can deny but the nourishment is his. I ask then, when did they begin to be his? . . . It is plain, if the first gathering made them not his, nothing else could. That *labour* put a distinction between them and common."[27] In his *Discourse on the Origin and Foundation of Inequality Among Men* (1755), Rousseau also uses the tree as a symbol of a nature transformed, but his appropriation is linguistic rather than economic; the tree stands for nature that must be worked on and worked over by the abstractive power of language:

> Abstractions are difficult and not particularly natural Operations. Each object was at first given a particular name without regard to kinds and Species, which these first Institutors were not in a position to distinguish; and all particulars presented themselves to their mind in isolation, just as they are in the picture of Nature. If one Oak was called A, another Oak was called B; for the first idea that one derives from two objects is that they are not the same, and it often takes a good deal of time to notice what they have in common: so that the more limited knowledge was, the more extensive did the Dictionary grow. The clutter of all this Nomenclature was not easily cleared.[28]

Victor Gourevitch's translation of this last sentence is interesting in our context. Rousseau writes, "L'embarras de toute cette nomenclature ne peut être levé facilement." "Clutter" for "l'embarras" and "cleared" for "levé" makes Rousseau's linguistic operations sound more like clear-cutting than does the original French, as though the abstract oaks A and B retained some of their refractory materiality not only for Rousseau's savage, but also for the "citoyen de Genève" himself. Gourevitch's interpretive freedom, however, honors the inextricable connection of abstract and concrete that is at stake in the figure of the tree.

Adam Smith brings Locke and Rousseau together—the story about gathering and the story about naming—in the opening of his "Considerations Concerning the Formation of First Languages, and the Different Genius of Original and Compound Languages" (1761). Smith had read Rousseau's *Discourse* immediately upon publication, and he disputes the latter's account of the role of naming in the development of "genera and species":

> The assignation of particular names, to denote particular objects, that is the Institution of nouns substantive, would probably, be one of the first steps towards the formation of languages. Two savages, who had never been taught to speak, but

> had been bred up remote from the societies of men, would naturally begin to form that language by which they would endeavour to make their mutual wants intelligible to each other, by uttering certain sounds, whenever they meant to denote certain objects. Those objects only that were most familiar to them, and which they had most frequent occasion to mention, would have particular names assigned to them. The particular cave whose covering sheltered them from the weather, the particular tree whose fruit relieved their hunger, the particular fountain whose water allayed their thirst, would first be denominated by the words cave, tree, fountain, or by whatever other appellations they might think proper, in that primitive jargon, to mark them. Afterwards, when the more enlarged experience of these savages had led them to observe, and their necessary occasions obliged them to make mention of other caves, and other trees, and other fountains, they would naturally bestow, upon each of those new objects, the same name, by which they had been accustomed to express the similar object they were first acquainted with.[29]

We have a tradition here in which an archaic, "savage" humanity first gathers itself together through a linguistic (nominative) and territorial appropriation of nature, the forests, the trees. Such a self-gathering is also, however, a self-negation, insofar as the prior humanity—humanity in a "state of nature," as the West will say—is understood as both continuous with, and decisively separated from, civilized, gathered, collective man. The single tree, in both its linguistic and its territorial dimensions, testifies to this ambivalence by at once marking and obscuring this mythic passage: linguistically, the single tree provides the provocation for its own negation, as, in Smith's version especially, it calls forth the nomination that will then render it merely one in a class. Territorially, the single tree, as we have seen, both exemplifies and negates, both remembers and forgets, as it were, the forest against which civilization defines itself, as a figure against a ground. To imagine primal acts of gathering—of acorns and fruits, or citizens and settlers—taking place beneath its umbrage is, again, to make the tree provide cover, as it were, for an ambivalent desire to be both natural and extranatural, rooted and uprooted.

My metaphors here—"ground," "cover," "rooted and uprooted"—are purposively "live," because part of what is at stake here is the extent to which the metaphor's origin in concrete particularity lingers on in its linguistic abstraction. One persistent dream of the West is that there is *no* metaphor live enough that it can gainsay the force of language's universalizing and abstracting vocation. When Hegel wishes to make the point that linguistic universality inhabits even the most apparently immediate sense certainties, his example is familiar: "'Here' is, e.g., the tree. If I turn round, this truth has vanished and is converted into its opposite: 'No tree is here, but a house instead.' 'Here' does not vanish; on the contrary, it abides constant in the vanishing of the house, the tree, etc. and is indifferently house or tree."[30] One can follow Hegel's general point here and still wonder about that word "opposite." In what world are house and tree opposites? Only in a world where the distinction between abstract and concrete is understood to be a digital one. It must have seemed to many over the generations that every time you turned around, the tree had become a house, and not everyone has felt quite so "indifferently" about it as Hegel does. Clear-cutting and the work of abstraction find themselves in close proximity. Derrida was right: "We should . . . study together, genetically and structurally, the history of the road and the history of writing."[31]

A different, but equally appropriative dream, was that of Giambattista Vico. Where Hegel projects dominion through language's divine power of negation, Vico's lexicon is a sedimented, cumulative word-hoard in which nothing is ever lost. Harrison reminds us that Vico took the burial of the dead, along with matrimony and religion, as the three universal institutions of humanity, and he offers this gloss on Vico's account of the primal appropriation of the earth: "The giants in their respective clearings claim dominion over the land by demonstration: We are sons of *this* earth, we are born from *these* oaks. Which earth? Which oaks? They point: this earth *here*, where the wooden graveposts mark the presence of our ancestors in the ground" (7). We too might well ask, "Which earth? Which oaks?" The problem—the stake—has all along been the "presence of our ancestors in the ground," how to find them, how to remember or forget them. Brown's "fatal Elm," the golden spruce, the pine tree in Oneida country, all attempt answers to the question of the relation between this earth and the ancestors in the ground. But Vico is a great believer in the embeddedness of language in concrete conditions. If humanity's entire history is virtually present in its lexicon, when considered etymologically, this is because language itself was, and is, an emanation of concrete settings. His version of the stories that we have been tracing breathtakingly completes the circle between tree and text:

> This was the order of human institutions: first the forests, after that the huts, then the villages, next the cities, and finally the academies. This axiom is a great

> principle of etymology, for this sequence of human institutions sets the patterns for the histories of words in the various native languages. Thus we observe in the Latin language that almost the whole corpus of its words had sylvan or rustic origins. For example, *lex*. First it must have meant a collection of acorns. Thence we believe is derived *ilex*, as it were *illex*, the oak (as certainly *aquilex* means collector of waters); for the oak produces the acorns by which the swine are drawn together. *Lex* was next a collection of vegetables, from which the latter were called *legumina*. Later on, at a time when vulgar letters had not yet been invented for writing down the laws, *lex* by a necessity of civil nature must have meant a collection of citizens, or the public parliament; so that the presence of the people was the *lex*, or "law," that solemnized the wills that were made *calatis comitiis*, in the presence of the assembled *comitia*. Finally, collecting letters, and making, as it were, a sheaf of them for each word, was called *legere*, reading.[32]

Our very concept of law is a form of gathering, binding, collecting, and includes in its magical reach the most primitive Lockean appropriations of acorns to our most rarefied alphabetic achievements, the written language. In light of Vico, that Clithero's pseudo-savage clawing beneath the tree involves the burial of a *manuscript*, and that the most fundamental questions involving law and legitimacy are coiled within this scene, begins to seem less anomalous. Hadwin's assault on the golden spruce is also in the grip of this short-circuiting relation between acorns and letters, concrete and abstract, life and language. Hadwin's act is at once an exuberantly embodied act of putting blade to trunk and a mythic enactment controlled by the despotism of the signifier. We need to see Hadwin as a character in a drama as much as an individual human. From the "forests" to the "academies," says Vico. How could Hadwin *not* see in this trajectory the revenge of "university-trained professionals" against "amateur life"? Hadwin's repudiation of "professionals" and their abominations is an attack on the hegemony of the symbol, but such an attack can only repeat and reinforce the logic of that hegemony.

That logic, as I have explored it in this book, depends on what Agamben describes as a "structural symmetry" between the exception and the example, between the sovereign and his abjected twin, the *homo sacer*. I have suggested throughout that the very availability of this logic has depended on a history, and a symbolism, of racialization, such that the convergence between these two figures could be both projected and denied. Race works like an alibi in this logic, an "exoneration," as Schmitt called it. Consider the dream of Hadwin: racial violence winds its tendrils round each detail in this bottomless story, and yet one also cannot help feeling, as the white man savages the albino tree, that the racial topos is ultimately something like a vanishing mediator in an affair among whites, as the historical Logan is in the all-white apocalypse of the "Logan" clan at the close of John Neal's novel. In the final analysis, I take this "symmetry" of exception and example to be a fiction and a dream. By being able to toggle back and forth between exception and example, sovereign and *homo sacer*, we surreptitiously subscribe to the illusion that such a binary logic is adequate to an analysis of the modes of belonging and inclusion. But there are, I believe, *only examples:* "Neither particular nor universal, the example is a singular object that presents itself as such. Hence its ambiguity, just when one has decided to take it really seriously. Being-called—the property that established all possible belongings . . . is also what can bring them all radically back into question."[33] I have proceeded in this chapter—and indeed in this book—on the assumption that literary analysis is at bottom a treatment of examples, a respecter of "singular objects that [present themselves] as such." Such a fidelity to the terms in which examples present themselves, to the tropes and figures and rhetoric specific to each, allows us to *be clear about ambiguity*, about the fact that, in our political belonging as elsewhere, all that most matters is neither particular nor universal. It seems fitting that in the passage just quoted from Agamben's book *The Coming Community*, his example of the example is the tree: "the antinomy of the individual and the universal has its origin in language. The word 'tree' designates all trees indifferently" (9).

"We're tired of trees!" exclaim Deleuze and Guattari, and who can blame them?[34] Perhaps Hadwin was tired of trees, too. But the tree, and the "arborescent culture" of which it is the symbol, is not to be gainsaid: it marks our home, it is our home: the " 'Here' "—*pace* Hegel—is at once tree and house. Deleuze and Guattari correctly observe that "the tree has dominated Western reality and all of Western thought, from botany to biology and anatomy, but also gnosology, theology, ontology, all of philosophy . . . : the root-foundation, *Grund*, *racine*, *fondement*. The West has a special relation to the forest, and deforestation" (18). Such "arborescence" is marked by an obsession with lineage, genealogy, and verticality—ultimately, the obsession is with identity itself, the fantasy or phantasm of unity, the one (even when, perhaps especially when, the one bifurcates to become two): "A first type of book is the root-book. The tree is already the image of the world, or the root-image of the world-tree. This is the classical book, as noble, signifying, and subjective organic interiority. . . . The law of the book is the law of reflection, the One that becomes two" (5). In place of such an identitarian logic, Deleuze and Guattari famously propose the rhizome—a kind of indiscernible multiplicity, always less than one and more than one. The rhizome resists the grip of the past, it "is an anti-genealogy . . . or antimemory" (21). It thereby also evades hierarchies of moral thought: "One can never posit a dualism or a dichotomy, even in the rudimentary form of the good and the bad" (9). Ultimately the rhizome stands against the fixation of identity itself: "The notion of unity appears only when there is a power takeover in the multiplicity by the signifier or a corresponding subjectification proceeding" (8). Something like this "power takeover" does indeed seem to be at work in the dream of Hadwin, and the logic of sovereignty that it so peculiarly exemplifies. There is a kind of mutually destructive binding between semiosis and embodied subjectivity—a correlation or "overcoding" between the subject (Hadwin) and a signifier (spruce). This "overcoding" leads to a kind of implosion, a symbolic black hole: the "notion of unity" here is pursued to the point of auto-destruction. Such is the (failed) "oneing of the West" exemplified by the dream of Hadwin.

But what is this "West," after all? If the "new world" has been the place of lingering and being last, a kind of dream space in which the contradictions of modern political imagination can be at once explored and disavowed, "the West" is one of the central phantasms of this imagination, its alibi or elsewhere. Deleuze and Guattari are themselves not immune to its appeal: "American books are different from European books, even when America sets off in pursuit of trees. The conception of the book is different, *Leaves of Grass*. And directions in America are different: the search for arborescence and the return to the Old World occur in the East. But there is the rhizomatic West, with its Indians without ancestry, its ever-receding limit, its shifting and displaced frontiers. There is a whole American 'map' in the West, where even the trees form rhizomes" (19). The two Frenchmen have been reading Leslie Fiedler here, as their footnote attests. *The Return of the Vanishing American*—a vanishing and returning we have described as the logic of the last—is a story that, like Hadwin's, takes "the peculiar form of madness which dreams, and achieves, and is the true West."[35] The problem, however, is that there is no "true West." There is no territory for which one might light out. The golden spruce is a landmark not on a "line of flight" but in a space folded over on itself, a pocket, an asylum, a preserve. In this sense the golden spruce operates less like an exception that founds an order than like Freud's "navel of the dream," an overdetermined node, neither particular nor universal, at which the rhizomatic network is knotted. If, indeed, in the "map" of the West, trees can form rhizomes, then the spruce does so not by instantiating the universal or the particular, but rather by presenting itself, singularly, as a matrix from which those dimensions subtract themselves. (The rhizome is that "from which the One is always subtracted (*n*—1)" [Deleuze and Guattari, *Thousand Plateaus*, 21]). The spruce marks out the folded-over zone of lingering and being last, where identity is purchased only at the price of subtraction, the one always shadowed, as it were, by Logan's "not one."

NOTES

INTRODUCTION

1. William Rasch, *Sovereignty and Its Discontents: On the Primacy of Conflict and the Structure of the Political* (London: Birkbeck Law, 2004); Aihwa Ong, *Neoliberalism as Exception: Mutations in Citizenship and Sovereignty* (Durham, NC: Duke University Press, 2006).

2. Stephen D. Krasner, *Sovereignty: Organized Hypocrisy* (Princeton, NJ: Princeton University Press, 1999).

3. James J. Sheehan, "The Problem of Sovereignty in European History," *American Historical Review* (February 2006): 1–15, quotes from 1–2.

4. Michel Foucault, "Governmentality" (1977), in *Power*, Vol. 3 of *Essential Works of Foucault, 1954–1984*, ed. James D. Faubion (New York: New Press, 2000), 220.

5. The recently translated courses offered by Foucault at the Collège de France show in great detail these ideas in development. See Michel Foucault, *"Society Must Be Defended": Lectures at the Collège de France, 1975–76*, ed. Mauro Bertani and Alessandro Fontana, trans. David Macey (Picador: New York, 2003); *Security, Territory, Population: Lectures at the Collège de France, 1977–78*, ed. Michel Senellart, trans. Graham Burchell (New York: Palgrave MacMillan, 2007).

6. Benedict Anderson, *Imagined Communities: Reflections on the Origin and Spread of Nationalism*, rev. ed. (London: Verso, 2006 [1983]), xiii.

7. Michael Hardt and Antonio Negri, *Empire* (Cambridge, MA: Harvard University Press, 2000), 70.

8. Edward Keene, *Beyond the Anarchical Society: Grotius, Colonialism, and Order in World Politics* (Cambridge: Cambridge University Press, 2002); Antony Anghie, *Imperialism, Sovereignty, and the Making of International Law* (Cambridge: Cambridge University Press, 2005).

9. Toni Morrison, *Playing in the Dark: Whiteness and the Literary Imagination* (New York: Vintage, 1992).

10. Eric Lott, *Love and Theft: Blackface Minstrelsy and the American Working Class* (New York: Oxford University Press, 1995).

11. Jacques Derrida, *Rogues: Two Essays on Reason*, trans. Pascale-Anne Brault and Michael Naas (Stanford, CA: Stanford University Press, 2005), 156.

12. Richard Tuck, *The Rights of War and Peace: Political Thought and the International Order from Grotius to Kant* (Cambridge: Cambridge University Press, 1999), 11.

13. Edwin DeWitt Dickinson, "The Analogy Between Natural Persons and International Persons in the Law of Nations," *Yale Law Journal* 26 (1916–17): 564–91, quote from 590.

14. Keene's *Beyond the Anarchical Society* is a full treatment of this idea, but here at least is a minimal elaboration of the merely gestural argument offered above: "The more lasting significance of Grotius' work . . . lies in its relevance to people who wanted to justify colonialism on the basis of individuals' rights in the law of nations to appropriate unoccupied or uncultivated lands, and to people who wanted to justify the assertion of public authority by European states in the extra-European world. . . . Over time an especially close relationship developed between the specific propositions of the Grotian theory of the law of nations—his ideas of divisible sovereignty and private property—and the modern practices of colonialism and imperialism. Certainly, there was more of an affinity here than there was between the Grotian theory and the practice of the 'Westphalian' states-system that developed within Europe" (60).

15. Michael Warner, "What's Colonial about Colonial America?" in *Possible Pasts: Becoming Colonial in Early America*, ed. Robert Blair St. George (Ithaca, NY: Cornell University Press, 2000), 63.

16. Thomas Hobbes, *Leviathan*, ed. Edwin Curley (Indianapolis: Hackett, 1994), 77.

17. Giorgio Agamben, *Homo Sacer; Sovereign Power and Bare Life*, trans. Daniel Heller-Roazen (Stanford, CA: Stanford University Press, 1998), 36; further references to this work will be included parenthetically in the main text. The idea that the experience and "idea" of the new world fundamentally changed political thought in the West is hardly novel, of course. Two studies that have been exemplary for me in demonstrating how one might approach the impact of new world experience on centuries-long conceptual traditions are Anthony Pagden, *The Fall of Natural Man: The American Indian and the Origins of Comparative Ethnography* (Cambridge: Cambridge University Press, 1982); and Ronald L. Meek, *Social Science and the Ignoble Savage* (Cambridge: Cambridge University Press, 1976).

18. Carl Schmitt, *The* Nomos *of the Earth in the International Law of the* Jus Publicum Europeaum, trans. G. L. Ulmen (New York: Telos, 2003), 96.

19. Carl Schmitt, *The Concept of the Political*, trans. George Schwab (Chicago: University of Chicago Press, 1996).

20. David Armitage, *The Ideological Origins of the British Empire* (Cambridge: Cambridge University Press, 2000), 4.

21. Eliga H. Gould, *The Persistence of Empire: British Political Culture in the Age of the American Revolution* (Chapel Hill: University of North Carolina Press, 2000); Brendan McConville, *The King's Three Faces: The Rise and Fall of Royal America, 1688–1776* (Chapel Hill: University of North Carolina Press, 2006), esp. Chap. 8; Dror Wahrman, *The Making of the Modern Self: Identity and Culture in Eighteenth-century England* (New Haven, CT: Yale University Press, 2004), Chap. 6.

22. Paul Downes, *Democracy, Revolution, and Monarchism in Early American Literature* (Cambridge: Cambridge University Press, 2002), ix. I mention here two other superb studies that have guided me as I tried to attend to historical and political pressures on the one hand, and the nuances of literary expression on the other: Elizabeth Maddock Dillon, *The Gender of Freedom: Fictions of Liberalism and the Literary Public Sphere* (Stanford, CA: Stanford University Press, 2004); and Julie Ellison, *Cato's Tears and the Making of Anglo-American Emotion* (Chicago: University of Chicago Press, 1999).

23. See Warner, "What's Colonial about Colonial Society?"; Ed White, *The Backcountry and the City: Colonization and Conflict in Early America* (Minneapolis: University of Minnesota Press, 2005); Ed White, "Early American Nations as Imagined Communities," *American Quarterly* 56, no. 1 (March 2004): 49–81; Peter S. Onuf, *Jefferson's Empire: The Language of American Nationhood* (Charlottesville: University of Virginia Press, 2000). See also David Kazanjian, *The Colonizing Trick: National Culture and Imperial Citizenship* (Minneapolis: University of Minnesota Press, 2003); Andy Doolen, *Fugitive Empire: Locating Early American Imperialism* (Minneapolis: University of Minnesota Press, 2005); Sean X. Goudie, *Creole America: The West Indies and the Formation of Literature and Culture in the New Republic* (Philadelphia: University of Pennsylvania Press, 2006).

24. David Waldstreicher, *Runaway America: Benjamin Franklin, Slavery, and the American Revolution* (New York: Hill and Wang, 2004).

25. John Wood Sweet, *Bodies Politic: Negotiating Race in the American North, 1730–1830* (Philadelphia: University of Pennsylvania Press, 2003), 19.

26. David Waldstreicher, "Racial Histories, Histories of Race: All or None of the Above?" *Reviews in American History* 32, no. 3 (September 2004): 347–51, quote from 348.

27. John Locke, *Second Treatise of Government* [1690], ed. C. B. Macpherson (Indianapolis: Hackett, 1980), 9.

28. Jacques Rancière, "Who Is the Subject of the Rights of Man?" *The South Atlantic Quarterly* 103, nos. 2–3 (Spring–Summer 2004): 297–310, quote from 301–2.

29. I have elaborated what I take to be the flaws in Agamben's (and others') anti-humanitarianism in "Torture and Hyperbole," *Law, Culture, and the Humanities* 3, no. 1 (2007): 18–34.

CHAPTER ONE

1. Susan Westbury, "Theatre and Power in Bacon's Rebellion: Virginia, 1676–77," *The Seventeenth Century* 19, no. 1 (April 2004): 69–86.

2. *Oxford English Dictionary*, Oxford Compact Edition, 1971, s.v. "postillion."

3. Aphra Behn, *The Fair Jilt*, in *Oroonoko and Other Writings*, ed. Paul Salzman (Oxford: Oxford University Press, 1994), 74. Further references to this story, and to *Oroonoko*, will be to the Salzman edition.

4. Janet Todd, *The Secret Life of Aphra Behn* (London: André Deutsch, 1996), 411.

5. Gilles Deleuze and Félix Guattari, *A Thousand Plateaus: Capitalism and Schizophrenia*, trans. Brian Massumi (Minneapolis: University of Minnesota Press, 1987), 508.

6. For accounts of Virginia's royalism under Governor Berkeley, see Westbury 71–73, 77. A rich sketch of the social makeup of seventeenth-century Virginia is provided by David Hackett Fischer, *Albion's Seed: Four British Folkways in America* (Oxford: Oxford University Press, 1989), 207–32.

7. See Michel Foucault, *Discipline and Punish: The Birth of the Prison*, trans. Alan Sheridan (New York: Vintage, 1977), Chap. 2.

8. Cited in Jennifer Hale Pulsipher, "*The Widow Ranter* and Royalist Culture in Virginia," *Early American Literature* 39, no. 1 (2004): 41–66, quote from 59.

9. Westbury 73. Kathleen Brown presents the richest account of the ways in which the rebellion flared up in a climate of increased worries about women's public unruliness. See Kathleen M. Brown, *Good Wives, Nasty Wenches, and Anxious Patriarchs: Gender, Race, and Power in Colonial Virginia* (Chapel Hill, NC: Omohundro Institute of Early American History and Culture, 1996), Chap. 5.

10. "A True Narrative of the Late Rebellion in Virginia, By the Royal Commissioners, 1677," in *Narratives of the Insurrections, 1675–1690*, ed. Charles M. Andrews (New York: Barnes and Noble, 1915), 135. Further references to the "True Narrative" will be to this edition.

11. Brown discusses the "white aprons" on pp. 165–66.

12. There is some debate about how Behn happened on Bacon's Rebellion as a topic for her last play. Wilber Henry Ward argued some time ago that Behn must have had access to the "True Narrative," because she references events of the rebellion, geographical details, and especially the depiction of Bacon himself, that are not present in the widely available pamphlet *Strange News From Virginia* (1677). See Wilber Henry Ward, "Mrs. Behn's 'The Widow Ranter': Historical Sources," *South Atlantic Bulletin* 41, no. 4 (November 1976): 94–98. More recently, Margaret Ferguson has suggested that such "intriguing" suggestions as Ward's "would be more persuasive if they dealt with the empirical problem of how Behn might have seen such a source." See Margaret Ferguson, "News from the New World: Miscegenous Romance in Aphra

Behn's *Oroonoko* and *The Widow Ranter*," in *The Production of English Renaissance Culture*, ed. David Lee Miller, Sharon O'Dair, and Harold Weber (Ithaca, NY: Cornell University Press, 1994), 154n6. The story of the "Scandalous Postillion" would have been even harder for Behn to have seen, because it was not included in the "True Narrative," but only in letters from the commissioners.

13. G. A. Starr, "Aphra Behn and the Genealogy of the Man of Feeling," *Modern Philology* 87, no. 4 (May 1990): 362–72, quote from 367.

14. This point is made in more detail by Jacqueline Pearson in "The Short Fiction (excluding *Oroonoko*)," in *The Cambridge Companion to Aphra Behn*, ed. Derek Hughes and Janet Todd (Cambridge: Cambridge University Press, 2004), 196.

15. The medieval two-bodies theory holds that the king had two bodies, one mortal and the other not. See Ernst H. Kantorowicz, *The King's Two Bodies: A Study in Medieval Political Theology* (Princeton, NJ: Princeton University Press, 1957).

16. Salzman 273, reporting the research of Maureen Duffy.

17. Julie Ellison, *Cato's Tears and the Making of Anglo-American Emotion* (Chicago: University of Chicago Press, 1999), 30.

18. See Ernest Bernbaum, "Mrs. Behn's *Oroonoko*," in *Anniversary Papers by Colleagues and Pupils of George Lyman Kittredge* (Boston: Ginn, 1913); and Bernbaum, "Mrs. Behn's Biography a Fiction," *PMLA* 28, no. 3 (1913): 432–53. For modern scholarship on the question, which makes use of documentary findings that show Bernbaum to have been wrong, see Katherine M. Rogers, "Fact and Fiction in Aphra Behn's *Oroonoko*," *Studies in the Novel* 20 (1988): 1–15; and Mary Ann O'Donnell, "Aphra Behn: The Documentary Record," *The Cambridge Companion*, 1–11. While Jennifer Hale Pulsipher persuasively argues that *The Widow Ranter* provides a "clear demonstration of the continuity of English royalist culture on both sides of the Atlantic," she does not bother to ask whether it might also demonstrate any discontinuities (Pulsipher 41).

19. Elliot Visconsi, "A Degenerate Race: English Barbarism in Behn's *Oroonoko* and *The Widow Ranter*," *ELH* 69 (2002): 673–701, quote from 697.

20. Janet Todd and Derek Hughes, "Tragedy and Tragicomedy," in *The Cambridge Companion*, 94.

21. "True Narrative," 112–13.

22. "Strange News from Virginia," reprinted as Appendix 7 in *The Widow Ranter, or, The History of Bacon in Virginia*, ed. Aaron R. Walden (New York: Garland, 1993), 165, 170, 169. I have used Walden's edition of Behn's play but give all citations by act, scene, and line numbers.

23. Walter Benjamin, *The Origin of German Tragic Drama*, trans. John Osborne (London: New Left, 1977), 142. In the beginning of the play, Friendly refers to Bacon's "Sullen Melancholly" (I.i.35). Because "Strange Newes" offers no such characterization, this detail has been seen as offering further evidence that Behn had access to the official commissioners' "True Narrative" (Ward 96).

24. See Catherine Gallagher, *Nobody's Story: The Vanishing Acts of Women Writers in the Marketplace, 1670–1820* (Berkeley and Los Angeles: University of California Press, 1994), 34, and Chap. 1 generally.

25. By emphasizing the ways in which theatricality is understood as productive of social stability for Behn, I offer a different interpretation than Heidi Hutner does: "Behn seems to want to supplement notions of male supremacy and authority with the concept that the white female performance of phallic power can supersede fact, history, or 'truth.' For Behn, then, above all else, the theater of history, gender, and race in *The Widow Ranter* marks the destabilization of fixed meaning, the blurring of categories and boundaries, and, hence, the impossibility of performing the always and already fictional 'real.'" See Heidi Hutner, *Colonial Women: Race and Culture in Stuart Drama* (Oxford: Oxford University Press, 2001), 106.

26. For thoughtful recent attempts to assess the critical appeal of Behn, and especially *Oroonoko*, see Laura Rosenthal, "*Oroonoko*: Reception, Ideology, and Narrative Strategy," in *Cambridge Companion*, 151–65; Joanna Lipking's collection of criticism in her Norton Critical Edition, Aphra Behn, *Oroonoko*, ed. Joanna Lipking (New York: Norton, 1997); and Srinivas Aravamudan, *Tropicopolitans: Colonialism and Agency, 1688–1804* (Durham, NC: Duke University Press, 1999), who remarks that "recent critical attention has bordered on the obsessional" (29).

27. The first phrase is William Spengeman's, and the second is from Janet Todd and Derek Hughes. See William Spengeman, "The Earliest American Novel: Aphra Behn's *Oroonoko*," *Nineteenth-century Fiction* 38, no. 4 (1984): 384–414; and Todd and Hughes 93.

28. Margaret Ferguson, "Juggling the Categories of Race, Class, and Gender: Aphra Behn's *Oroonoko*," in *Aphra Behn: Contemporary Critical Essays*, ed. Janet Todd (New York: St. Martin's, 1999), 209–33, quote from 218.

29. Laura Brown, "The Romance of Empire: *Oroonoko* and the Trade in Slaves," in *The New Eighteenth Century: Theory, Politics, English Literature*, ed. Felicity Nussbaum and Laura Brown (New York: Methuen, 1987), 57.

30. Absolutist convictions were of course perfectly capable of flipping over into something like their opposite. For example, as Catherine Gallagher shows, Margaret Cavendish's absolutism was inflected in such a way as to reveal a radical relativism as its other side. Gallagher's conclusion is that "absolutist imagination . . . paradoxically supplied the terms of 'emancipated' subjectivity." See "Embracing the Absolute: The Politics of the Female Subject in Seventeenth-century England," *Genders* 1 (Spring 1988): 25–39, quote from 38.

31. Wylie Sypher, *Guinea's Captive Kings: British Anti-Slavery Literature of the XVIIIth Century* (Chapel Hill: University of North Carolina Press, 1942), 110.

CHAPTER TWO

1. Two canonical surveys of such influence are Sypher; and Edward D. Seeber's "Oroonoko in France in the XVIIIth Century," *PMLA* 51, no. 4 (December 1936): 953–59.

2. Barry Weller, "The Royal Slave and the Prestige of Origins," *Kenyon Review* 14, no. 3 (Summer 1992): 65–79, quote from 68.

3. The best-known example would be the kidnapped and eventually ransomed prince of Annamaboe, whose tears during a performance of Southerne's staging of *Oroonoko* was reported in the *Gentleman's Magazine* in 1749. See Sypher 166–68. See also Aravamudan 250–53; and Felicity A. Nussbaum, *The Limits of the Human: Fictions of Anomaly, Race, and Gender in the Long Eighteenth Century* (Cambridge: Cambridge University Press, 2003), 189ff. Given the uncertainties about whether the origins of Behn's hero, and those of the texts I examine in this chapter, should be taken as historical or mythical, it is worth noting that the anonymous pamphlet *The Royal African: or, Memoirs of the Young Prince of Annamaboe* (London: W. Reeve, ca. 1749), sees the need, when describing the prince's social status, to censure "that strange Principle of Incredulity, which induces [People] to question the Veracity of every thing that does not fall immediately within the Compass of their own Observation" (iii).

4. Elizabeth Maddock Dillon makes a related point about the world of contingency that Behn's text opens to view. She suggests that the royal slave passes over into his generically posthumous life-after-romance precisely when Oroonoko hears that Imoinda is pregnant, which, as Behn writes, "made Caesar even adore her, knowing he was last of his great race" (44). "While this sentence constitutes closure with respect to romance," writes Dillon, "Behn's text continues past the end-point which would represent full knowledge—full elaboration of divine principle—in romance." See Elizabeth Maddock Dillon, "The Original American Novel; Or, The American Origin of the Novel," in *A Companion to The Eighteenth Century Novel*, ed. Paula Backscheider and Catherine Ingrassia (Oxford: Blackwell, 2005), 235–60. The text continues, as we saw in the last chapter, into a weirdly suspended state agitated by the instabilities of contract and promise, a lingering condition between life and death rendered concrete by the grisly attenuations of Oroonoko's death. Overflowing the "closure" of romance, Oroonoko finds himself stranded in a world marked by the dynamics of what Dillon calls an "actuarial logic": "Contractual logic is *actuarial* in both the vernacular and etymological sense of the word—predicated, that is, upon the Latin *actum*, 'things done' in the world, and linked to the capacity to aggregately predict, on the basis of empirical observation of such acts, what may unfold in the future" (242). If Oroonoko closes out romance as the "last of his great race," he nevertheless lingers on in this new generic space defined simultaneously by facticity and contingency, by the indisputable fact of certain "things done" in the world, and the equally certain fact that they could have been different, and may be different in the future. In place of romance, then, we get something more unstable: the "Romantic," by which Behn means a hybrid discourse between fiction and fact. She implies to Lord Maitland in her dedication that this is the only resource available to her in this new world: "I wanted power to preserve this great man. If there be anything that seems Romantic, I beseech your Lordship to consider these countries do, in all things, so far differ from ours, that they produce unconceivable wonders" (5).

5. The authenticity of Equiano's African past has for some time been the subject of doubt. In a critical review of Linebaugh and Rediker's *Many-headed Hydra*, David Brion Davis claims that Equiano's authenticity has been in doubt "for years," but his only citation is to Vincent Carretta's 1999 article in *Slavery and Abolition*. See David Brion Davis, "Slavery—White, Black, Muslim, Christian," *The New York Review of Books* (July 5, 2001), 54. The article Davis refers to is Vincent Carretta, "Olaudah Equiano or Gustavus Vassa? New Light on an Eighteenth-century Question of Identity," *Slavery and Abolition* 20, no. 3 (1999): 96–105. In the course of his editorial and biographical research on Equiano, Carretta unearthed two documents—a baptismal record and a ship's muster roll—that list Equiano's birthplace as South Carolina, or Carolina. In his recent biography, Carretta puts the question this way: "Recent biographical discoveries have cast doubt on Equiano's story of his birth and early years. The available evidence suggests that the author of *The Interesting Narrative* may have invented rather than reclaimed an African identity. If so, Equiano's literary achievements have been vastly underestimated. Baptismal and naval records say that he was born in South Carolina around 1747. If they are accurate, he invented his African childhood and his much-quoted account of the Middle Passage on a slave ship." Carretta, *Equiano, the African: Biography of a Self-made Man* (Athens: University of Georgia Press, 2005), xiv. Carretta goes on to clarify that he *does* consider these baptismal and naval records to be accurate, and that he thus must take Equiano's account of his life in Africa—everything from his relationship to his mother, the Embrenché, his having been "hurried away amongst the uncircumcised," to his terror-stricken introduction to white people—as a "literary achievement," albeit an extraordinary one. But can we really accept this way of rescuing Equiano? As I argue in this chapter, Equiano's rehabilitation and canonization is powerfully connected with what we take to be his status as historical witness. Carretta himself is interested in the historical man Gustavus Vassa, and not a character named Olaudah Equiano: if we might as well be reading a novel, why bother with research into baptismal records and the like? For an interesting debate on these issues, see the forum on "Teaching Equiano's *Interesting Narrative*," *Eighteenth-century Studies* 34, no. 4 (2001), where Adam Potkay uses Carretta's evidence as a way to criticize "fundamentally poststructuralist approaches" for failing to recognize that "even literature professors are apt to crave veridicality" (602). But Potkay then does an about-face and asserts that "whether or not Equiano is from Africa is beside the point because *The Interesting Narrative* is far less significant as a factual account of one man's life than as a rhetorical performance of considerable skill" (604). Responding to Potkay, Srinivas Aravamudan sees that "a bizarre divorce between 'facts' and 'rhetoric' [in Potkay's account] only allows an old-fashioned division of labor between history and literature" (617). The challenge of Equiano's text, I would argue, is to resist a division between rhetoric and facts, the literary and the historical, and instead to see how "the craving for veridicality"

is implicated in "the rhetorical and religious slipperiness of the text" (618). The debate has continued, of course. See, for example, Paul Lovejoy, "Autobiography and Memory: Gustavus Vassa, Alias Olaudah Equiano, the African," *Slavery and Abolition* 27, no. 3 (2006): 317–47; and the exchange on this article between Lovejoy and Carretta, *Slavery and Abolition* 28, no. 1 (2007): 115–25.

6. Olaudah Equiano, *The Interesting Narrative and Other Writings*, ed. Vincent Carretta (Harmondsworth: Penguin, 1995), 32–33. Further references will be to this edition.

7. John Marrant, *A Narrative of the Lord's Wonderful Dealings with John Marrant, a Black* (1785), in *Unchained Voices: An Anthology of Black Authors in the English-speaking World of the 18th Century*, ed. Vincent Carretta (Lexington: University Press of Kentucky, 1996), 120. Further references to Marrant's text are to Carretta's edition.

8. Phillis Wheatley, "On Being Brought From Africa," in *Unchained Voices*, 62.

9. I am using the text reprinted in *Unchained Voices*, 32. Future references to Gronniosaw will be to this edition.

10. Dale B. Martin, *Slavery as Salvation: The Metaphor of Slavery in Pauline Christianity* (New Haven, CT: Yale University Press, 1990).

11. Jean-François Lyotard, "The Grip (*Mainmise*)," in *Political Writings*, trans. Bill Readings and Kevin Paul (Minneapolis: University of Minnesota Press, 1993), 148.

12. Jacques Derrida, *Monolingualism of the Other; Or, the Prosthesis of Origin*, trans. Patrick Mensah (Stanford, CA: Stanford University Press, 1998), 59–60.

13. A. E. Afigbo, *Ropes of Sand (Studies in Igbo History and Culture)* (Oxford: Oxford University Press, 1981), 145.

14. See *Equiano's Travels; The Interesting Narrative of the Life of Olaudah Equiano, or Gustavus Vassa, the African*, ed. Paul Edwards (New York: Praeger, 1967). As early as 1969, Equiano was being anthologized. See *Great Slave Narratives*, ed. Arna Bontemps (Boston: Beacon, 1969).

15. Charles T. Davis and Henry Louis Gates Jr., eds., *The Slave's Narrative* (Oxford: Oxford University Press, 1985); Henry Louis Gates Jr., *The Signifying Monkey: A Theory of African-American Literary Criticism* (Oxford: Oxford University Press, 1988). As early as 1990, Equiano began to be included in the huge teaching anthologies of American literature. See, for example, *The Heath Anthology of American Literature*, ed. Paul Lauter et. al. (Lexington: D. C. Heath, 1990).

16. Abiola Irele, "African Letters: The Making of a Tradition," *Yale Journal of Criticism* 5, no. 1 (1991): 69–100, quote from 70.

17. Carretta, "Olaudah Equiano or Gustavus Vassa?", 96.

18. See Paul Gilroy, *The Black Atlantic: Modernity and Double Consciousness* (Cambridge, MA: Harvard University Press, 1993), 38; Equiano appears again

as an exemplary figure in Gilroy's more recent *Against Race: Imagining Political Culture Beyond the Color Line* (Cambridge, MA: Harvard University Press, 2000), 115–22. Let me also mention here another sophisticated poststructuralist interpretation of Equiano: Ronald A. T. Judy, *(Dis)forming the American Canon: African-Arabic Slave Narratives and the Vernacular* (Minneapolis: University of Minnesota Press, 1993), esp. 85–98. Peter Linebaugh and Marcus Rediker develop this focus on the itinerant lives of sailors more historically, describing the maritime world of the eighteenth century as the matrix for a multiracial, revolutionary underclass: they, too, give Equiano a significant role in their story, calling him an "éminence grise" of the abolitionist movement. See Peter Linebaugh and Marcus Rediker, *The Many-headed Hydra: Sailors, Slaves, Commoners, and the Hidden History of the Revolutionary Atlantic* (Boston: Beacon, 2000), 243.

19. Carretta, *Equiano, the African*, 119. Carretta titles his chapter on Equiano's manumission "Freedom of a Sort."

20. Jean-François Lyotard, "Time Today," in *The Inhuman: Reflections on Time* (Stanford, CA: Stanford University Press, 1991), 68.

21. Adam Potkay, "Olaudah Equiano and the Art of Spiritual Autobiography," *Eighteenth-century Studies* 27, no. 4 (Summer 1994): 677–92.

22. Derrida, *Monolingualism*, 27.

23. In his biography of Equiano, Carretta implies that Equiano's treatment of this topic represents a literary license: "Equiano's reference to uncircumcised Africans is odd, since ethnographers believe that probably all peoples in what is now southern Nigeria practiced circumcision." And later, "Equiano's successful refusal to be scarified by his latest owners is remarkable to the point of incredibility. Like many of the details in his account of his forced journey from 'Eboe' to the sea, if not simply unbelievable, his ability to resist his masters is unrepresentative of the experiences of the vast majority of enslaved Africans destined for the Americas" (26, 27).

24. The rhetorical salience of flogging in the abolitionist record is hardly a point of controversy, but for one subtle interpretation of just how affectively labile such scenarios could be, see Mary A. Favret, "Flogging: The Anti-slavery Movement Writes Pornography," in *Essays and Studies 1998: Romanticism and Gender*, ed. Anne Janowitz (Cambridge: D. S. Brewer, 1998). The display of scars as authentication procedure was more prominent in U.S. abolitionism.

25. Already in 1994, Joan Scott had noted a dialectical turn in this story, "a turn to foundation even by antifoundationalists": "What is most striking these days is the determined embrace, the strident defense, of some reified, transcendent category of explanation by historians who have used insights drawn from the sociology of knowledge, structural linguistics, feminist theory, or cultural anthropology to develop sharp critiques of empiricism." Joan W. Scott, "The Evidence of Experience," in *Questions of Evidence: Proof, Practice, and Persuasion Across the Disciplines*, ed. James Chandler, Arnold I. Davidson, and Harry Harootunian (Chicago: University of Chicago Press, 1994), 370. In his discerning

reply to Scott, Thomas C. Holt acknowledges the force of her "deconstruction of any possible claim for a foundational status for experience" while simultaneously pointing out how that deconstruction imperils the contemporary validation of "diversity" in academic and other institutions: "Absent this claim to the value of a diversity of experience, what authorizes a claim to a diversity of representation?" Holt's conclusion suggests that multiculturalism and deconstruction are bound in an uneasy but necessary alliance: "The contradictions of so-called identity politics . . . are, it seems to me, *necessary* ones; they demand not an abrupt denial of that form of politics but more reflexivity and sensitivity in its exercise." Thomas C. Holt, "Experience and Intellectual Inquiry," in *Questions of Evidence*, 389, 395. Contradictions of this kind, Holt implies, are an invitation to further (deconstructive) reflexivity, not an abandonment of the terms.

26. Cathy Caruth, *Unclaimed Experience: Trauma, Narrative, and History* (Baltimore: Johns Hopkins University Press, 1996), 18. The way in which Caruth's deconstructive-psychoanalytical procedure manages to preserve the terms it calls into question might be viewed as an instance of what it describes. The crucial concept here is Freud's notion of latency, a paradoxical memory concept that subjects the concepts of both event and experience to a structural belatedness. Just as the psychological experience of an event is maintained by its inaccessible location in the unconsciousness of latency, so the terms *event* and *experience*, in Caruth's analysis, are oddly secured and enforced by their very deconstruction: "The space of unconsciousness is, paradoxically, what preserves the event in its literality" (16).

27. I have pursued some of the resonances of Equiano's text for trauma theory in more detail in Jonathan Elmer, "Olaudah Equiano and the Poetics of the Archive," in *Berichten, Erzählen, Beherrschen: Wahrnehmung und Repräsentation in der frühen Kolonialgeschichte Europas* (Klostermann: Frankfurt am Main, 2003), 240–61.

28. Maurice Halbwachs, *On Collective Memory*, ed. and trans. Lewis A. Coser (Chicago: University of Chicago Press, 1992), 51.

CHAPTER THREE

1. Herman Melville, *Billy Budd, Sailor (An Inside Narrative)* (New York: Library of America, 1984), 1423–24. Further references to *Billy Budd* (*BB*) and *Benito Cereno* (*BC*) will be to this edition and will be included in the text.

2. See Morrison, *Playing in the Dark*.

3. Reginald Horsman, *Race and Manifest Destiny: The Origins of American Racial Anglo-Saxonism* (Cambridge, MA: Harvard University Press, 1981), 74. *The Anglo-Saxon*, according to Horsman, purveyed a species of sanitized—because aestheticized and Christianized—racism, keeping its distance, for example, from the notorious racial theories of Robert Knox, even as it popularized

them: "The magazine quoted Knox, yet also referred to his 'erratic and frequently . . . unsteady pen.' Whereas Knox dealt with the cruel realities of power, the *Anglo-Saxon* stressed the Christian mission of the Anglo-Saxon race" (74). We might say that the Pope is to Germanicus, in Melville's passage, as *The Anglo-Saxon* is to Knox's "cruel realities of power," but with this difference: Melville's rhetoric clearly draws attention to the continuity between imperial and missionary forms of racial domination, and *The Anglo-Saxon* strives to mystify that connection. Ralph Waldo Emerson, in his famous essay "Fate," invokes Knox in the style of *The Anglo-Saxon*, referring to his "pungent" theses even as he quarantines them: "Look at the unpalatable conclusions of Knox, in his 'Fragment of Races,'—a rash and unsatisfactory writer, but charged with pungent and unforgettable truths. 'Nature respects race, and not hybrids.' 'Every race has its own *habitat*.' 'Detach a colony from the race, and it deteriorates to the crab.' " Ralph Waldo Emerson, "Fate," in *Essays and Lectures* (New York: Library of America, 1983), 950.

4. H. Bruce Franklin, *The Wake of the Gods: Melville's Mythology* (Stanford, CA: Stanford University Press, 1963), 195.

5. In the "Editor's Introduction" to their study of the genetic text of *Billy Budd*, Harrison Hayford and Merton Sealts Jr. place the interpolation of the "Negro sailor" as having taken place in Stage D, or at the tail end of the second major development of the text. The final development returns to Captain Vere and makes him more central than he had been before. See Harrison Hayford and Merton M. Sealts Jr., *Herman Melville, Billy Budd, Sailor (An Inside Narrative), Reading Text and Genetic Text, Edited from the Manuscript with Introduction and Notes* (Chicago: University of Chicago Press, 1962), 7.

6. Carolyn L. Karcher, *Shadow over the Promised Land: Slavery and Violence in Melville's America* (Baton Rouge: Louisiana State University Press, 1980), 302–3.

7. See Eric J. Sundquist, "Suspense and Tautology in Benito Cereno," *Glyph* 8 (1981): 103–26. Sundquist's formalist argument in this essay is largely incorporated into his better-known, historically more textured treatment of the story in *To Wake the Nations: Race in the Making of American Literature* (Cambridge, MA: Harvard University Press, 1993), 135–82.

8. Herman Melville, *Moby-Dick; or, The Whale* (New York: Penguin, 1992), 88. Further references to *Moby-Dick (MD)* will be to this edition and will be included in the text.

9. Hobbes, *Leviathan*, 109.

10. Wai-Chee Dimock, *Empire for Liberty: Melville and the Poetics of Individualism* (Princeton, NJ: Princeton University Press, 1989), 117.

11. C. L. R. James, *Mariners, Renegades, and Castaways: The Story of Herman Melville and the World We Live In* (Hanover, NH: Dartmouth College/University Press of New England, 2001 [1953]), 54, 13.

12. Cesare Casarino, *Modernity at Sea: Melville, Marx, Conrad in Crisis* (Minneapolis: University of Minnesota Press, 2002), 109.

13. To be precise, James's point here is that Ishmael's structural alienation from the working crew only becomes fully visible on board the *Pequod*. But the transition from land-based, "modern" homosexuality, to an oceangoing, all-male laboring collective free from such problems animates the turn of his thinking here.

14. Merrell R. Davis and William H. Gilman, eds., *The Letters of Herman Melville* (New Haven, CT: Yale University Press, 1960), 124–25.

15. Dickinson, "The Analogy Between Natural Persons and International Persons in the Law of Nations," 564.

16. Dickinson considers this influence a largely baleful one, but Carl Schmitt, writing some thirty-five years later, disagrees: "A decisive step toward this great, new institution called 'state' and the new interstate international law was taken in that these new, contiguous, and contained power complexes were represented as persons. This is how they obtained the quality that made the analogy between war and a duel meaningful. These states were conceived of as *magni homines*. In human fantasy, they actually were sovereign persons, because they were the representative sovereigns of human persons, of the agents of old and newly crowned heads, of kings and princes not precisely specified. These kings and princes now could be 'great men,' because they had become absolute. They separated themselves from church, feudal, estate, and all other medieval ties, thereby entering into ties of a new spatial order" (Nomos, 143–44). Hobbes had underscored, as Schmitt does here, the indispensable role of personification, or "personation," in the functioning of the state: "A multitude of men are made *one* person, when they are by one man, or one person, represented so that it be done by the consent of every one of that multitude in particular. For it is the *unity* of the representer, not the *unity* of the represented, that maketh the person one. And it is the representer that beareth the person, and but one person, and *unity* cannot otherwise be understood in multitude" (104). Person here is an *achievement* of representation: it is what secures the possibility of treating with all upon an equal basis. But such unity is also of course a *presupposition* of the work of representation, inasmuch as the consent of the individual, of all individuals, must be assumed to be unproblematically attached to "every one of that multitude." There is, in other words, a pre-representational "one" before the multitude, and there is also a one after that multitude—namely the "person" of the sovereign (which need not, of course, be a singular human being, but can easily be a group—a "person" of absolute authority). This is a familiar aporia brought forward by the "methodological individualism" of social contract theory. See, for one, Louis Dumont, *Essays on Individualism: Modern Ideology in Anthropological Perspective* (Chicago: University of Chicago Press, 1986), Chap. 2. My main point is that Melville's tendency to embed questions of state power in analyses of the dynamics of selfhood and personification is consistent with the development of one influential mode of political imagination in the West.

17. Royall Tyler, *The Algerine Captive; Or, the Life and Adventures of Doctor Updike Underhill*, ed. Caleb Crain (New York: Modern Library, 2002), 119.

18. Amasa Delano, *A Narrative of Voyages and Travels in the Northern and Southern Hemispheres: Comprising Three Voyages Round the World; Together with a Voyage of Survey and Discovery, in the Pacific Ocean and Oriental Islands* [1817] (New York: Praeger, 1970). Both Babo and Atufal are mentioned by name in Delano's account, and named as ringleaders (335, 337), though nothing is anywhere said about Atufal's royal origins. And it is a slave named Mure, Babo's son, who performs "the office of an officious servant, with all the appearance of the humble slave" (338). In Melville's version of the deposition, Atufal's royalty is again asserted, but doubtfully, and still within the context of the investment of the white world in this idea: "A powerful negro named Atufal, who, being supposed to have been a chief in Africa, his owners set great store by him" (740).

19. Paul Downes, "Melville's *Benito Cereno* and the Politics of Humanitarian Intervention," *South Atlantic Quarterly* 103, nos. 2–3 (Spring–Summer 2004): 465–88, quote from 472.

20. Another strong reading of the complex thematics of Catholicism can be found in Jenny Franchot, *Roads to Rome: The Antebellum Protestant Encounter with Catholicism* (Berkeley and Los Angeles: University of California Press, 1994), 172–81.

21. William Robertson, *The History of the Reign of the Emperor Charles the Fifth, with An Account of the Emperor's Life After His Abdication by William H. Prescott* [1856], 3 vols. (Philadelphia: J. B. Lippincott, 1871). Prescott's "Account" comes at the end of Vol. 3, pp. 325–510. The explosion of interest in Charles V was in part ignited by William Stirling's tracking down the Gonzalez MS (after he had already finished his articles for *Fraser's*, and before releasing his book). Prescott mentions (327–30) a number of French scholars—the MS was housed in Paris—working also during this same short span of years: M. Mignet's *Charles-Quint; son Abdication, son Séjour, et sa Mort au Monastère de Yuste* appeared in 1854, for example. In a contemporary account, M. J. Rodríguez-Salgado has noted that "interest in the emperor's life in the monastery at Yuste has not been lacking" over the past century, but says of the "common assumption" in these accounts that Charles "continued to influence . . . his son's policies" that it was "not the case." See M. J. Rodríguez-Salgado, *The Changing Face of Empire: Charles V, Philip II and Habsburg Authority, 1551–1559* (Cambridge: Cambridge University Press, 1988), 132.

22. I am quoting from the Harper and Brothers's edition of 1833. See William Robertson, *The History of the Reign of the Emperor Charles V., with a View of the Progress of Society in Europe; from the Subversion of the Roman Empire, to the Beginning of the Sixteenth Century, Complete in One Volume* (New York: Harper and Brothers, 1833), v.

23. Mark Salber Philips, *Society and Sentiment: Genres of Historical Writing in Britain, 1740–1820* (Princeton, NJ: Princeton University Press, 2000), 90.

24. Carl Schmitt, *Ex Captivitate Salus: Erfahrungen der Zeit, 1945–47* (Cologne: Greven, 1950), 75. The German reads: "Ich bin der letzte, bewusste Vertreter des *jus publicum Europeaum* . . . und erfahre sein Ende so, wie Benito Cereno die Fahrt des Piratenschiffs erfuhr."

25. Thomas O. Beebee, "Carl Schmitt's Myth of Benito Cereno," *seminar* 42, no. 2 (May 2006): 114–33. Beebee quotes Schmitt's letter—"Ich denke an Benito Cereno als *Situations*-Symbol"—on p. 117.

26. Beebee points out just how indeterminate such an impersonation is: "Once Schmitt assumes the mask of Benito Cereno, it becomes impossible to ground or establish the sincerity of any of his statements, since each can later be claimed to have been a coerced performance. In publishing the *Waschzettel*, is Schmitt disclaiming some of what he wrote in *Leviathan*—for example, he had identified the Leviathan as 'jüdisches Kampfsymbool'—because he was under the control of the Nazis at the time? Or is he winking at the reader and giving him mysterious signs, the way the Spanish sailors do to Amasa Delano, in order to indicate that his warning against reading *Leviathan* is not to be taken seriously, because it is made in conformity with the American occupation and the postwar regime?" (121). Whatever expedient reasons Schmitt may have had, the act bespeaks a nearly febrile identification with Melville, as if in signing as Cereno about a book called *Leviathan* Schmitt had finally become Melville's confidence man.

27. Schmitt develops some of these contrasts in greater speculative depth in the three appendixes included in the English translation of *The* Nomos *of the Earth*. See Pt. 5, 323–55.

28. For another perspective on Schmitt's thinking about land and sea, see Christopher L. Connery, "Ideologies of Land and Sea: Alfred Thayer Mahan, Carl Schmitt, and the Shaping of Global Myth Elements," *boundary 2* 28, no. 2 (2001): 173–201.

29. My emphasis. Beebee gives the German: "Das Meer als Element ist nur durch Melville fassbar zu machen. Ein sehr aktuelles Thema" (117).

30. Jon Beasly-Murray, "The Common Enemy: Tyrants and Pirates," *South Atlantic Quarterly* 104, no. 2 (Spring 2005): 218–25, quote from 220.

31. See Jay Fliegelman's brilliant reading of the play of agency and passivity in the Declaration, *Declaring Independence: Jefferson, Natural Language, and the Culture of Performance* (Stanford, CA: Stanford University Press, 1993).

32. Thomas Jefferson, *Writings* (New York: Library of America, 1984), 22.

33. Paul Downes has offered the best assessment of how Delano's humanitarianism in *Benito Cereno* exemplifies a contemporary blindness about "the relationship between sovereignty and *right*," about how the form of the modern democratic citizen maintains—and represses—a "founding relationship to sovereign violence and thus to the sovereign's constitutive other (the rightless human being)" (484).

34. Herman Melville, *White-Jacket; or, The World in a Man-of-War* (New York: Signet, 1979), 16.

35. Paul Gilroy, *The Black Atlantic: Modernity and Double Consciousness* (Cambridge, MA: Harvard University Press, 1993).

36. Ian Baucom, *Specters of the Atlantic: Slavery, Finance Capital, and the Philosophy of History* (Durham, NC: Duke University Press, 2005).

37. See Linebaugh and Rediker, *The Many-headed Hydra*; Rediker, *Between the Devil and the Deep Blue Sea: Merchant Seamen, Pirates, and the Anglo-American Maritime World, 1700–1750* (Cambridge: Cambridge University Press, 1989); and Rediker, *Villains of All Nations: Atlantic Pirates in the Golden Age* (Boston: Beacon, 2005).

38. See Eve Kosofsky Sedgwick, *Epistemology of the Closet* (Berkeley and Los Angeles: University of California Press, 1990), Chap. 2.

39. A cogent critique of how Agamben sutures Schmitt's theories of sovereignty to Foucault's analysis of biopower can be found in Jacques Rancière, "Who Is the Subject of the Rights of Man?" *South Atlantic Quarterly* 103, nos. 2–3 (Spring–Summer 2004): 297–310.

40. Barbara Johnson's great investigation into the mutual deconstruction of cognition and performance in *Billy Budd* can be understood to be concerned with the "figure of an action": the "deadly space" traced out by Melville marks "that which, within cognition, functions as an act; [and] that which, within action, prevents us from ever knowing whether what we hit coincides with what we understand." See Johnson, "Melville's Fist: The Execution of *Billy Budd*," in *The Critical Difference: Essays in the Contemporary Rhetoric of Reading* (Baltimore: Johns Hopkins University Press, 1980), 107.

41. See Reginald Horsman, "The Paradox of Dartmoor Prison," *American Heritage* 26 (February 1975): 12–17, 85; and W. Jeffrey Bolster, *Black Jacks: African American Seamen in the Age of Sail* (Cambridge, MA: Harvard University Press, 1998), Chap. 4.

42. Nathaniel Hawthorne, ed., "Papers of an Old Dartmoor Prisoner," *U.S. and Democratic Review* (March 1846), 210–11. The series ran from January to September 1846, with the following pages: January: 31–39 (where it is incorrectly titled "Papers of an Old Dartmouth Prisoner"); February: 97–111; March: 200–212; May: 360–68; June: 467–65; August: 141–48; September: 209–17).

CHAPTER FOUR

1. See Dimock, *Empire For Liberty*, Chap. 4.

2. Thomas Jefferson, *Notes on the State of Virginia* [1954], ed. William Peden (Chapel Hill: University of North Carolina Press, 1982), 63. All subsequent references are to this edition.

3. Lewis K. Gannett lists "Chief Logan the eloquent" along with Squanto, Pocahontas, Crazy Horse, and "The Last of the Mohicans" in his brief preface to Thoedora Kroeber, *Ishi in Two Worlds: A Biography of the Last Wild Indian in*

North America (Berkeley and Los Angeles: University of California Press, 1961). For other informative accounts of Logan's speech, and especially its afterlife, see Edwin W. Seeber, "Critical Views of Logan's Speech," *Journal of American Folklore* 60 (April 1947): 130–46; Edward G. Gray, "The Making of Logan, the Mingo Orator," in *The Language Encounter in the Americas, 1492–1800*, ed. Edward G. Gray and Norman Fiering (New York: Berghahn, 2000); Anthony F. C. Wallace, *Jefferson and the Indians: The Tragic Fate of the First Americans* (Cambridge, MA: Harvard University Press, 1999), 1–20; and David Murray, *Forked Tongues: Speech, Writing, and Representation in North American Indian Texts* (Bloomington: Indiana University Press, 1991). The best and most detailed recent treatment of Logan can be found in Gordon M. Sayre, *The Indian Chief as Tragic Hero: Native Resistance and the Literatures of America, from Moctezuma to Tecumseh* (Chapel Hill: University of North Carolina Press, 2005), Chap. 5.

4. Lynn Festa has some words on this distinction that are helpful: "Romance *recognizes* characters; sentimentality *creates* recognition between groups that are not already the same. Thus although the sentimental novel and the romance share a loose peripatetic structure depicting serial encounters with quasi-allegorical figures, the sentimental community is elastic in a way that romance does not permit: its similitude is not grounded in the preexisting likeness of its members (the community of aristocrats featured in romance), but in their shared relation to a common object (a slave, a prostitute, a child) *unlike* themselves." See Lynn Festa, *Sentimental Figures of Empire in Eighteenth-century Britain and France* (Baltimore: Johns Hopkins University Press, 2006), 55. Behn's *Oroonoko*, by this account, offers a titular hero that is neither enough alike nor enough unlike to be susceptible to either strategy: Surinam can no longer be a site for romance, nor is it yet the scene for a working sentimental operation. Parham is proto-sentimental—it *creates* a group where none had been—but Behn's text clearly depicts Parham's failure to consolidate the rest of the English into an "elastic" community.

5. Jacques Derrida, "Archive Fever," trans. Eric Prenowitz, *diacritics* 25, no. 2 (1995): 9–63, quote from 10.

6. Charles A. Miller, *Jefferson and Nature: An Interpretation* (Baltimore: Johns Hopkins University Press, 1988), 41.

7. For a history of the transition from "incorporation" to "removal" in early national America, see Bernard W. Sheehan, *Seeds of Extinction: Jeffersonian Philanthropy and the American Indian* (New York: Norton, 1974), especially Chap. 5.

8. See Lacan's comments on this genealogy in Jacques Lacan, *The Four Fundamental Concepts of Psychoanalysis*, trans. Alan Sheridan (New York: Norton, 1978), 29–41.

9. Jefferson's appropriative relation to this scene is even more in evidence in the other sublime landscape in *Notes*, the Natural Bridge, which he purchased in 1774, between his original drafting of the passage on it in *Notes* and the

volume's publication: the Natural Bridge thus gets archived twice over (Miller 105). The scene at Harper's Ferry is also still held to emblematize some essential relation between the American nation and the land, as its choice as backdrop for President Clinton's appearance on Earth Day 1998 made clear. The translation of geological into political history is suggested by the fact that Jefferson uses "avulsion" rather than his more usual "convulsion" to describe the rocks' "disrupture . . . from their beds" (19). The *OED* defines avulsion as the "action of pulling off, plucking out, or tearing away; forcible separation" (Compact *OED*, 1971), and cites Jefferson himself in 1777 referring to the "condition of everlasting avulsion from Great Britain." "Avulsion" seems available to Jefferson as a term for a kind of historical parthenogenesis.

10. I refer to the key concept of Peter S. Onuf's important book *Jefferson's Empire: The Language of American Nationhood* (Charlottesville: University of Virginia Press, 2000). In his second chapter, Onuf offers a compelling account of Jefferson's political imagination and its territorial foundations, commenting that "*Notes on the State of Virginia* constituted both a promotional tract, celebrating the state's and the nation's prospects for economic development, and Jefferson's blueprint for completing the republican Revolution in his beloved Commonwealth" (67–68).

11. A similar moment in which culture must come to supplement nature concerns women's "natural" equality with men. Referring to native women's role as laboring drudges in Indian societies, Jefferson avows that "it is civilization alone which replaces women in the enjoyment of their natural equality" (60).

12. Writing to his Genevan correspondent François d'Ivernois in 1795, Jefferson touted the advantages of American territorial expanse as productive of the kind of self-abstraction from particular interests that leads to political peace: "The smaller the societies," by contrast, "the more violent and more convulsive their schisms" (quoted in Onuf 54). We see here again how convulsions become manageable once one has taken up the proper abstracted distance, here the distance created naturally by the expanse of the republican empire.

13. Ed White, *The Backcountry and the City: Colonization and Conflict in Early America* (Minneapolis: University of Minnesota Press, 2005), 113.

14. Homi K. Bhabha, *The Location of Culture* (London: Routledge, 1994), 245.

15. *Democratic Review* 14 (1844), cited in Lucy Maddox, *Removals: Nineteenth-century American Literature and the Politics of Indian Affairs* (Oxford: Oxford University Press, 1991), 30–31.

16. Lewis Henry Morgan, *League of the Iroquois* [1851] (Secaucus, NJ: Carol, 1996), 143. See also Roy Harvey Pearce, *Savagism and Civilization: A Study of the Indian and the American Mind* [1953] (Berkeley and Los Angeles: University of California Press, 1988), Chap. 4.

17. The words are William Peden's, editor of the modern edition of Jefferson's text. See Jefferson, *Notes*, 281n8.

18. It is suggestive that in "Traits of Indian Character," a kind of digest of received ideas on Indian character and history circa 1820, Washington Irving invokes this Jeffersonian scene in order to codify Native American mourning as a "sublime and holy feeling": "The Indians are remarkable for the reverence which they entertain for the sepulchres of their kindred. Tribes that have passed generations exiled from the abodes of their ancestors, when by chance they have been traveling in the vicinity, have been known to turn aside from the highway, and, guided by some wonderfully accurate tradition, have crossed the country for miles to some tumulus, buried perhaps in woods, where the bones of their tribe were anciently deposited; and there have passed hours in silent meditation." See Washington Irving, *History, Tales, and Sketches* (New York: Library of America, 1983), 1005–6. Jefferson's doubtful "expressions of sorrow" are here simplified to a stoical "silent meditation": mourner and mourned are equally silent as the tomb, which makes sense given that the present-day mourners are "buried . . . in woods" as effectively as their forebears are in the "tumulus."

19. Indeed, Anthony F. C. Wallace says that the barrow is the same in both episodes: "A little band of mourners visited a burial mound near Charlottesville around 1750 by Jefferson's reckoning. This was most likely a family of Tutelos visiting the grave of their ancestors one last time before leaving Virginia forever. Jefferson would later excavate the mound in an early exercise in archaeological research" (28).

20. Dumas Malone, *Jefferson the Virginian* (Boston: Little, Brown, 1948), 392. For a particularly rich study of links between Scotland and America in the colonial and early national periods, see Susan Manning, *Fragments of Union: Making Connections in Scottish and American Writing* (Houndmills: Palgrave, 2002), especially Chap. 4, which explores the connections between Ossian and Jefferson's Logan.

21. Katie Trumpener, *Bardic Nationalism: The Romantic Novel and the British Empire* (Princeton, NJ: Princeton University Press, 1997).

22. Anthony F. C. Wallace presents an excellent historical contextualization of Lord Dunmore's War and Logan's place in it, drawing attention both to Jefferson's land interests in the region, and to Logan's thoroughly typical placement within a cycle of frontier violence that moves from (white) provocation, to (Indian) retaliation, (state-sponsored) pacification—in this case, Lord Dunmore's forces—and concluding in (Indian) land cession. Wallace calls the goals and effect of this cycle "ethnic cleansing" (10; he describes the four-part cycle on pp. 19–20). Gordon Sayre provides a succinct summary of some of the conflicting biographical evidence and speculation on Logan. We know he was the son of Shickellamy, a noted Oneida negotiator and friend—or perhaps business associate would put it more accurately—of James Logan, his Quaker counterpart in Pennsylvania, the man after whom Logan was named. Whether Logan's Indian name was Tah-ga-jute, Soyechtowa, or Tachnechdorus, and whether the Logan of the speech was Shickellamy's eldest or younger son is not clear (see Sayre 183–84).

23. It appears that, through the agency of James Madison, Logan's speech was first published in the *Pennsylvania Journal* on February 1, 1775, with copies or alternate versions quickly following in the *New York Gazette* and *Virginia Gazette*. For details about Madison's role, as well as a copy of the version of Logan's speech that he sent in a letter as early as January 20, 1775, see Irving Brant, *James Madison, The Virginia Revolutionist* (Indianapolis: Bobbs-Merrill, 1941), 281–91. As Brant points out, Jefferson's version in *Notes* is a near-verbatim copy of Madison's.

24. Peden comments (298) that the speech maintained this special pedagogical function well into the nineteenth century, via McGuffey's *Readers* and Irving's *Sketch-Book*, whose "Traits of Indian Character" has an epigraph from the speech. Roy Harvey Pearce (79) says the speech was a test piece in McGuffey's Fourth and Fifth *Readers*.

25. Richard White, *The Middle Ground: Indians, Empires, and Republics in the Great Lakes Region, 1650–1815* (Cambridge, MA: Harvard University Press, 1991), 358. For an overview of hybridization from an ethnohistorical perspective, see Colin G. Calloway, *New Worlds for All: Indians, Europeans, and the Remaking of Early America* (Baltimore: Johns Hopkins University Press, 1997).

26. It is perhaps worth remarking that even in this transaction there remains some doubt about the suture between archives. Although proficient in English, Logan chose to have Gibson serve as translator. Jefferson has difficulty tracking the material identity of this speech, however: Logan "gave" the speech to Gibson, who then "carried" it to Dunmore (228). Both terms could refer either to oral or written communications, but later Jefferson suggests a material object when he writes that Gibson claims to have "received" the speech "from Logan's hand" (252).

27. There is of course a psychoanalytic theorization of identification that, like White's here, resists an overly psychologizing discourse. Identification, as a glance at Freud's *Group Psychology and the Analysis of the Ego* will make clear, is a concept that necessarily concerns itself with the conjunction of *psyche* and *socius*. Identification can of course also be aggressive in its essence. Lacan's extension of Freud's ideas about identification led him, as is well known, to distinguish imaginary and symbolic identification. We might suggest that the mimetic antagonism by which a white settler "identifies" with his Indian enemy conforms more or less to imaginary identification, while the level at which Jefferson "identifies" with Logan "as an American man" pertains to the level of symbolic identification. I briefly explore such an idea in Jonathan Elmer, "Inclusion and Exclusion of the Indian in the Early American Archive," *Soziale Systeme* 8, no. 1 (2002): 54–68.

28. Paul Downes, *Democracy, Revolution, and Monarchism in Early American Literature* (Cambridge: Cambridge University Press, 2002), 48. For more on "Tammany," see also Philip J. Deloria, *Playing Indian* (New Haven, CT: Yale University Press, 1998), Chap. 1.

29. Frances Ferguson, *Solitude and the Sublime: Romanticism and the Aesthetics of Individuation* (New York: Routledge, 1992), 32.

30. Alain Badiou, *Being and Event*, trans. Oliver Feltham (New York: Continuum, 2005), 93, 95.

31. Locke, *Second Treatise of Government*, 29.

CHAPTER FIVE

1. Anne Anlin Cheng, *The Melancholy of Race: Psychoanalysis, Assimilation, and Hidden Grief* (Oxford: Oxford University Press, 2000), 12, 11, 10.

2. Morton Paley, "The Last Man: Apocalypse Without Millenium," in *The Other Mary Shelley: Beyond* Frankenstein, ed. Audrey A. Fisch, Anne K. Mellor, and Esther H. Schor (New York: Oxford University Press, 1993), 107–8. See Fiona Stafford's monograph *The Last of the Race: The Growth of a Myth from Milton to Darwin* (Oxford: Oxford University Press, 1994) for a good sense of the range and reach of this topos in English literary history.

3. Barbara Johnson, "The Last Man," in *The Other Mary Shelley* (258).

4. Numerous critics have explored the symbolic place of the Indian in American culture in terms of haunting, uncanny returns, and other gothic motifs. See Susan Scheckel, *The Insistence of the Indian: Race and Nationalism in Nineteenth-century American Culture* (Princeton, NJ: Princeton University Press, 1998); Teresa A. Goddu, *Gothic America: Narrative, History, and Nation* (New York: Columbia University Press, 1997); Leslie A. Fiedler, *The Return of the Vanishing American* (New York: Stein and Day, 1968); Renée L. Bergland, *The National Uncanny: Indian Ghosts and American Subjects* (Hanover, NH: University Press of New England, 2000); Werner Sollors, *Beyond Ethnicity: Consent and Descent in American Culture* (New York: Oxford University Press, 1986).

5. Cited in Jill Lepore, *The Name of War: King Philip's War and the Origins of American Identity* (New York: Vintage, 1999), 221.

6. Ian Baucom, *Specters of the Atlantic: Finance Capital, Slavery, and the Philosophy of History* (Durham, NC: Duke University Press, 2005).

7. Cited in Mary Shelley, *The Last Man*, ed. Anne McWhir (Peterborough, ON: Broadview, 1996), xiv. Further references to the novel will be included in the main body of the text.

8. While Shelley's novel is not racialized in the sense that my American examples are, it is fundamentally structured by the civilized/savage dyad on which American racialization is also erected, suggesting that this antinomy is in fact the invariant feature of the trope of the last. Toward the end of the novel, Lionel Verney, the last living man on earth, looks in a mirror and sees a "wild-looking, unkempt, half-naked savage" (354). As Alan Richardson has remarked, Lionel's situation here is less a regression to savagery than a subsumption of it: "Lionel will preserve civilization (his accessories include a Homer and a Shakespeare once he resumes a more kempt outfit) yet his own survival depends on

skills learned as a Wordsworthian 'savage' in his 'uncouth' pre-Adrian years. The polarities of savage and civilized are finally reconciled, but only because there is in the end a single subject to fill both positions." See Alan Richardson, "*The Last Man* and the Plague of Empire," at http://www.rc.umd.edu/villa/vc97/richardson.html.

9. For a strong analysis of Shelley's political skepticism, see Lee Sterrenburg, "*The Last Man*: Anatomy of Failed Revolutions," *Nineteenth-century Fiction* 33 (1978): 324–47.

10. Gilles Deleuze and Félix Guattari, *Anti-Oedipus, Capitalism, and Schizophrenia*, trans. Robert Hurley, Mark Seem, and Helen R. Lane (Minneapolis: University of Minnesota Press, 1983), 265.

11. See David Kazanjian, *The Colonizing Trick: National Culture and Imperial Citizenship in Early America* (Minneapolis: University of Minnesota Press, 2003), Chap. 3; Andy Doolen, *Fugitive Empire: Locating Early American Imperialism* (Minneapolis: University of Minnesota Press, 2005), chaps. 2 and 3; Sean X. Goudie, *Creole America: The West Indies and the Formation of Literature and Culture in the New Republic* (Philadelphia: University of Pennsylvania Press, 2006), Chap. 5; Jared Gardner, "Alien Nation: Edgar Huntly's Savage Awakening," *American Literature* 66, no. 3 (September 1994): 429–61; Luke Gibbons, "Ireland, America, and Gothic Memory: Transatlantic Terror in the Early Republic," *boundary 2* 31, no. 1 (2004): 25–47; Bryan Waterman, "The Bavarian Illuminati, the Early American Novel, and Histories of the Public Sphere," *William and Mary Quarterly* 62, no. 1 (January 2005): 9–30; Philip Gould, *Barbaric Traffic: Commerce and Antislavery in the 18th Century Atlantic World* (Cambridge, MA: Harvard University Press, 2003), Chap. 5.

12. Downes, *Democracy, Revolution, and Monarchism*. In an article on *Edgar Huntly* published prior to his book, Downes pursues arguments quite close to my own. Attentive to the lingering structures of what he calls a "monarchic mentality," Downes suggests that Huntly explores the "persistence of a feudal or monarchic logic within a post-feudal social order." Interested, as I am, in the "continuities between a sentimental radicalism and an autocratic conservatism," Downes also points to Brown's having absorbed the "Godwinian critique that saw the arbitrary tyranny of monarchy repeated in the bureaucratic violence of a legal state," the critique whose fictional embodiment and influence on Brown I explore here in more detail than Downes was able to do in his excellent article. See Paul Downes, "Sleep-walking out of the Revolution: Brown's *Edgar Huntly*," *Eighteenth-century Studies* 29, no. 4 (1996): 413–31, quotes from 420, 414, 417.

13. Sigmund Freud, *Totem and Taboo: Some Points of Agreement Between the Mental Lives of Savages and Neurotics*, trans. James Strachey (New York: Norton, 1950), 143.

14. F. R. Ankersmit, *Political Representation* (Stanford, CA: Stanford University Press, 2002), 60–90; Philippe Lacoue-Labarthe and Jean-Luc Nancy, "La

Panique Politique," trans. Céline Surprenant, in Lacoue-Labarthe and Nancy, *Retreating the Political*, ed. Simon Sparks (London: Routledge, 1997), 11.

15. The importance of Freud's commitment to such a psycho-politics of "brutal egoism" has been analyzed in painstaking detail by Phillipe Lacoue-Labarthe and Jean-Luc Nancy, and then, in their wake, Mikkel Borch-Jacobsen. See Lacoue-Labarthe and Nancy, "Panique," as well as "The Unconscious Is Destructured like an Affect," trans. Brian Holmes, *Stanford Literature Review* 6 (Fall 1989): 191–208. In *The Freudian Subject*, an assessment of Freud's political theses in *Group Psychology and the Analysis of the Ego* (1922), Borch-Jacobsen contends that the point of convergence between Freud's psychological and sociohistorical writings is the figure of Narcissus. It was in order to save this "completely egoistic" subject as the irreducible element of his system that Freud was led, despite his personal politics and despite a number of alternative conceptions he had himself opened to view, to concoct his own brand of authoritarian doctrine by insisting that the prehistorical counterpart to the individual narcissus must have been a "primal" father—the original despot. See Mikkel Borch-Jacobsen, *The Freudian Subject*, trans. Catherine Porter (Stanford, CA: Stanford University Press, 1988). Lacoue-Labarthe and Nancy had written that "the Narcissus is the ultimate object of the *theory*, it offers the theory its absolute figure as a visible form, and so assures the identity of psychoanalysis" ("Unconscious" 201), and Borch-Jacobsen draws out the consequence: "The Leader . . . is a subject. Strictly speaking, he is even *the* subject. . . . Political unity is equivalent here . . . to the unity of a subject. . . . There would be no body politic if there were no individual at the outset; and if this is so, it is because the body politic is defined as a supra-individual" (145). In reading Freud on politics, on the evolution of civilization, on the murder of the primal father, we are once again witnessing the "complicity between the political form and the Subject-form" (Borch-Jacobsen 145).

16. Sigmund Freud, *Moses and Monotheism* [1939], trans. Katherine Jones (New York: Vintage, 1967), 63.

17. Quoted in Pamela Clemit, *The Godwinian Novel: The Rational Fictions of Godwin, Brockden Brown, Mary Shelley* (Oxford: Oxford University Press, 1993), 107.

18. William Godwin, *An Enquiry Concerning Political Justice*, Vol. 3 of *The Political and Philosophical Writings of William Godwin*, ed. Mark Philp (London: William Pickering, 1993), 142.

19. Charles Brockden Brown, *Edgar Huntly; Or, Memoirs of a Sleep-Walker*, ed. Norman S. Grabo (New York: Penguin, 1988), 3.

20. Maurice Hindle describes these events in the introduction to the Penguin edition. See William Godwin, *Things as They Are; or the Adventures of Caleb Williams*, ed. Maurice Hindle (Harmondsworth: Penguin, 1987), xi, xxxviii. Further references to the novel, however, will be to William Godwin, *Caleb Williams; or, Things as They Are*, ed. George Sherburn (New York: Holt, Rinehart, and Winston, 1960). An informed and discerning treatment of legal issues

in the novel is Nicholas Williams, " 'The Subject of Detection': Legal Rhetoric and Subjectivity in *Caleb Williams*," *Eighteenth-century Fiction* 9, no. 1 (July 1997): 475–92.

21. Foucault, "*Society Must Be Defended*," 240–41.

22. Antony's speech over the murdered body of Caesar comes in William Shakespeare, *Julius Caesar*, and concludes with the following words:

> And Caesar's spirit, ranging for revenge,
> With Ate by his side, come hot from hell,
> Shall in these confines, with a monarch's voice,
> Cry "Havoc!" and let slip the dogs of war,
> That this foul deed shall smell above the earth
> With carrion men, groaning for burial. (III.i.369–75)

23. Gilles Deleuze and Félix Guattari argue that the state emerges from the "horizon of despotism," as its complement or twin, in just the way that Brown ties Euphemia's liberality to Arthur's tyranny. In ideological terms, Euphemia's advent fundamentally *requires* Clithero's inexpiable guilt in having killed her despotic twin. Thus do Clithero's gratitude to his patron and his melancholic guilt at Wiatte's death unite in the infinitization of his debt: "In a word, money—the circulation of money—*is the means for rendering the debt infinite.* And that is what is concealed in the two acts of the State: the residence or territoriality of the State inaugurates the great movement of deterritorialization that subordinates all the primitive filiations to the despotic machine (the agrarian problem); the abolition of debts and their accountable transformation initiates the duty of an interminable service to the State that subordinates all the primitive alliances to itself (the problem of debts). The infinite creditor and infinite credit have replaced the blocks of mobile and finite debts. There is always a monotheism on the horizon of despotism: the debt becomes a *debt of existence* of the subjects themselves. A time will come when the creditor has not yet lent while the debtor never quits repaying" (197).

24. Sydney J. Krause, "Penn's Elm and *Edgar Huntly*: Dark 'Instruction to the Heart,' " *American Literature* 66, no. 3 (September 1994): 463–84.

25. Gardner, "Alien Nation."

26. Eric Slauter, "Being Alone in the Age of the Social Contract," *William and Mary Quarterly* 62, no. 1 (January 2005): 31–66, quote from 64–65.

27. See Agamben, *Homo Sacer*, esp. 91–103; and Downes, *Democracy, Revolution, and Monarchism*, Chap. 1.

28. See Dillon, *The Gender of Freedom*, 161–83. Dillon's searching argument has a number of points of contact with my own. Like those critics listed in the next note, Dillon focuses on the foundational importance of embodiment in the production of the novel's meaning. Huntly's swerve away from marriage, for Dillon, as well as his profoundly somatic relation to Clithero, are ultimately

dictated by his desire to "produce himself as embodied" (167), and more specifically, as an embodied republican American man. But "killing Indians thus does not seem to prove Huntly's credentials as a white civilized American; rather, it seems to steep him in the gore of his own body and that of those around him, dissolving boundaries between white and Irish, and white and Indian bodies in the flow of bodily fluids across and between them" (178). Dillon also links the identificatory energies in the novel to what I analyze as the peculiarly deterritorialized soil status of Brown's Norwalk: "American land never had the same role in producing republican identity as did British land" (174).

29. Chad Luck has written about how Edgar's time in the pit amounts to a recapitulation of some classics of sensation theory in eighteen-century philosophy: Edgar exploring his senses in the pitch blackness of the pit is a version of Condillac's "statue" in *Traité de la Sensation*, for example. Timothy Sweet may be overly particular in arguing that Brown is "taking aim at [Benjamin] Rush," specifically in having Edgar lay waste to the rationale of frontier stages theory, but his general point seems right to me. See Chad Luck, "Re-walking the Purchase: *Edgar Huntly*, Embodiment, and Property on the Frontier," in *Early American Literature* (forthcoming); and Timothy Sweet, *American Georgics: Economy and Environment in Early American Literature* (Philadelphia: University of Pennsylvania Press, 2002), 117.

30. Walter J. Ong, *Ramus, Method, and the Decay of Dialogue: From the Art of Discourse to the Art of Reason* (Cambridge, MA: Harvard University Press, 1958).

31. The connection between memory and spatialization is the subject of Frances A. Yates's classic account *The Art of Memory* (Chicago: University of Chicago Press, 2001). A. R. Luria's *The Mind of a Mnemonist* offers some remarkable anecdotes of S's "method" of remembering a list of items by "seeing" them as he walked in his mind through the city. See A. R. Luria, *The Mind of a Mnemonist: A Little Book about a Vast Memory* (Cambridge, MA: Harvard University Press, 2006).

32. Jacques Derrida, "Freud and the Scene of Writing," in *Writing and Difference*, trans. Alan Bass (Chicago: University of Chicago Press, 1978), 214.

33. John Neal, *American Writers: A Series of Papers Contributed to Blackwood's Magazine (1824–25)*, ed. Fred Lewis Pattee (Durham, NC: Duke University Press, 1937), 57, 61.

34. Harold C. Martin, "The Colloquial Tradition in the Novel: John Neal," *The New England Quarterly* 32, no. 4 (1959): 455–75, quote from 458. The full quote is worth reproducing: "What holds this farrago together is a fermented syrup of romanticism. If ever man was intoxicated by the spirit of a literary movement, Neal is the one. The arrogance, the sentimentality, the near-paranoia, the humanitarianism; the exuberance and the melancholy; the rage against order and the frenzy in chaos—all the poses of the romantic are played to the hilt" (458).

35. According to Baucom, Scott figured out how to convert romantic melancholy back into a mourning that honors the past, experiments in sympathetic

identification with history's losers, *and then moves on*. In Scott's novels "what might appear at first glance as an invitation to melancholy, or even to a politics of resentment or revenge . . . converts itself . . . into the exact opposite. To revise an earlier formula then: where melancholy classically encrypts what mourning proves willing to exchange, here it is melancholy (or at least the experiment of melancholy) that generates exchange. . . . Refashioned as a romance convention, melancholy emerges not as liberalism's negation but as liberalism's transitory precondition" (280–81). The primary device Scott uses to effect this is the sympathetic observer of other's sorrows (e.g., Edward Waverly) with whose *sympathy* the reader is made to sympathize, rather than with the inassimilable *fate* of the characters, groups, or clans with whom Waverly himself sympathizes.

36. Dana D. Nelson, *National Manhood: Capitalist Citizenship and the Imagined Fraternity of White Men* (Durham, NC: Duke University Press, 1998), 90.

37. John Neal, *Our Country: An Address Delivered Before the Alumni of Waterville College, July 29, 1830* (Portland: S. Colman, 1830), 34.

38. John Neal, *Logan, The Mingo Chief: A Family History* (London: J. Cunningham, 1840), 45.

39. The phrase gives the title to the second chapter of Mario Praz, *The Romantic Agony*, 2nd ed., trans. Angus Davidson (Oxford: Oxford University Press, 1970).

40. Sigmund Freud, *The Ego and the Id* [1923], trans. Joan Riviere (New York: Norton, 1960), 24.

41. Dana Nelson has also suggested the appropriateness of Deleuze and Guattari's "politicized understanding of oedipalization" (97) for Neal's novel.

42. Richard Van Alstyne, *The American Empire: Its Historical Pattern and Evolution* (London: Routledge and Kegan Paul, 1960), 4.

43. For a rich description of this world, as well as further details regarding Shickellamy, see James H. Merrell, *Into the American Woods: Negotiators on the Pennsylvania Frontier* (New York: Norton, 1999).

44. John Neal, "Mr John Dunn Hunter; The Hero of Hunter's Captivity Among the Indians, &c.," *London Magazine* 5 (1826): 317–43, quote from 341. In his story "Otter-Bag" (1829), Neal writes, "Perhaps the best specimen of Indian oratory that we have now, is the speech of Logan the Mingo chief; and yet Mr Jefferson, to whom we are indebted for it, knows very well, that instead of being a true speech, or the translation of a true speech, it is altogether untrue." See John Neal, "Otter-Bag, The Oneida Chief," in *The Genius of John Neal: Selections from his Writings*, ed. Benjamin Lease and Hans-Joachim Lang (Frankfurt: Peter Lang, 1978), 13.

CHAPTER SIX

1. Jacques Derrida, *Of Grammatology*, trans. Gayatri Chakravorty Spivak (Baltimore: The Johns Hopkins University Press, 1974), 101.

2. John Vaillant, *The Golden Spruce: A True Story of Myth, Madness, and Greed* (New York: Norton, 2005), 135. Further references to Hadwin's story will be to Vaillant's wonderful book, and included in the main body of the text. I borrow the paradoxical "west of everything" from Jane P. Tompkins, *West of Everything: The Inner Life of Westerns* (New York: Oxford University Press, 1992).

3. Roland Barthes, *The Grain of the Voice: Interviews 1962–1980*, trans. Linda Coverdale (Berkeley and Los Angeles: University of California Press, 1985), 127.

4. *The American Pioneer* 1, no. 1 (January 1842), 5. Further references will be included in the text.

5. Cormac McCarthy, *Blood Meridian* (New York: Vintage, 1985), 140.

6. Sigmund Freud, *The Interpretation of Dreams*, trans. James Strachey (New York: Avon, 1965), 564.

7. Elizabeth Gilbert, *The Last American Man* (New York: Viking, 2002), 1.

8. Vaillant records one of Hadwin's former supervisors describing Hadwin as a "person who, with very few resources, could be dropped anywhere on earth and come up smelling like a rose" (209).

9. Philip J. Deloria, *Playing Indian* (New Haven, CT: Yale University Press, 1998).

10. See Mark Twain, "Fenimore Cooper's Literary Offenses," in *Great Short Works of Mark Twain*, ed. Justin Kaplan (New York: Harper and Row, 1967), 169–90. The story about the grizzlies can be found in Vaillant.

11. James Fenimore Cooper, *The Last of the Mohicans* (New York: Penguin, 1986), 349.

12. D. H. Lawrence, *Studies in Classic American Literature* [1923] (New York: Penguin, 1977), 61.

13. James Hall, "The Indian Hater," in *Stories of the Early American West*, ed. Peter Bischoff (Essen: Die Blaue Eule, 1989), 72.

14. Catherine Maria Sedgwick, *Hope Leslie; or, Early Times in Massachusetts* [1827], ed. Mary Kelley (New Brunswick, NJ: Rutgers University Press, 1987), 84.

15. On Mononotto's mention in Winthrop and Hubbard, see notes 4 and 5 in Sedgwick, *Hope Leslie*, 356–57. The Pequots were not extinct in Melville's time, of course, nor are they today. See William Apess, *A Son of the Forest, and Other Writings*, ed. Barry O'Connell (Amherst: University of Massachusetts Press, 1992).

16. The phrase is from the Book of Job in the King James Version, where it serves as the plangent refrain (four times iterated) of the messenger informing Job of the destruction of his family and estate (Job 1:14–19). The echoes between Melville's mythopoeisis and the "dream of Hadwin" are uncanny and striking. I mentioned already (in Chapter 4) Melville's likening of Ahab to "that wild Logan of the woods." In offering some sense of the world in which Hadwin worked, Vaillant brilliantly described West Coast logging as "a kind of terrestrial whaling: determined, poorly paid men working in remote areas were using

temperamental machinery and simple hand tools to subdue enormous, often unpredictable creatures that could squash them like bugs—and did" (73). Most bizarrely, Vaillant reports that Hadwin spent the night before he cut down the golden spruce in The Moby Dick Inn (135).

17. See *Major Problems in American Indian History: Documents and Essays*, ed. Albert L. Hurtado and Peter Iverson (Lexington, MA: D. C. Heath, 1994), 340.

18. Despite the fact that Abiram White deserves his hanging, I cannot agree, for the reasons suggested above, with Sandra M. Gustafson's view that the scene of White's hanging represents "Cooper's desire to discipline U.S. territorial expansion." See Sandra M. Gustafson, "Histories of Democracy and Empire," *American Quarterly* 59, no. 1 (March 2007): 107–33, quote from 125.

19. See Krause, "Penn's Elm and *Edgar Huntly*."

20. See Francis Paul Prucha, *American Indian Treaties: The History of a Political Anomaly* (Berkeley and Los Angeles: University of California Press, 1994), 3.

21. Francis Jennings, William N. Fenton, Mary Druke, and David R. Miller, eds., *The History and Culture of Iroquois Diplomacy: An Interdisciplinary Guide to the Treaties of the Six Nations and Their League* (Syracuse, NY: Syracuse University Press, 1985), 16.

22. James H. Merrell, *Into the American Woods: Negotiators on the Pennsylvania Frontier* (New York: Norton, 1999), 180.

23. *Indian Treaties Printed by Benjamin Franklin, 1736–1762*, with an introduction by Carl Van Doren, and historical and bibliographical notes by Julian P. Boyd (Philadelphia: Historical Society of Pennsylvania, 1938), 280. Carl Van Doren calls particular attention to this speech in his introduction, calling it "an enormous image" (xv). Thomas King is identified as Saghughsuniunt in Merrell, *Into the American Woods*, 213. Prucha observes that, as in most details of the earlier treaty agreements, the Euro-Americans adopted Indian usage. He quotes from a report on a treaty in 1775 that has one of the white representatives addressing the assembly as follows: "Brethren with these strings we dry up your Tears for the Loss of your Freinds who have died since your last assembly at this Place we remove all Greif from your hearts on this Account that your minds may be at ease whilst we deliver our Embassy to you from our great United Council of Wise men now Assembled at Philadelphia which we hope you will hear with as much pleasure as we shall deliver it and we Collect the Bones of your Deceased freinds and Bury them deep in the Earth and Transplant the Tree of Peace over them that our Freindship may not be Interrupted nor our Minds disturbed at the Sight of them" (29).

24. Robert Pogue Harrison, *Forests: The Shadow of Civilization* (Chicago: University of Chicago Press, 1992), 69.

25. Gayle Brandow Samuels, *Enduring Roots: Encounters with Trees, History, and the American Landscape* (New Brunswick, NJ: Rutgers University Press, 1999), 8.

26. The intensity with which such trees of legitimation continue to be revered is suggested by a recent story from Texas, as recounted by Vaillant: "It

was set around the state capital's famed Treaty Oak, one of a group of trees known as the Council Oaks. Local Comanche Indians had once performed ceremonies within this sacred grove, and it was under the sole survivor that Stephen F. Austin, the founder of the state, allegedly signed the first border agreement between Indians and settlers. Once declared the most perfect specimen of a North American tree by the Forestry Association Hall of Fame for Trees, the 500-year-old live oak was poisoned in 1989 by a man named Paul Cullen; his motive, he claimed, was unrequited love. After extensive rescue efforts (financed with a blank check by the billionaire industrialist Ross Perot), a third of the tree was saved. Cullen was charged with a felony and sentenced to nine years in prison. Given that he tried to kill the Lone Star State's most venerable symbol, some might say that he got off easy, and relatively speaking, he did: a life sentence had been seriously considered" (140–41).

27. Locke, *Second Treatise of Government*, 19.

28. Jean-Jacques Rousseau, "Discourse on the Origin and the Foundations of Inequality among Men," in *The Discourses and Other Early Political Writings*, ed. and trans. Victor Gourevitch (Cambridge: Cambridge University Press, 1997), 147.

29. Adam Smith, "Considerations Concerning the Formation of First Languages, and the Different Genius of Original and Compound Languages," in *Lectures on Rhetoric and Belles Lettres*, ed. J. C. Bryce, Vol. 4 of *The Glasgow Edition of the Works and Correspondence of Adam Smith* (Indianapolis: The Liberty Fund, 1985), 203. "Genera and species" is from p. 205. So insistent is this story about savage vocabularies, the power of nomination and abstraction, and trees, that Claude Lévi-Strauss invokes it in the opening salvo of *The Savage Mind* (1962): "It has long been the fashion to invoke languages which lack the terms for expressing such a concept as 'tree' or 'animal,' even though they contain all the words necessary for a detailed inventory of species and varieties." Lévi-Strauss disputes this "fashion" first by saying that "savage" languages do, of course, have abstractions, and then by making the point that, from a linguistic point of view, "Words like 'oak,' 'beech', 'birch', etc. are no less entitled to be considered abstract words than the word 'tree"; and a language possessing only the word 'tree' would be, from this point of view less rich in concepts than one which lacked this term but contained dozens or hundreds for the individual species." Claude Lévi-Strauss, *The Savage Mind* (Chicago: University of Chicago Press, 1966), 1–2. Walter J. Ong records an especially amusing version of this story about abstraction, literacy, and trees. During his research in Uzbekistan, A. R. Luria's "requests for definitions of even the most concrete objects met with resistance. 'Try to explain what a tree is.' 'Why should I? Everyone knows what a tree is, they don't need me telling them,' replied one illiterate peasant, aged 22. Why define, when a real-life setting is infinitely more satisfactory than a definition? Basically the peasant was right. There is no way to refute the world of primary orality. All you can do is walk away from it into literacy."

Walter J. Ong, *Orality and Literacy: The Technologizing of the Word* (London: Routledge, 1982), 53. One implication of my argument is that it is less easy than Ong imagines to find a country of "literacy" that is not still rooted in the territoriality from which it presumes to be free.

30. G. W. F. Hegel, *The Phenomenology of Spirit*, trans. A. V. Miller (Oxford: Oxford University Press, 1977), 60–61.

31. Derrida, "Freud and the Scene of Writing," 214.

32. *The New Science of Giambattista Vico*, ed. and trans. Thomas Goddard Bergin and Max Harold Frisch (Ithaca, NY: Cornell University Press, 1970), 36. Harrison comments on this passage at *Forests* 35. Also see Isaiah Berlin, *Three Critics of the Enlightenment: Vico, Hamann, Herder*, ed. Henry Hardy (Princeton, NJ: Princeton University Press, 2000), 5–167. Berlin cites the same passage on p. 68.

33. Giorgio Agamben, *The Coming Community*, trans. Michael Hardt (Minneapolis: University of Minnesota Press, 1993), 10.

34. Deleuze and Guattari, *A Thousand Plateaus*, 15.

35. Fiedler, *The Return of the Vanishing American*, 7.

INDEX